Body Temperature Control

in Anaesthesia, Surgery
and Intensive Care

Body Temperature Control

in Anaesthesia, Surgery and Intensive Care

Anita Holdcroft, MB, ChB, FFARCS

Professor of Anaesthesia, University of Jos, Nigeria
formerly Senior Lecturer and Honorary Consultant, Charing Cross Hospital
Medical School, London

with a chapter on Malignant Hyperthermia by
G. M. Hall, MB, BS, PhD, MIBiol, FFARCS
Senior Lecturer and Honorary Consultant, Hammersmith Hospital and Royal
Postgraduate Medical School, London

Baillière Tindall·London

A BAILLIÈRE TINDALL book
published by Cassell Ltd,
35 Red Lion Square, London WC1R 4SG

and at Sydney, Auckland, Toronto,
Johannesburg

an affiliate of
Macmillan Publishing Co. Inc.
New York

© 1980 Baillière Tindall
a division of Cassell Ltd

First published 1980

ISBN 0 7020 0789 7

Printed in Great Britain by Spottiswoode
Ballantyne Ltd., Colchester and London

**British Library
Cataloguing in Publication Data**
Holdcroft, Anita
Body temperature control.
1. Body temperature—Regulation
I. Title
612'.01426   QP135
ISBN 0-7020-0789-7

Contents

Preface

An understanding of the measurement of body temperature is a necessity for anaesthetists, surgeons and physicians as well as for other medical and nursing staff. This book attempts to provide a rational basis for monitoring body temperature in clinical practice and to bring together the previously scattered information on body temperature changes, induced and spontaneous, which can occur during anaesthesia, surgery and intensive care.

Anaesthesia involves the pre- and postoperative management of patients as well as their care in the operating suite, yet the measurement of body temperature in most patients is a routine clinical investigation, performed by the nursing staff, to which the anaesthetist pays little attention. It is rarely included in the anaesthetist's preoperative assessment and often the decision to use temperature monitoring equipment is taken by the anaesthetist after a cursory touch with the back of the hand on the patient's forehead. Yet clinical indications for temperature monitoring, such as hyperthermia, hypothermia or an unstable cardiovascular system, may not be obvious and neither may the most suitable site for temperature recording nor the most appropriate measuring apparatus. An anaesthetist should be aware of the disease states that may affect normal thermoregulatory mechanisms and the problems of temperature regulation which may occur during anaesthesia. These are subjects not only of theoretical interest for professional examinations but also of practical importance to the patient.

Cellular metabolism is affected by tissue temperature, and deviations from the normal temperature may have adverse effects. The use of these effects in induced hypothermia has been practised for many years in cardiothoracic surgery but recently a resurgence of interest in them has occurred. The principles underlying the technique are considered here, not least because they can be applied in various other situations, such as cold exposure.

In a tropical environment, heat gain may be more important than heat loss; the effect of high environmental temperatures on metabolism and fluid balance is discussed in this book. It is worth remembering that such conditions are not always produced by natural environments, for similar ambient conditions may be encountered in the theatre or the intensive care ward when the ventilation system fails.

An understanding of the temperature regulation of neonates is necessary for all who care for them, especially when their environment or energy sources are disordered, as occurs during surgery. With this age group an anaesthetist may need guidance with regard to maintaining an adequate body temperature and consideration has been given in this monograph to problems which may arise during neonatal surgery and intensive care.

The use of specialized equipment specifically to maintain body temperature during anaesthesia, for example blood-warming apparatus or a water blanket, is now of prime concern to the anaesthetist. Not all this equipment operates satisfactorily and an attempt has been made here to assess the essential characteristics of equipment rather than to provide a shopping list of 'best buys'.

The effect of drugs and anaesthetic agents themselves on body temperature also requires consideration and this book attempts to piece together the available information so that the anaesthetist, physician or surgeon is presented with a clear picture of the way in which he may affect temperature homeostasis.

Any book owes its existence to the input of many people over a period of time, and it is with great pleasure that I record the contribution of my colleagues in the Department of Anaesthetics at the Hammersmith Hospital and especially that of Dr George Hall who has contributed the chapter on malignant hyperthermia. The constructive criticisms of Mr Sean Cavanagh, Mr Alan Sapsford and Dr J. L. H. Laity are gratefully acknowledged. I thank the members of the Department of Medical Illustration of Charing Cross Hospital for their advice and photographic skills. The permission of Blackwell Scientific Publications to reproduce Figure 38 is gratefully acknowledged. Finally I thank the publishers for their long-suffering and painstaking editing.

March 1980   ANITA HOLDCROFT

Control of body temperature

Man is a homeotherm, that is, he maintains his temperature within limits of approximately ±2°C despite much larger variations in ambient temperature. Temperature regulation is maintained by both behavioural and physiological mechanisms.

Behavioural temperature regulation involves a complex pattern of responses of the skeletal muscle to heat or cold which modify the rates of heat production and heat loss, e.g. by exercise or changing clothing. This allows man to live in environments with which physiological control of body temperature would not be able to cope, such as the Arctic (−60°C) or the moon (+200°C). The physiological regulation of body temperature in man involves both peripheral and central mechanisms which detect the body's temperature and a control system which is able to effect the necessary measures to counteract changes in temperature.

PHYSIOLOGICAL TEMPERATURE REGULATION

The hypothalamus is the main thermosensitive structure in the central nervous system: warming or cooling the hypothalamus elicits typical physiological responses (Hensel 1973). Other thermosensitive structures in the central nervous system include the mid-brain and the spinal cord: the existence of deep body thermosensors outside the central nervous system is still questionable.

Peripheral sensors of environmental temperature relay temperature sensations in conscious human subjects, allow behavioural responses to thermal stimulation and initiate peripheral and central thermoregulatory reflexes in man. Cutaneous thermoreceptors are divided, on the basis of their response, into warm and cold receptors. A few cold receptors have been identified in the skin of human subjects. In primates it seems certain that warm receptors exist and are served by unmyelinated nerve fibres.

Any thermoregulatory response can be initiated by temperature stimuli from various parts of the body in man, and a combination of

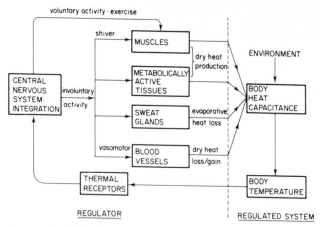

Fig. 1. Integration of the Thermoregulatory Response

thermal inputs leads to an integrated response (Figure 1). The question is not whether interaction of temperature signals takes place but where and how it occurs. Variations in hypothalamic temperature occur under natural conditions and may or may not be associated with corresponding thermoregulatory responses, suggesting that hypothalamic temperature is not the single controlled variable. If the posterior hypothalamus is damaged experimentally an animal cannot conserve heat when it is cold but loses heat normally when in a warm environment. The posterior hypothalamus appears to control the mechanisms for metabolic heat production, including increases in metabolic rate and shivering. When the anterior hypothalamus in the preoptic region near the optic chiasma and internal carotid artery is destroyed experimentally, an animal can maintain a normal temperature in a cold environment but when placed in a hot environment cannot bring into play its mechanisms for losing heat.

There are inputs to the hypothalamus from the spinal cord and other parts of the central nervous system and the role of central neurotransmitters has to be considered. In primates micro-injections of noradrenaline into the hypothalamus activate heat loss mechanisms which lower body temperature; 5-hydroxytryptamine has the opposite effect. The prostaglandins E_1 and E_2 can cause a rapid rise in body temperature and may have a physiological role in temperature regulation. Pyrogens cause an increase in prostaglandin activity in the brain which is reduced by prostaglandin inhibitors such as aspirin, indomethacin and paracetamol (Feldberg et al. 1973).

The following hypothesis has been put forward for the integration of peripheral and central temperature signals: the anterior hypothalamus is responsible for temperature sensing and the posterior hypothalamus

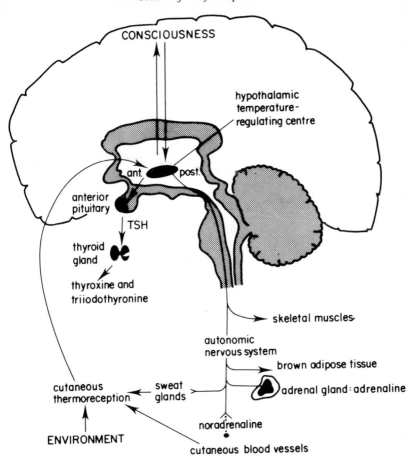

CONSCIOUSNESS

hypothalamic
temperature-
regulating centre

ant.   post.

anterior
pituitary

TSH

thyroid
gland

thyroxine and
triiodothyronine

skeletal muscles

autonomic
nervous system

brown adipose tissue

cutaneous   sweat
thermoreception   glands

adrenal gland: adrenaline

ENVIRONMENT

noradrenaline

cutaneous blood vessels

Fig. 2. *The Mechanisms of Central and Peripheral Temperature Regulation*
The effect of hot environments is to produce a pleasant sense of warmth in the
skin and to initiate centrally, via the anterior hypothalamus, the mechanisms
which produce heat loss. The autonomic response is dominant and stimulates
sweating and vasodilatation. The sensation of cold on the skin is more
unpleasant and the peripheral cutaneous receptors are stimulated to produce a
strong behavioural defence response which is augmented in the long term by an
increase in the hormones which stimulate basal metabolism

for eliciting the response (Figure 2). The central mechanisms activate the
thermoregulatory responses to warmth and the peripheral cool-sensing
mechanisms inhibit these responses (Figure 3). The application of
cooling to a body will, therefore, stimulate the peripheral receptors and
centrally inhibit vasodilation (Benzinger 1970). Short-term control of

thermoregulation is initiated by the nervous pathways: hormonal factors play a role only in long-term alterations of the system.

CORE TEMPERATURE

Body temperature is a nebulous term. Temperature can be measured in a number of different sites in the body and each has its normal range. We may usefully employ the rather simplified concept that in man the body consists of a central warm core, within which the temperature varies only between narrow limits (Figure 4), and a peripheral region throughout which there are various temperature gradients (Cooper 1969). The central core includes the contents of the skull, thorax and abdomen, i.e. most of the vital organs, and a variable amount of the deep tissues of the limbs. The core temperature is the mean temperature of the tissues within the body which are not affected directly by changes in the temperature gradient through peripheral tissues. The mean core temperature cannot be measured accurately and is generally represented by a specified temperature. The true core temperature should probably be regarded as that of the hypothalamus; Benzinger and

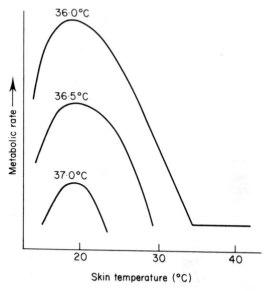

Fig. 3. The Relation between Metabolic Rate and Skin Temperature at Different Tympanic Temperatures

The metabolic response to cold is maximal at a mean skin temperature of 20°C. As the central temperature rises, central inhibition of heat generation increases so that lower skin temperatures elicit the same response in metabolic rate.

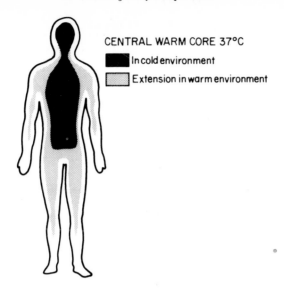

CENTRAL WARM CORE 37°C

■ In cold environment

▨ Extension in warm environment

Fig. 4. The 'Core' Temperature (after Mclean & Emslie-Smith 1977)

Taylor (1963) have shown that in man the temperature recorded from the tympanic membrane closely approximates to the temperature of the blood supplying the hypothalamus and tympanic temperature is also recommended by Benzinger (1969a) as the most reliable core temperature in clinical practice. The temperatures taken in external auditory meatus, the oesophagus, the closed mouth or the rectum, give adequate but less accurate indications of the core temperature and may vary between sites by about 1°C.

THERMAL BALANCE

Heat exchange between man and his environment maintains homeothermy and if man is to remain in thermal equilibrium his body must gain as much heat as it loses. The heat balance equation can be written down according to the first law of thermodynamics (Monteith 1974):

$$M - W = E + R + C$$
$$(\text{gains} = \text{losses})$$

where

M = rate of metabolism
W = physical work
E = evaporative loss
R = radiation loss
C = convective and conductive loss

The rate of metabolism is related to the respiratory quotient, the oxygen consumption and the evaporation from the respiratory tract. Radiation, conduction and convection may cause heat gain to a body as well as heat loss (Figure 5), so that a better form of the equation would be:

$$\text{Heat storage} = M - W - E \pm C \pm R$$

This equation is able to describe only the generalized heat balance of a body and takes no account of the variations in ambient temperature near a body surface, changes of heat storage in peripheral tissues and other facets of heat exchange between an organism and its environment.

Set Point

The set point of a regulatory system is that value of the controlled variable at which the control action is zero. Any change in core temperature away from this set point initiates heat production or dissipation mechanisms (Figure 6). The set temperatures of the various effector responses, e.g. shivering and panting, are not identical. Intracranial pathology in man can set this temperature at a different point and the patient becomes hypothermic or hyperthermic. There is a normal diurnal variation in the set point and fluctuation in this rhythm

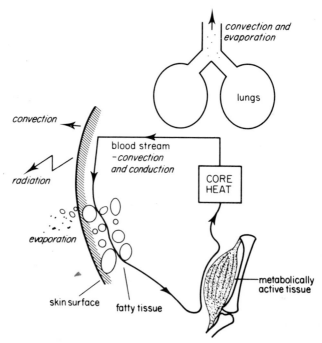

Fig. 5. Heat Exchange between Man and his Environment

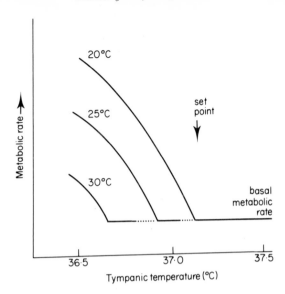

Fig. 6. The Set Point
Temperatures on the graph refer to mean skin temperatures. The inhibition of metabolic action in man becomes complete at the set point.

can occur during travel or when man is isolated from his environment. The feedback system in the central nervous system has been discussed by Hensel (1973) and he proposed a simple positive feedback loop.

MECHANISMS FOR HEAT GAIN

Basal Metabolism

The basal metabolic rate is measured in a resting, fasting, awake person in a thermoneutral environment with 50% relative humidity. In infants this measurement is not possible, so the minimum observed metabolic rate is used.

The basal metabolism of the body forms heat which must be lost if the body temperature is not to rise. Heat is not produced uniformly but mainly in the muscles, liver and glands. There is a range of environmental temperatures—the zone of thermal neutrality in Figure 7—where the body temperature and the basal metabolic rate both remain steady despite increasing ambient temperatures. This is achieved by the conduction of warmth through the tissues so that heat can be lost to the environment. It is impossible to reduce heat production in the tissues to less than the basal metabolic rate and so when the ambient temperature exceeds the body temperature, heat can no longer be passively lost by conduction, convection or radiation but only through the evaporation

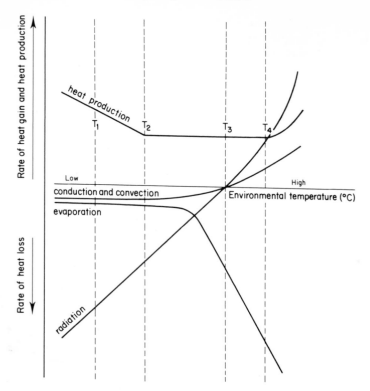

Fig. 7. Heat Production and Heat Loss in Naked, Healthy Resting Man in Relation to the Environmental Temperature

T_{1-4} Range of environmental temperature over which deep body temperature can be maintained within normal range.

T_{2-4} Range of environmental temperature over which thermal neutrality is maintained. T_2 is the critical temperature.

T_3 Environmental temperature at which the body begins to gain heat by radiation, conduction and convection. This gain can be balanced by evaporative losses unless the temperature rises above T_4.

Temperatures T_{1-4} are not constant and vary from individual to individual.

of water. Many powerful physiological mechanisms that lead to cooling by evaporation, such as sweating and panting, involve metabolic work, thereby reducing their apparent effectiveness.

Increased Heat Production

The main mechanism for increasing heat production is increased skeletal muscle activity either by voluntary movement or by shivering. Skeletal muscle makes up about 50% of the body mass but at rest it contributes about 20% of the heat production (Carlson & Hsieh 1965).

During activity it may increase its heat production ten times but because the core is thereby shifted towards the body surface there is a greater heat loss through convection.

Shivering

Shivering can increase the rate of metabolism as much as five-fold, but the increase in temperature is not maintained because of the loss of insulation by increased convection due to movement of the body. Shivering is inhibited by vigorous exercise.

Cooling the spinal cord leads to an increased excitability of the motor neurones and hence to shivering, so that the spinal cord is not only a site of thermosensitive structures transmitting impulses centrally, but also contains thermosensitive motor neurones that can reinforce the effected mechanisms of the system regulating against cooling (Hensel 1973). Visible shivering is preceded by muscle movements that can be demonstrated by electromyography (Burton & Bronck 1937). This change in muscular tone can increase basic heat production by up to 100%.

Hormonal Activity

Cold stimulates the release of thyrotrophin-releasing hormone from the hypothalamus. Consequent upon this, the thyroid secretes thyroxine and triiodothyronine which can produce prolonged increases in the metabolic rate (Doniach 1975).

The pituitary and adrenal glands are also involved in the central hypothalamic mechanisms of heat gain. Noradrenaline is produced in response to cold: it increases the concentration and utilization of glucose.

Radiation and Conduction

Heat gain occurs by the absorption of long wave radiant energy from the surroundings, the ingestion of hot drink and food and the ventilation of the lungs with warm gases.

Peripheral Cold Receptors

In man, the peripheral cold receptors in skin seem to be much the most important receptors involved in the human defence mechanism against cold so long as the nervous system is intact (Benzinger 1970). A skin temperature of about 20°C seems to produce the maximum firing rate of the cutaneous cold receptors and a full metabolic reaction at the central set point. At skin temperatures higher than this the action is weaker and begins only after the central temperature has fallen below the set point. At core temperatures below the set point metabolic heat production falls, so that it cannot maintain the human body temperature in a cold environment without the mechanisms for increasing body heat activated by the peripheral cold receptors.

Much weaker central cold receptors such as have been shown in animal experiments also exist in man, and have been demonstrated in paraplegic patients. They only come into action at a temperature lower than 35·6°C (Downey et al. 1967). The mechanisms with which these central cold receptors are involved can raise the metabolic rate by about 40 J/sec/°C, compared with the increase of about 800 J/sec/°C that is the result of the normal mechanism involving the release of central warmth inhibition.

Non-shivering Thermogenesis

Non-shivering thermogenesis is an effective means of heat production in neonates, where it occurs mainly in brown fat, and in the adult after prolonged exposure to the cold (Davis 1963). Metabolically active tissues are stimulated by the sympathetic nervous system in response to prolonged cooling of the hypothalamus. This mechanism can be depressed by ganglionic blockade and adrenergic beta-blocking agents. Direct local heating of the anterior hypothalamus in the presence of external cooling totally inactivates non-shivering thermogenesis (Davis & Mayer 1955). The tissues which increase their heat production in cold-induced stress are those that produce the basal metabolic heat, such as the liver and, in the neonate, brown fat. Davis (1963) suggests that cold stress may induce the adult fatty tissues to revert to the neonatal state, but evidence for this hypothesis is incomplete. Brown fat has been demonstrated anatomically in man around the kidneys, in the supra-renal area and in the aortic regions (Heaton 1972), but its role in normal thermogenesis is still under investigation.

Brown Fat

The newborn and young infant have in certain sites highly vascular multilocular deposits of brown adipose tissue which are histologically different from ordinary white adipose tissue. The brown adipose cell contains many small vacuoles of fat surrounded by a large number of mitochondria, the organelles of cellular oxidation thus lying close to a source of fuel. It has been said that whereas white fat plays the role of an insulating blanket in thermoregulation, brown fat, being actively thermogenic, can be regarded as an electric blanket (Renold & Cahill 1965). The tissue is not brown to the naked eye and so is difficult to distinguish from normal adipose tissue. The brown coloration, which only becomes apparent after fat depletion, is caused by the presence of an iron-containing cytochrome.

Brown fat accounts for about 1–6% of body weight of the human infant at birth (Hey 1974). Deposits of brown fat occur subcutaneously, after twenty-eight weeks gestation, between the scapulae, around the major blood vessels in the thorax, abdomen and the neck, and in large deposits in and around the kidney. The brown fat has a rich blood supply and adrenergic innervation and the production of heat from it involves the stimulation of cyclic AMP by noradrenaline. Cyclic AMP activates lipase which splits triglycerides into glycerol and free fatty acids. These free fatty acids are not released from the cell but are either resynthesized or oxidized to carbon dioxide and water, releasing energy. Heim and Hull (1966) infused noradrenaline into anaesthetized one-week-old rabbits and showed that 1 g of brown adipose tissue was capable of producing more than 10 J/minute of heat. If human tissues are capable of generating heat as rapidly as this then non-shivering thermogenesis could be responsible for more than half the increase in heat production that occurs when a newborn baby is subject to acute cold stress. Brown adipose tissue is almost always totally depleted of fat in babies dying of neonatal cold injury (Aherne & Hull 1966) and this may explain the impaired response of the malnourished child to cold (Brooke et al. 1973).

The significance of brown fat to non-shivering thermogenesis is not only in its relation to the amount of heat it produces, but also to its presence around the great vessels in the core of the body (Smith & Horwitz 1969) and the spinal cord.

THERMAL NEUTRALITY AND OPTIMAL THERMAL ENVIRONMENT

There is an optimal thermal environment in which the animal's health is optimal and its growth maximal, but this is not necessarily a thermoneutral environment. Hey (1975) limits the use of the term 'thermal neutrality' to those environments in which body temperature is normal and remains normal while heat production and evaporative water loss both remain at a minimum. For instance, heat production in a one-week-old baby is at a minimum when the ambient temperature lies between 32·5°C and 36°C, but thermal neutrality occurs only from 32·5°C to 33·5°C, since higher temperatures cause increased evaporative heat loss. As an infant becomes older, basal heat production increases so that the temperature of the thermally neutral environment falls. It is probably reasonable to define any environment as comfortable which does not require either heat production or evaporative heat loss to increase by more than 25% above basal. Provision of clothes and bedding lowers the minimum tolerable temperature. In practice thermal comfort (Fauger 1973) depends on:

1. Air temperature
2. Mean radiant temperature
3. Relative air velocity
4. Vapour pressure in ambient air
5. Activity level (i.e. internal heat production)
6. Thermal resistance of clothing

The investigation of the optimal thermal environment is of practical significance for the planning and operating of heating and ventilation systems for hospital wards and operating theatres.

MECHANISMS FOR HEAT LOSS

Radiation

The naked human body has an effective radiating surface of about 85% of its total surface area because surfaces that are frequently opposed, such as the inner aspect of the thighs, radiate not to the environment but to each other. The amount of radiation produced by the body is affected by cutaneous vasodilatation.

Conduction

Heat loss from the body occurs by conduction when it is in contact with a cold object and is dependent on blood flow to the area of contact. It is usually important only during immersion in cold water.

Convection

The surface area of the body and the amount of clothing worn can alter the effect of ambient temperature and air movement on heat loss by convection currents. Convection is minimized by high ambient temperatures and still air conditions at the surface of the skin. This may be achieved by trapping a layer of stagnant air between the skin and the environment.

Evaporation

Evaporation of water from the body is an important mechanism of heat loss. It occurs not only from the skin but also from the respiratory tract. Factors such as a large surface area of the body being available for evaporation, low relative humidity, movement of the surrounding air and hyperventilation will all tend to raise heat loss from its basal level. Evaporation contributes about a quarter of the total heat loss from man (Hey & Katz 1969) under basal conditions in a moderately humid environment (the majority of the heat loss is by convection and radiation). A third of the evaporative heat loss is via the respiratory tract and the remainder from the skin surface (Burton & Edholm 1955).

In thermally neutral environments man does not sweat but vapour continually diffuses through the skin without wetting it. Under such conditions insensible perspiration usually accounts for about 25% of the evaporative loss. This, combined with the loss of water from the respiratory tract, is called the insensible water loss, and amounts to about 30 g of water every hour. Every gram of water evaporated is equivalent to the loss of 24 KJ. Since sweat is derived from blood an adequate blood volume is necessary to maintain evaporative heat loss.

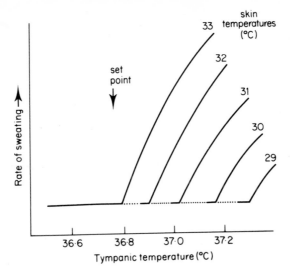

Fig. 8. The Relation between Sweating and the Tympanic Membrane Temperature
Sweating begins at a set point, indicating a threshold phenomenon of the central neurones involved. The intensity of sweating rises in a linear fashion with temperature. *(after Benzinger 1969b)*

When the body is exposed to heat, sweating appears first on the lower extremities with recruitment proceeding cranially. Eccrine thermal sweating is controlled by cholinergic sympathetic pathways, although adrenergic sweating also occurs in humans. Local effects of temperature on sweat secretion are limited to the area affected by the temperature change. General sudomotor activity occurs only in the presence of adequate central drive. At skin temperatures above about 33°C the rate of sweat secretion can be described as a function of tympanic temperature (Benzinger 1969b). Reduction of skin temperature below 33°C causes a reduction in the rate of sweat secretion unless counteracted by an increase in deep body temperature (Figure 8). Sudomotor responses can be elicited at skin temperatures above 33°C before any increase in tympanic temperature occurs.

Women tend to sweat less than men and this smaller sweating capacity can result in a more rapid rise in body temperature when women are exposed to a hot environment (Fox 1974). Women also have a lower heat production.

Evaporative heat loss is increased in a warm environment and control of this mechanism is an efficient means of controlling body temperature when environmental temperature is high: sweating can cause a tenfold increase in evaporative heat loss in man. This factor is reduced in the newborn, and in pre-term babies Hey and Katz (1969) found that sweating was almost impossible, presumably because of glandular immaturity.

Circadian Rhythms

In man there is *circadian rhythm* in the total conductance which is maximal in the late afternoon and minimal soon after midnight (Figure 9). The internal conductance, core-to-skin, has another rhythm with a maximal level at night and a minimum during the day so that the external conductance, skin-to-air, also varies systematically with the time of day, being lower at night. Core temperatures are lowest in the early morning and reach a peak in the early evening. Heat loss varies throughout the day not only according to the diurnal rhythm of conductance but between different regions of the body (Aschoff 1974). As the ambient temperature falls from 28 to 20°C, the heat loss decreases in the feet more than in the hands and in the toes more than in the fingers. It is interesting that the heat loss from the fingers and toes seems to be minimal in the afternoon and starts to rise in the evening just before the onset of sleep. On the other hand the rhythm of the heat loss from the trunk is almost the opposite, decreasing just as sleep begins. This diurnal variation is affected by the transitory effects of bathing, exercise, food intake and ovulation. Henane et al. (1977) observed that in ambient temperatures of more than 35°C no diurnal variation occurred, but they did not use acclimatized subjects.

VASCULAR CONTROL OF BODY TEMPERATURE

Homeothermic animals normally maintain a core temperature higher than that of the ambient air but heat is lost to the environment from the

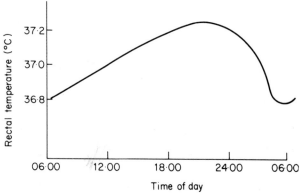

Fig. 9. The Circadian Rhythm of Core (Rectal) Body Temperature at 32°C Ambient Temperature

surface of the body (i.e. the skin and respiratory tract) which thus becomes cooled. There is therefore a temperature gradient between the core and the surface which can be varied by changes in the thermal conductivity of the subcutaneous tissues and fluid, but most importantly by the circulating blood which has a high heat capacity because of its large water content. Cutaneous arteriolar and venous blood flow can be so reduced that the thermal conductivity of the outer inch of the body becomes very low. This control over vasomotor tone is fully operational, even in newborn babies. However there is a basal conductance of about 21J/sec/°C and this persists despite further falls in central temperature (Benzinger 1969*b*). Total flow of heat from the core to the surface cannot be much reduced below this basal conductance no matter what the temperature gradient between the core and the surface may be.

Generalized cooling therefore produces a redistribution of circulating blood: blood flow to the skin diminishes while the muscle blood flow increases. However, the effects of moderate local cooling may be different in that it can produce vasoconstriction in blood vessels of nearby muscles, but this effect is of minor significance except that it induces muscle cramps. Severe cold applied locally may produce extra vasoconstriction, especially of the fingers and toes, and this is mediated by sympathetic vasoconstrictor nerves releasing noradrenaline. This is a direct peripheral effect on the blood vessels (Keatinge 1969).

In warm environments vasodilatation may increase the superficial blood flow to as much as one hundred times the minimum. This virtually abolishes the gradient between the deep tissues and the surface, allowing greater heat loss by radiation and convection.

A countercurrent phenomenon has been described in mammals (Carlson & Hsieh 1965) in which heat exchange is directly related to blood flow. During circulation through the arterial system, warm blood from the centre of the body or limb is in close proximity to colder venous blood, which is returning to the central veins, and some heat is transferred from the arterial to the venous circulation. This may cool the arterial blood before it reaches the peripheral tissues and, where environmental temperatures are low, prevent excessive heat loss. This 'countercurrent' phenomenon is not as significant in man as in mammals.

THERMOREGULATION IN THE NEWBORN

The exposed surface of the small mammal is much greater relative to its body weight than that of a large mammal of similar shape. Significant factors concerned in the infant's ability to withstand cold include patterns of behaviour, the amount of motor development at birth determining its activity, the maximum rate of endogenous heat production, thermal insulation and the hypothalamic set point of the critical temperature. In a cold environment babies are restless and cry, but only if the cold stress is very severe do they shiver. In the newborn the metabolism of the brain is normally responsible for about 70% of the total body heat production (Cross & Stratton 1974).

A light-for-dates baby is a full-term baby whose birth weight is 750 g or more below the mean weight for its gestation. It has a high metabolic rate but normal vasomotor control, unlike the pre-term baby who may be vasodilated all the time. Pre-term and light–for–dates newborn infants begin life with very small energy stores and are at a grave risk of failing to develop and maintain an adequate metabolic response when challenged by cold stress. In such cases, fat deposits are sufficient only to meet the energy demands for bare survival without growth, i.e. 210 KJ/kg per day, for two to four days. Fat stores can be preserved and the rate of lipolysis slowed by providing energy from an infusion of glucose (Sinclair 1972; Hey 1975). The smaller the baby the higher its critical temperature and the lower its rate of heat production when compared with surface area.

The factors which impair the metabolic response to cold through interference with thermoregulation include hypoxaemia, brain damage, drugs and latent hypothyroidism (Calvert 1962). Newborn infants and mothers who have been given more than 30 mg of diazepam in the fifteen hours prior to delivery may also have an impaired metabolic response to cold which can persist for up to eight days (Cree et al. 1973). When the infant has sustained intra-cranial haemorrhage or cerebral damage at birth the thermoregulatory centres in the hypothalamus may not function normally and a moderate degree of hypothermia may result. Neonatal hypothermia may also be precipitated by excessive heat loss during procedures such as resuscitation, exchange blood transfusion or artificial ventilation.

Hypothermia in Neonates and Infants

Causes
The following conditions have all been found to contribute to the development of hypothermia in neonates and infants (Bower et al. 1960; Cross et al. 1971; Appenzeller et al. 1970).

　　Prematurity
　　Cerebral birth injury
　　Severe infection
　　Congenital heart disease
　　Perinatal asphyxia
　　Malnutrition
　　Central nervous system abnormalities (craniopharyngeomas and hydrocephaly)

Clinical Features

The hypothermic infant does not look ill but he lies still and may not feed. There is erythema of the skin of the nose, face and extremities and coldness to the touch. Oedema gives place to sclerema (Yu & Jackson 1974). Most deaths are caused by respiratory failure associated with broncho-pneumonia or massive pulmonary haemorrhage. The intrapulmonary haemorrhage is associated with massive capillary damage and is almost specific for a neonatal cold injury especially in infants whose clotting mechanisms are immature (Chadd & Gray 1972; Brooke et al. 1973).

Management

Monitoring of body temperature, acid–base and electrolyte status, blood glucose level, platelet count, blood pressure, weight and urine output is required. The rate of re-warming the baby depends on the rate at which it cooled. Anderson et al. (1970) found various neurological sequelae after very rapid rewarming which fortunately disappeared in a few months. It is safe to raise the temperature by 1°C/hour. Pre-term babies may become apnoeic in response to re-warming (Maxwell 1967). Recommendations for oxygen therapy should be made on the basis of the arterial Po_2 level (Macintosh & Walker 1973). There is a need for glucose provided the temperature is above 30°C: it is best given intravenously (Ellis et al. 1974).

In infants the combination of rhinorrhoea, nasal obstruction and adventitious sounds in the chest cannot be taken as reliable evidence of chest infection. These signs often develop after re-warming, probably as a result of transudation from the mucous surfaces of the respiratory tract. Steroids are of doubtful value in the general management of hypothermic neonates and may encourage the spread of unrecognized infection.

Prevention

Warmth is necessary in the delivery room, nursery and incubator. The optimal environmental temperature is at least 24°C. The baby must be adequately dried on delivery and bathed only when necessary. If it has to be transported, even between hospital departments, extra pre-cautions are necessary to prevent heat loss, such as a silver swaddler and cellular blanket (Baum & Scopes 1968) or plastic wrapper (Besch et al. 1971). Radiant heat may be required (Price et al. 1971). The mortality of babies less than 2 kg in weight can be reduced by more than a quarter if their body temperature is maintained above 36°C, but the mortality rises with temperatures above 37·8°C.

EFFECTS OF ALTERATIONS IN BODY TEMPERATURE ON BODILY SYSTEMS

Cardiovascular System

The effect of cooling on the body is to increase those thermoregulatory responses which will tend to reduce heat loss and increase heat gain. There is stimulation of the autonomic nervous system. Peripheral vasoconstriction occurs, increasing the peripheral resistance. The demands of shivering muscles are met by an increase in heart rate and systolic blood pressure. Blood which is displaced from the superficial vessels is accommodated in the deep capacitance vessels (liver and lungs) and overdistended vessels can be seen on chest radiographs (Hervey 1973). This increase in circulating blood volume may contribute to a diuresis. When central cooling occurs bradycardia develops with an increase in systolic/diastolic time (Hervey 1973) due to a direct effect of cold on the sino-atrial pacemaker (Bigelow et al. 1954) and the blood pressure is lowered despite high peripheral resistance. Myocardial work is increased by the intense vasoconstriction. If the body temperature is reduced to 30°C the cardiac output falls by as much as 30% (Keatinge 1969).

Abnormalities of conduction occur at temperatures below 31°C; the PR and QT intervals are prolonged and the QRS complex widened. In many studies a notched downstroke called the junctional or J wave has been recorded from the right precordial leads and the AVR leads. It may appear as part of the QRS complex or separately from it (Fleming 1956). There is no consistent pattern of T-wave changes. Arrhythmias may develop as a result of changes in acid–base status and local oxygen supply.

Tachycardia occurring during hypothermia may be a manifestation of haemorrhage, hypoglycaemia or poisoning with the tricyclic anti-depressants or carbon monoxide. Ventricular fibrillation can occur at rectal temperatures below 30°C (Cooper & Ross 1960). It is more likely to occur if there are pathological abnormalities of the myocardium, and may be precipitated by endotracheal intubation (Fell & Dendy 1968). Spontaneous reversion to sinus rhythm can occur at temperatures between 33°C and 36°C.

Exposure to a hot environment, sufficient to produce a rise in body temperature, produces widespread superficial vasodilatation and distribution of blood to non-essential tissues. In shocked patients protective reflexes are lost, tissue oxygenation requirements are increased, and dehydration can create a vicious cycle that will lead to the death of the patient.

Venous return to the heart is diminished in warm ambient temperatures and there is a lowering of blood pressure. Warmth also relaxes the voluntary muscles and reduces their pumping action so that syncope may follow a failure of adequate venous return.

In hyperthermia the pulse rate rises by 20 beats for every 1°C (Wakim 1964) but up to 40°C little change in cardiac output occurs because stroke volume is reduced. A warm dry environment may in fact be beneficial to patients with left ventricular failure, but a warm humid environment can increase cardiac work.

Central Nervous System

In hypothermia cerebral blood flow decreases as a result of a combination of factors including a fall in cardiac output and blood pressure and increases in blood viscosity and cerebrovascular resistance. The fall in brain blood flow is accompanied by a reduction in cerebral oxygen consumption and lowered cerebrospinal fluid pressure. Cerebral oxygen consumption may fall to 75% of normal at 28°C, but at this temperature shivering can increase cerebral metabolism by more than 100%. Consciousness may be maintained to a temperature as low as 29°C.

A flat EEG during hypothermia is not a certain indicator of death. In man, electrical cortical activity diminishes as the brain temperature falls until at 18°C electrical silence occurs (Vandam & Burnap 1959). This reduced electrical activity is consistent with the diminished metabolic activity of the brain cells induced by cold, but cerebral hypoxia may also play a part. Ichiyanagi et al. (1969) found that the addition of carbon dioxide did not affect the pattern of slowing EEG activity during cooling, but they did not demonstrate that hypoxia did not occur. EEG activity may in any case cease at higher temperatures when a patient is anaesthetized.

Acid–Base Balance and Respiration

Hypothermia might be expected to protect the cells from the effects of hypoxaemia because it reduces their requirements for oxygen, but unless the metabolism of all tissues is reduced enough to enable all their oxygen demands to be met, some parts of the body acquire an oxygen debt. Tissue cooling is never uniform during surface exposure to cold: the skin and muscles always cool more rapidly than the tissues of the body core (Nisbett 1964). In addition, inadequate tissue perfusion during hypothermia can more than offset the benefit derived from the tissue's lower demand for oxygen.

Adequacy of tissue perfusion depends on many factors, including cardiac output, peripheral resistance and blood viscosity. During hypothermia the fall in cardiac output will obviously reduce perfusion of some tissues but the rise in blood viscosity is of much greater relevance to tissue oxygen supply. If the viscosity can be reduced the tissue perfusion increases and more oxygen is extracted from the blood

(McNicol & Smith 1964). Arterial hypoxaemia may also contribute to metabolic acidosis during hypothermia. As the core temperature falls the oxygen dissociation curve shifts progressively to the left. The amount of oxygen in physical solution increases during hypothermia but this dissolved oxygen alone is insufficient to fulfil the tissue oxygen requirements until the temperature falls to 16°C.

Hepatic metabolism of lactic, pyruvic and other organic acids is decreased during hypothermia, especially if the oxygen supply to the liver is impaired causing metabolic acidosis. When circulatory failure prevents tissue acids from being fully buffered in the circulating blood, acidosis can increase. When the microcirculation improves during rewarming and acid products are returned to the general circulation, metabolic acidosis may increase rapidly, particularly in the presence of other factors such as previous overventilation and increased metabolism because of shivering. Normally the kidney responds to metabolic acidosis by excreting more hydrogen ions, but hypothermia enhances sodium excretion: the impaired acid excretory capacity of the kidneys at low body temperatures may be explained by reduced sodium–hydrogen exchange. A normal renal response to metabolic acidosis is increased reabsorption of bicarbonate ions. There is no evidence of any modifying influence of hypothermia on this mechanism. Nevertheless, hypothermia presumably blocks many of the enzymatic processes in the renal tubular cells with the result that the role of the kidneys in maintaining the acid–base balance is virtually lost.

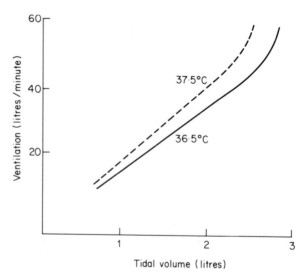

Fig. 10. The Effect of Core Temperature on the Relation between Minute Ventilation and the Tidal Volume (after Hey et al. 1966)

Changes in body temperature have a marked effect on tidal volume and respiratory frequency (Figure 10). When body temperature is raised, the tidal volume is reduced and the respiratory frequency increases (Hey et al. 1966; Euler et al. 1970) until the panting threshold is reached. Bradley et al. (1974) found that the threshold for inspiration to cut off was reached earlier at higher temperatures. In the absence of vagal feedback on the degree of distension of the lung this effect persisted. This indicates that the temperature effects are mainly of central origin. Peterson and Vejby-Christensen (1977) also postulate that the inspired time is shortened by an alteration in the central respiratory regulating mechanisms and the expiratory time change is consequent upon a change in end-inspiratory volume. These workers also demonstrated increased hypercapnic ventilatory response to hyperthermia (Vejby-Christensen & Peterson 1973) which they suggested was a multiplication in response between the effect of carbon dioxide and temperature. Natalino et al. (1977) measured the human ventilatory response to hypoxia during hyperthermia to $39.5°C$ and normocapnia and found that ventilation was significantly increased.

The mechanism of heat-induced changes in breathing in man is poorly understood. The contribution of temperature receptors can only be speculated upon. Direct thermal effects on the carotid body have been found in the dog by Bernthal and Weeks (1939). Hypermetabolic states are associated with hyperventilation but the respiratory changes correspond to the metabolic demands for oxygen. In the study of Natalino et al. (1977) there was increased ventilation at high oxygen tensions during hyperthermia. Hyperventilation and the washing out of carbon dioxide may shift the oxygen dissociation curve so that less oxygen is supplied to the tissues and during a fever the metabolic demands and the effects of hypocapnia may necessitate the administration of oxygen.

With the onset of cooling, minute ventilation is increased with a consequent reduction in $P_a co_2$, but this is not maintained and respiration becomes depressed despite an increase in oxygen consumption from shivering muscles. Low arterial oxygen tensions which accompany hypothermia were thought to be caused mainly by a severe reduction in pulmonary ventilation, but McNichol (1967) suggests that a reduction in alveolar–capillary oxygen transfer occurs, and Severinghaus and Stupfel (1955) have shown that the physiological and anatomical dead spaces increase by bronchial dilatation so that at $25°C$ the anatomical dead space has increased by 50%. The respiratory drive of hypothermic patients may be from the stimulus of hypoxia and the administration of oxygen may remove this stimulus and necessitate artificial ventilation. Respiration ceases at $24°C$.

Benumof and Wahrenbrock (1977) tested the hypoxic pulmonary vasoconstrictor response to temperature in open-chested dogs. Hypothermia was associated with a significantly increased pulmonary vascular resistance, which was more than could be explained by an increase in blood viscosity alone. Hypoxic pulmonary vasoconstriction was diminished during hypothermia, but increased during hyperthermia. This mechanism may aggravate the other causes of hypoxia which have been suggested, and the inability of the lung to maintain normal ventilation-to-perfusion ratios at low body temperatures may be potentiated by the effect of anaesthetics themselves.

The solubility of gases in liquids is inversely related to temperature and appreciably more oxygen and carbon dioxide can be carried in physical solution in the blood under hypothermia than normothermia. A patient ventilated with 100% pure oxygen will carry 2 ml of oxygen in solution in 100 ml of blood at 38°C: this amount will be increased to 3·2 ml at 10°C, which should meet tissue oxygen requirements. There is a shift to the left of the oxygen dissociation curve at low temperatures to the extent that at the tissue tension of 5·3 kPa (40 mmHg) the blood can unload 25% of its oxygen, whereas at 10°C, less than 10% will be unloaded. Hypercapnia and acidosis can reverse this shift and encourage the dissociation of oxygen at low temperatures (Figure 11).

Carbon dioxide is more soluble than oxygen in blood so that at a P_aCO_2 of 5·3 kPa arterial blood will carry 2·7 ml of carbon dioxide per 100 ml of blood at 37°C and 5·4 ml at 10°C. The additional carbon dioxide, in solution as the weak acid carbonic acid, is readily buffered,

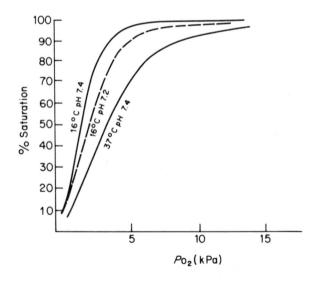

Fig. 11. *Oxygen Dissociation Curves of Haemoglobin when Temperature and pH are Varied (after Osborn et al. 1961)*

mainly by haemoglobin, and providing the buffer systems are functioning acidosis is unlikely to develop.

Measurement of acid–base disturbances during body temperature alterations can present difficulties. Rosenthal (1948) measured the change in pH when blood was cooled anaerobically in a sealed vessel and derived the following equation:

$$pH_{38} = pH_t - 0.0147(38 - t)$$

where t was the temperature of the measurement. The equation is valid only for anaerobic cooling. Severinghaus et al. (1956) have constructed a nomogram which relates changes in pK to variations in serum temperature and pH. In the Henderson–Hasselbalch equation

$$pH = pK + \log \frac{(HCO_3^-)}{(H_2CO_3)}$$

pK varies with temperature and pH. Nisbet (1964) suggests that calculated values may not correspond with those obtained with direct measurement, but Bergman (1968) confirmed experimentally that these theoretical discrepancies are too small to be of practical importance. If direct measurement of pH is undertaken, a constant temperature should be maintained and several electrodes may have to be used to correspond to the variations in patient temperature. This is difficult and in practice the pH is usually calculated by using nomograms such as those given by Kelman and Nunn (1966) after making measurements at normal body temperature.

Renal System
Urine output is indirectly affected by changes in the blood flow to the kidney. Morales et al. (1957) found that the glomerular filtration rate at 30°C is about half normal and tubular function is directly influenced by hypothermia. The active transport systems are depressed so that there is a reduced absorption of sodium, water (in the proximal and distal tubules) and glucose, and an impaired excretion of hydrogen ions. Polyuria develops with increased sodium and glucose excretion (Slotkoff et al. 1963; McKean et al. 1970).

Gastrointestinal Tract
Acute dilatation of the stomach may occur in hypothermia both in the newborn and in adults and can be confirmed by a plain radiograph of the abdomen. Multiple acute submucosal haemorrhages and erosions are common in the stomach.

Liver
Hepatic metabolism is reduced as body temperature falls and this will affect the metabolism and detoxification of endogenous and exogenous

substances. The hypothermic liver is less able to reutilize glucose, but the metabolism of fructose is unimpaired (Cooper 1968).

Glucose Metabolism

Glucose utilization is decreased during hypothermia and at core temperatures below about 30°C it is severely reduced. This impairment persists even in the presence of large amounts of circulating insulin and seems to result from an inhibition of the glucose carrier systems of the cell membranes but this mechanism cannot account for all of the disturbances in blood glucose during generalized hypothermia. A raised blood glucose level may also result from severe haemoconcentration, increased adrenaline, reduced insulin activity (Bickford & Mottram 1958) or pancreatitis. The roles played by glucagon and growth hormone are unknown.

Fat Metabolism

Initial exposure to cold considerably depletes body fat stores and produces a large rise in the level of free fatty acids in the plasma (Masoro 1966). High plasma FFA levels may precipitate serious cardiac arrhythmias in euthermic patients with acute myocardial infarction. It is not known whether a similar mechanism operates in hypothermic man (Opie 1974).

Endocrine Glands

The function of the adrenal gland (Wilson et al. 1970; Swan et al. 1957) and the thyroid gland (Hervey 1973) are both affected by changes in body temperature. Adrenaline and noradrenaline are potent mediators of thermogenesis and in hypothermia when shivering has ceased they may be the main determinants of heat production. They mobilize free fatty acids from adipose tissue and affect the rate of lipolysis by stimulating adenyl cyclase activity. Their metabolic effects may require blocking during hyperthermia.

At low temperatures free cortisol becomes increasingly protein-bound and the effect which it has in hypothermia has not been fully worked out in man.

Serum thyroid-stimulating-hormone levels rise with cooling, quickly in children but only after a delay in adults. The half-life of circulating thyroxine is about a week, so a deficiency is unlikely, but the free fraction of the hormone which is available to stimulate thermogenesis is reduced in a similar fashion to cortisol.

Fluid Balance

Thermal sweating is a threat to fluid and electrolyte balance. Body stores of water, sodium, chloride and potassium are depleted. Severe water depletion rarely occurs because it is usually prevented by thirst and subsequent water intake. Relative salt depletion or water intoxication is the basis of heat cramps.

When body temperature is reduced the intake of fluid may be minimal and absorption from the gastrointestinal tract is impaired. There is polyuria and the plasma volume is further reduced by redistribution into the interstitial fluid and the intracellular fluid. In animals there is a 60% reduction in blood volume after six hours at 15°C. An increase in blood volume on rewarming indicates successful recovery from hypothermia and the indications for the administration of fluid during hypothermia as judged by the usual criteria should not be too readily accepted (Hockaday & Fell 1969).

Sweating

A man rewarming from hypothermia sweats very little and the capacity for normal sweating may not be restored until several days after rewarming has been completed (Bloch et al. 1961).

Electrolytes and Protein

In hypothermia, sodium and chloride levels in the serum have been found to be essentially normal whereas in myxoedemic coma or cases of pituitary insufficiency the levels may be abnormal to start with. Potassium levels are frequently normal (Rosenfeld 1963) in hypothermia and neither calcium nor protein serum levels seem to be consistently or significantly altered. There is an increase in plasma magnesium which may be beneficial at low basal metabolism (Popovic & Popovic 1974) for maintenance of cellular functions.

Summary of Ionic Changes in the Plasma during Hypothermia

$$K^+ \quad \text{fluctuates}$$
$$Na^+ \quad \text{reduced at temperatures below 25°C}$$
$$Ca^{2+} \quad \text{unchanged}$$
$$Mg^{2+} \quad \text{increased}$$
$$PO_4^{2-} \quad \text{increased}$$

Haemopoetic System

Haemoglobin and white cell counts will be influenced by coexisting diseases and fluid shifts between the various compartments of the body. Platelet counts fall at temperatures between 28 and 32°C but normal counts are rapidly restored on rewarming after induced hypothermia. Thrombocytopenia may be associated with platelet clumping.

Blood viscosity increases with a reduction of body temperature (Figure 12) (Rand et al. 1964). The phenomenon is not wholly static: it appears to be related to a loss of plasma into the tissues. It varies with the velocity of the blood and the packed cell volume so that the effect of temperature is exaggerated at high packed cell volumes. An increase in

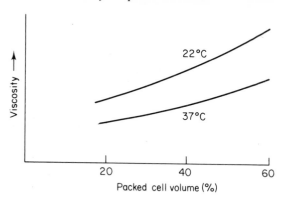

Fig. 12. The Effect of Variations in Core Body Temperature on the Relationship between Packed Cell Volume and Blood Viscosity

Viscosity increases with temperature but at higher packed cell volumes low temperatures have greater effect.

blood viscosity interferes with the microcirculation and favours hypoxia by delaying the passage of red blood cells.

The presence or absence of cold agglutinins should be determined before surgery which requires hypothermia although their presence does not preclude surgery. Transfused blood should preferably be warmed.

Muscles and Nerves

Cold produces progressive slowing of conduction along nerve fibres until at about 4°C reversible paralysis occurs. Katz and Miledi (1965) showed a prolongation of the synaptic delay time when the neuro-muscular junction was cooled. During induced hypothermia in anaes-thetized patients in whom no muscle relaxants had been used, twitch height was reduced during cooling to 25°C. The effect is reversed by the administration of edrophonium or tetanic stimulation (Feldman 1971). This suggests that acetylcholine release is the most important factor in this effect.

HYPOTHERMIA

Hypothermia is defined as that condition of a temperature-regulating animal when the core temperature is more than one standard deviation below the mean core temperature of the species in resting conditions in a thermoneutral environment (Bligh & Johnson 1973). The clinical signs of hypothermia are listed in Table I.

Cold produces physiological and behavioural responses in man. Sympathetic nervous activity is increased and mental activity can lead to

Table I: Clinical Signs of Hypothermia

Core temperature	Clinical condition
32–34°C	Dysarthria, ataxia
<30°C	Ventricular fibrillation
28–29°C	Delay in answering questions (Bloch 1961)
24–29°C	Myoclonia, facial spasm
<26°C	Failure to respond to stimuli
<24°C	Loss of corneal reflex (McQueen 1956)

more movement, changes of clothing, etc. In an artificial situation, if respiratory and circulatory functions are maintained by mechanical means, cellular function diminishes gradually in relation to bodily needs and death does not occur until the cells undergo crystallization (Fuhrman & Field 1943). The extent to which a human can withstand acute low environmental temperatures is illustrated by the case of a woman in Chicago who, in an alcoholic stupor, exposed herself to subfreezing temperatures overnight. When she was found the next morning her rectal temperature was 18°C. She survived after being gradually warmed in a room at 20°C (Laufman 1951).

Prolonged exposure to cold leads to acclimatization: shivering does not occur so frequently, the evaporative water loss from the respiratory tract is reduced and the physiological hormonal responses (pituitary and thyroid) come to play a larger role in thermoregulation.

HYPERTHERMIA

Fever is defined as a pathological condition in which there is an abnormal rise in core temperature of more than one standard deviation above the mean core temperature in resting conditions in a thermo-neutral environment. Hyperthermia is defined in the same manner, but is not a pathological condition.

The threat of hyperthermia may represent a more serious problem than that of hypothermia. Both temperature and humidity are impor-tant: fit individuals are unharmed if exposed to 130°C for 20 minutes in dry air. Sauna bath temperatures can rise to 110°C. However, hyperthermia is a problem, not only in the field of medicine but also in industry, sports and military training. Illness due to heat can be regarded as primary or secondary (Minard et al. 1957). Primary hyperthermia may either be physiological due to a lack of acclimatization, a deficiency of body salt or lack of water, or behavioural, if clothing is worn which does not allow dissipation of heat or there is an excessive amount of physical work performed during exposure to heat. Secondary hyperthermia is related to intercurrent illness (such as the reticuloses), nutrition (malnutrition or obesity), fatigue and post-prandial heat exposure.

A pyrogen is the generic term for any substance, whether exogenous or endogenous, which causes a fever when introduced into or released in the body (Gk. *pur* = fire; *gen* = become). An endogenous pyrogen is a heat-labile substance, formed in body tissues, which when released causes fever by an action upon the central nervous system. An example is leucocyte pyrogen. Bacteria can produce pyrogens and endotoxins. These latter substances are heat-stable and are derived from the cell walls of Gram-negative bacteria.

ACCLIMATIZATION TO HEAT

Acclimatization is a physiological change in an organism which reduces the strain caused by stressful changes in the natural climate.

Most of the research into this important mechanism in the avoidance of heat stroke has been performed in a controlled-climate laboratory (Fox 1965). There are various routines of acclimatization which can be used in the pre-treatment of personnel from temperate climates. In the past volunteers were kept for a fixed period of time during the day in the laboratory and then returned to their normal environment for the rest of the day. During the period in the laboratory, heart rate, body temperature and sweat loss were measured during resting and working. This cycle continued for up to a week. More modern researchers keep the volunteers inside the laboratory continuously and they perform no active work.

Features of Acclimatization

The major physiological change which occurs during acclimatization is an alteration in the amount of sweat produced. There are also changes in the endocrine, cardiovascular and respiratory systems.

Endocrine Changes

Initially, exposure to heat causes active retention of water. Antidiuretic hormone is increased and the sweat rate is reduced to give minimal water losses (1–2% of body weight). The loss of sodium ions and water is finely controlled by an increase in pituitary adrenocorticotrophic hormone providing there is an adequate salt intake (5 g per day) (Fox 1965). Cyclic adenosine monophosphate (cAMP) increases significantly in the hypothalamus after heat exposure (Kornbluth & Siegel 1977). cAMP is an intermediary in the neurotransmitter process: the effect of prostaglandins on this process requires evaluation. There is little evidence of alteration in thyroid activity (Fox 1974).

Cardiovascular System

This is the most important system in which acclimatization changes occur. There is an increase in blood volume and venomotor tone.

Increased peripheral blood flow occurs at a lower temperature and is greater for a given rise in temperature than in unacclimatized man. The pulse rate is also reduced. This was thought to be a sensitive index of acclimatization, but is probably a result of training in physical work.

Respiratory Changes

Hyperventilation occurs, increasing evaporative water loss, and arterial carbon dioxide tension is lowered.

Problems of Acclimatization

Problems of acclimatization occur when, for instance, military troops are moved at short notice from temperate to tropical conditions and have to be prepared for immediate work, or when expatriate professionals are employed in a hot environment and precise work has to be performed immediately on entry into this environment. Although the techniques of preparatory physical acclimatization can be of great assistance in such instances, their effectiveness cannot be guaranteed for any particular case. The length of pretreatment required is debatable and retention of acclimatization in the temperate climate may vary from individual to individual. Most studies of acclimatization have been performed in fit young adults and the influence of the subject's physical condition on the effectiveness of pretreatment is not yet clear. Moreover when fine skills are required, e.g. mental activity or manipulation, the use of pretreatment acclimatization programmes may be inappropriate (Wilkinson et al. 1964).

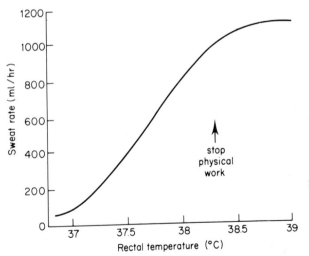

Fig. 13. The Relationship between Sweating and Core (Rectal) Temperature, and the Time at which Physical Work must be Stopped to Prevent Hyperpyrexia

In a hot climate, work should be stopped when there is still a reserve capacity left in the sweat rate, i.e. when the body temperature reaches 38·3°C (Figure 13); the maximum sweat rate for an acclimatized man is reached at a body temperature of 38·9–39·4°C (Wyndham et al. 1965).

Physiology of Exercise in the Heat

Skin vasodilatation occurs in a warm environment and reduces the circulatory blood volume. This in turn reduces venous return and hence the mean blood pressure, stimulating the baroreceptors which trigger visceral vasoconstriction by liberating adrenaline. Erect posture and exercise exaggerate any deficiency in blood volume as up to 800 ml of blood can pool in the lower limbs and increased demand by the muscles for blood will reduce circulatory blood volume even further (Keatinge 1970). There will also be a need for increased intestinal blood flow to transport water from the gut to the skin. Thermally induced circulatory fluid shifts are related to the severity of the heat stress and to the rate of cutaneous water loss. Compensation for these demands is made by an increase in blood volume and a reduced renal blood flow.

Dehydration will lead to reduction in the blood pressure and to hyperpyrexia because of a reduced circulatory blood flow. However, increased fluid intake before exercise in the heat may not protect a person from heat stroke: haemoconcentration occurs even when evaporative fluid loss is replaced (Myhre & Robinson 1977). Heat exchange from cutaneous vessels in hyperthermia differs from that in hypothermia. There is no countercurrent heat exchange but blood is diverted from the deep to the superficial veins so that blood is cooled as it returns to the heart.

Heat Disorders

Whether acclimatized or not, workers who exert themselves in hot conditions can develop heat cramps which respond to supplementation of the diet with salt. In the unacclimatized individual syncope can occur following acute exposure to high environmental temperatures.

The heat exhaustion syndrome is more serious and develops insidiously. Typically the patient is either unacclimatized or ill (e.g. following brain surgery and during a thyroid crisis: Silverman and Wilson 1950). Initially the body temperature remains normal, but complaints of vague malaise are common. Confusion and circulatory collapse are associated with a rise in body temperature and finally gross neurological change occurs with a core body temperature of more than 41°C and an absence of sweating. The patient has then lost all ability to lose heat and death ensues.

Heat stroke is a disorder of thermoregulation characterized by total absence of sweating, hyperthermia of more than 41°C and severe disturbances of consciousness and brain function.

Heat stroke requires more vigorous cooling measures than heat exhaustion. Occasionally hot weather is not the only cause. Bacon et al. (1979) report the development of heat stroke in five infants who were 'swaddled' during a mild fever. Predisposing factors for heat stroke are old age and alcoholism.

Acute heat stroke with no prodromal symptoms is characterized by tachycardia, fainting, unconsciousness and hypotension. It is emerging as a medical emergency in marathon runners ('joggers'). Bassler (1979) reports four deaths due to myocardial failure in the last eleven years, and unconsciousness and shock have occurred in unacclimatized runners (Hughson & Sutton 1978).

Apart from heat stroke occurring in joggers, the other common hyperthermic emergency is myocardial ischaemia during sauna bathing. Saunas increase catecholamine secretion and secondarily the cardiac output in both normal and ischaemic hearts. A tachycardia is mainly responsible for this: Taggart et al. (1972) noted progressive ischaemic changes in an ECG study. This is probably because coronary artery filling pressure is low due to a generally reduced blood pressure and reduced diastolic filling time. Tall pointed T waves can occur in the ECG. Their cause is unknown: they are unrelated to the serum potassium level. There is tenuous evidence that hyperthermia (from fever, saunas, etc.) plays a part in the causation of neural tube defects (Lancet 1978).

Hyperthermia of 41–42°C is lethal to some tumour cells but not to normal cells. This effect has been applied in the treatment of human tumours either by induced whole body hyperthermia or isolated limb hyperthermia (Pettigrew et al. 1974). Anaesthesia is required: the technique is described in Chapter 5.

DISORDERS PREDISPOSING TO ALTERATIONS IN BODY TEMPERATURE

The body temperature of man is maintained within narrow limits but the normal thermoregulatory mechanisms involved may be deranged by disease or drugs. Regulation is in any case inefficient in the human neonate as has been mentioned earlier.

Abnormal Heat Production

Reduced heat production will tend to induce hypothermia; increased heat production, hyperthermia. The basic problem is the regulation of cellular energy production.

Hypoglycaemia and Starvation

Hypothermia above 32°C associated with low blood sugar levels may be improved simply by the administration of glucose. The elimination of hypoglycaemia before active rewarming is started is important.

Immobility

Patients who are unable to move because of conditions such as myocardial infarction, poisoning or neurological disorders often do not generate enough energy from their muscles to maintain body temperature. Occasionally hypothermia has multiple causes, as when cerebral haemorrhage occurs; not only may limb movement be reduced but also the central temperature regulating centres may be damaged.

Thyroid Gland – Hypothyroidism and Hyperthyroidism

Thyrotoxic crises are fortunately rare, but when they do occur they may be complicated by hyperpyrexia which should be treated by mild cooling.

Hypothermia may be precipitated in hypothyroid patients by drugs such as chlorpromazine, by trauma or by exposure to cold. Maclean and Emslie-Smith (1977) found that the rate of rewarming of hypothermic hypothyroid patients correlated with the serum level of protein-bound iodine. Where hypercapnic narcosis complicates severe hypothermic myxoedema, intermittent positive pressure ventilation may be prolonged to allow the respiratory centre to regain normal function under the influence of thyroid hormone replacement. In patients who develop hypothermia following long standing hypothyroidism or hypopituitarism there may be abnormal water retention, haemodilution and low serum electrolyte concentrations. The excess water will induce cerebral oedema. Water intake should be restricted accordingly and if this fails to improve the patient, diuretics should be given.

Hyperkalaemia may develop secondarily to acute renal tubular necrosis, complicating the myopathy that can be associated with hypothermic hypothyroidism.

Hypopituitarism

This multihormone disease will precipitate hypothyroidism and hypoglycaemia.

Adrenal Gland

Adrenal cortical carcinoma may present with periodic fevers.

Adrenal insufficiency may be acute or chronic (Addison's disease) The clinical picture is due to a lack of aldosterone, which will reduce plasma volume, and/or glucocorticoid deficiency, resulting in hypoglycaemia and weakness. These are precisely the conditions that lead to hypothermia if the patient is in a cold environment.

Malignant Hyperthermia

This subject is dealt with in Chapter 4.

Heat Loss

Heat loss can be increased or decreased by any mechanism that affects the transfer of heat from the core to the skin, and by behavioural and environmental changes. Sweating may be decreased by drug action, e.g. atropine, or there may even be a congenital absence of sweat glands. Clothing or other insulative materials can increase body temperature to abnormal levels, especially if there is increased heat production. Malnutrition is less acute than starvation, but it can lead to a reduction in body insulation and is associated with a reduction in available energy stores so that it predisposes to hypothermia. Exposure of the body surface is considered in more detail later.

Vasodilating Drugs (Ethyl Alcohol)

Alcohol causes vasodilatation and may accelerate the fall in body temperature of men exposed to cold (Pickering et al. 1977). The effect is probably dose-related because Keatinge and Evans (1960) found that a moderate dose (75 ml) of absolute alcohol did not significantly increase the heat loss of human volunteers immersed in water at 24–27°C but the alcohol did reduce the discomfort of the cold water. Hewer (1964) records the use of 1750 ml of 10% solution given parenterally over six hours to induce hypothermia, i.e. a total dose of 175 ml.

Erythroderma

In this condition the skin is red and brawny, especially on exposed areas. Hypothermia may occasionally develop as a result of increased heat loss from the skin.

Paget's Disease of Bone

There is an extensive blood flow through bones affected by this disease. The skull and legs are commonly affected and if care is not taken to protect these areas during cold weather hypothermia may result.

Burns

The area of skin involved in a burn will determine the likelihood of hypothermia developing, but patients with burns should be nursed in a warm humid atmosphere to minimize heat loss and energy expenditure.

Impaired Thermoregulation

Diabetes

Gale and Tattersall (1978) warn that the association of unstable diabetes and hypothermia should receive more attention: they recorded an incidence of more than 10% of ketoacidosis complicating severe accidental hypothermia (defined as a rectal temperature of 33°C or below). The mechanisms suggested to explain this association are that insulin secretion is impaired at low temperatures, peripheral utilization of glucose is reduced and resistance to endogenous insulin develops as the body temperature falls. The release of catecholamines and cortisol may aggravate the metabolic disturbance. This, however, is not a complete picture because central temperature regulation may be affected.

The initial requirement of a patient in such a condition is rapid rewarming because blood glucose is not utilized at low body temperatures and administered insulin has little or no effect: the core temperature should be above 31°C before insulin is given. Fluid and potassium replacement should be administered cautiously and based on arterial blood sampling because stasis and pooling make venous samples unreliable.

Infection may not produce fever in patients with diabetic coma.

Central Thermoregulatory Failure

There are two types of chronically hypothermic individuals: those who have lost all or most of their temperature-regulating ability and those who regulate their temperatures at a subnormal level. There is no suggestion that hypothermia itself affects thermoregulation (Macmillan et al. 1967).

Periodic hypothermia is often associated with epilepsy (Hoffman & Pobirs 1942; Duff et al. 1961; Thomas and Green 1973). The episodes of hypothermia reported were characterized by depression, ataxia, mental slowness and sweating and could easily have been misdiagnosed as a psychotic illness.

Where pathological injuries, for example trauma, tumours and vascular occlusion, affect the brain stem and hypothalamus, hyperpyrexia may complicate other manifestations of brain stem injury, e.g. coma and decerebrate rigidity. Other abnormalities indicating hypothalamic dysfunction include precocious puberty or hypogonadism, diabetes insipidus, somnolence and obesity.

The effect of drugs on central temperature regulation is discussed in Chapter 3.

Uraemia

The patient who develops renal failure may become hypothermic not only because of central nervous system depression and coma, but also because of multi-system disorders.

Peripheral Thermoregulatory Failure

This can occur in spinal cord lesions as a result of trauma or other pathology: the sympathetic pathways controlling sweating and vasomotor activity are interrupted and hyperthermia can occur in a warm climate. Acute spinal cord transection is likely to lead to severe hypothermia in temperate climates.

Patients with Parkinson's disease may suffer from excessive vaso-dilatation and sweating and the incidence of accidental hypothermia is increased in this disorder (Johnson & Spalding 1974).

Other Disorders

Pancreatitis and cirrhosis of the liver can predispose to hypothermia. Infections precipitate hyperpyrexia, especially in children.

References

Aherne, W. & Hull, D. (1966) Brown adipose tissue and heat production in the newborn infant. *J. Path. Bact., 91*, 223–234.

Anderson, S., Herbring, B. G. & Widman, B. (1970) Accidental profound hypothermia. *Br. J. Anaesth., 42*, 653–655.

Appenzeller, O., Snyder, R. & Kornfeld, M. (1970) Autonomic failure in hydroencephaly. *J. Neurol. Psychiat., 33*, 532–543.

Aschoff, J. (1974) Circadian rhythm. In: *Heat Loss from Animals and Man*, ed. J. L. Monteith & L. E. Mount, p. 156. London: Butterworths.

Bacon, C., Scott, D. & Jones. P. (1979) Heat stroke in well wrapped infants. *Lancet, 1*, 422–425.

Baum, J. D. & Scopes, J. W. (1968) The silver swaddler. *Lancet, 1*, 672–673.

Bassler, T. J. (1979) Heat stroke in a 'run for fun'. *Br. med. J., 1*, 197.

Benumof, J. L. & Wahrenbrock, E. A. (1977) Dependency of hypoxic pulmonary vasoconstriction on temperature. *J. appl. Physiol., 42*, 56–58.

Benzinger, T. H. (1969a) Clinical temperature: new physiological basis. *J. Am. med. Ass., 209*, 1200–1206.

Benzinger, T. H. (1969b) Heat regulation: homeostasis of central temperature in man. *Physiol. Rev., 49*, 671–759.

Benzinger, T. H. (1970) Peripheral cold reception and central warm reception; sensory mechanisms of behavioural and autonomic thermostasis. In: *Physiological and Behavioural Temperature Regulation*, ed. J. D. Hardy, A. P. Gagge & J. A. J. Stolwijk, pp. 831–855. Springfield, Ill.: Charles C. Thomas.

Benzinger, T. H. & Taylor, G. W. (1963) Cranial measurements of internal temperature in man. In: *Temperature: its Measurement and Control in Science and Industry*, Vol. 3, p. 11. New York: Reinhold.

Bergman, N. A. (1968) Temperature coefficients for PCO_2 and PO_2 in bloods with varying acid–base status. *J. appl. Physiol., 24*, 225–228.

Bernthal, T. & Weeks, W. F. (1939) Respiratory and vasomotor effects of variations in carotid body temperature. *Am. J. Physiol., 127*, 94–105.

Besch, N. J., Perlstein, P. H., Edwards, N. K., Keenan, W. J. & Sutherland, J. M. (1971) The transparent baby bag. *New Engl. J. Med., 284*, 121–124.

Bickford, A. F. & Mottram, R. F. (1958) Glucose metabolism during periods of induced hypothermia. *J. Physiol., Lond., 143*, 37P–38P.

Bigelow, W. G., Mustard, W. T. & Evans, J. G. (1954) Some physiologic concepts of hypothermia and their applications to cardiac surgery. *J. thorac. cardiovasc. Surg., 28*, 463–480.

Bligh, J. & Johnson, K. G. (1973) Glossary of terms for thermal physiology. *J. appl. Physiol., 35*, 941–961.

Bloch, M., Bloom, H. J. G., Penman, J. & Walsh, L. (1961) Irradiation of cerebral astrocytoma under whole body hypothermia. *Lancet, 2*, 906–909.

Bower, B. D., Jones, L. F. & Weeks, M. M. (1960) Cold injury in the newborn: a study of 70 cases. *Br. med. J., 1*, 303–309.

Bradley, G. W., von Euler, C., Martilla, I. & Roos, B. (1974) Steady state effects of CO_2 and temperature on the relationship between lung volume and inspiratory duration. *Acta physiol. scand.*, *92*, 351–363.

Brooke, O. G., Harris, M. & Salvosa, C. B. (1973) The response of malnourished babies to cold. *J. Physiol., Lond., 233*, 75–91.

Burton, A. C. & Bronck, D. W. (1937) Motor mechanism of shivering and thermal muscular tone. *Am. J. Physiol., 119*, 284.

Burton, A. C. & Edholm, O. G. (1955) *Man in a Cold Environment*. London: Edward Arnold.

Calvert, D. G. (1962) Inadvertent hypothermia in paediatric surgery and a method for its prevention. *Anaesthesia, 17*, 29–45.

Carlson, L. D. & Hsieh, A. C. L. (1965) Cold. In: *The Physiology of Human Survival*, ed. O. G. Edholm & A. L. Bacharach, p. 19. London: Academic Press.

Chadd, M. A. & Gray, O. P. (1972) Hypothermia and coagulation defects in the newborn. *Arch. Dis. Child., 47*, 819–821.

Cooper, K. E. & Ross, D. N. (1960) *Hypothermia in Surgical Practice*. Philadelphia: Davis.

Cooper, K. E. (1968) Temperature regulation and its disorders. In: *Recent Advances in Medicine*, ed. D. N. Barron, N. Compston & A. W. Dawson, 15th ed., pp. 343–350. London: Churchilll.

Cooper, K. E. (1969) Regulation of body temperature. *Br. J. Hosp. Med., 2*, 1064–1067.

Cree, J. E., Meyer, J., & Hailey, D. M. (1973) Diazepam in labour: Its metabolism and effect on the clinical condition and thermogenesis of the newborn. *Br. med. J., 4*, 251–255.

Cross, K. W., Hey, E. N., Kennaird, D. L., Lewis, S. R. & Urich, H. (1971) Lack of temperature control in infants with abnormalities of central nervous system. *Arch. Dis. Child., 46*, 437–443.

Cross, K. W. & Stratton, D. (1974) Aural temperature of the newborn infant. *Lancet, 2*, 1179–1180.

Davis, T. R. A. & Mayer, J. (1955) Demonstration and quantitative determination of the contributions of physical and chemical thermogenesis on acute exposure to cold. *Am. J. Physiol., 181*, 675–678.

Davis, T. R. A. (1963) Nonshivering thermogenesis. *Fedn Proc. Fedn Am. Socs exp. Biol., 22*, 777–782.

Doniach, D. (1975) Possible stimulation of thermogenesis in brown adipose tissue by thyroid-stimulating hormone. *Lancet, 2*, 160–161.

Downey, J. A., Chiodi, H. P. & Darling, R. C. (1967) Central temperature regulation in the spinal man. *J. appl. Physiol., 22*, 91–94

Duff, R. S., Farrant, P. C., Leveaux, V. M. & Wray, S. M. (1961) Spontaneous periodic hypothermia. *Q. Jl. Med., 30*, 329–338.

Ellis, R. J., Hoover, E., Gay, W. A. & Ebert, P. A. (1974) Metabolic alterations with profound hypothermia. *Arch. Surg., Chicago, 109*, 659–662.

von Euler, C., Herrero, F. & Wexler, I. (1970) Control mechanisms determining rate and depth of respiratory movements. *Resp. Physiol., 10*, 93–108.

Fanger, P. O. (1973) Assessment of man's thermal comfort in practice. *Br. J. indust. Med., 30*, 313–324.

Feldberg, W., Gupta, K. P., Milton, A. S. & Wendlant, S. (1973) Effect of pyrogen and antipyretics on prostaglandin activity in cisternal CSF of unanaesthetised cats. *J. Physiol. Lond., 234*, 279–303.

Feldman, S. A. (1971) *Muscle Relaxants*, pp. 117–128. Philadelphia: W. B. Saunders.

Fell, R. H. & Dendy, P. R. (1968) Severe hypothermia and respiratory arrest in diazepam and glutethimide intoxication. *Anaesthesia*, *23*, 636–640

Fleming, P. R. (1956) The electrocardiogram and induced hypothermia. *Br. Heart J.*, *18*, 288.

Fox, R. H. (1965) Heat. In: *The Physiology of Human Survival*, ed. O. G. Edholm & A. L. Bacharach, pp. 53–79. London: Academic Press.

Fox, R. H. (1974) Heat acclimatisation and the sweating response. In: *Heat Loss from Animals and Man*, ed. J. L. Monteith & L. E. Mount, pp. 290–292. London: Butterworth.

Fuhrman, F. A. & Field, J. (1943) Reversibility of inhibition of rat brain and kidney metabolism by cold. *Am. J. Physiol.*, *139*, 193.

Gale, E. A. M. & Tattersall, R. B. (1978) Hypothermia: A complication of diabetic ketoacidosis. *Br. med. J.*, *2*, 1387–1389.

Heaton, J. M. (1972) The distribution of brown adipose tissue in the human. *J. Anat.*, *112*, 35–39.

Heim, T. & Hull, D. (1966) The blood flow and oxygen consumption of brown adipose tissue in the newborn rabbit. *J. Physiol. Lond.*, *186*, 42–55.

Henane, R., Buguet, A., Roussel, B. & Bittel, J. (1977) Variations in evaporation and body temperatures during sleep in man. *J. appl. Physiol.*, *42*, 50–55.

Hensel, H. (1973) Neural processes in thermoregulation. *Physiol. Rev.*, *53*, 948–1017.

Hervey, G. R. (1973) Physiological changes encountered in hypothermia. *Proc. R. Soc. Med.*, *66*, 1053–1057.

Hewer, A. J. H. (1964) Hypothermia for neurosurgery. *Int. Anesth. Clin.*, *2*, 919–939.

Hey, E. N., Lloyd, B. B., Cunningham, D. J. C., Jukes, M. G. M. & Bolton, D. G. P. (1966) Effects of various respiratory stimuli on the depth and frequency of breathing in man. *Resp. Physiol.*, *1*, 193–205.

Hey, E. N. & Katz, G. (1969) Evaporative water loss in the newborn baby. *J. Physiol., Lond.*, *200*, 605–619.

Hey, E. N. (1974) Physiological control over body temperature. In: *Heat Loss from Animals and Man*, ed. J. L. Monteith & L. E. Mount, pp. 77–95. London: Butterworth.

Hey, E. N. (1975) Thermal neutrality. *Br. med. Bull.*, *31*, 69–74.

Hockaday, T. R. D. & Fell, R. H. (1969) Accidental hypothermia. *Br. J. Hosp. Med.*, *2*, 1083–1093.

Hoffman, A. M. & Pobirs, F. W. (1942) Intermittent hypothermia with disabling hyperhydrosis. *J. Am. med. Ass.*, *120*, 445–447.

Hughson, R. L. & Sutton, J. R. (1978) Heat stroke in a 'run for fun'. *Br. med. J.*, *2*, 1158.

Ichiyanagi, K., Matsuki, M., Masuko, K., Nishisaka, T., Wantanabe, R. & Horikawa, H. (1969) Effect of altered arterial carbon dioxide tensions on the electroencephalogram during hypothermia. *Acta anaesth. scand.*, *13*, 173–183.

Johnson, R. H. & Spalding, J. M. K. (1974) *Disorders of the Autonomic Nervous System*. Oxford: Blackwell.

Katz, B. & Miledi, R. (1965) The effect of temperature on the synaptic delay at the neuromuscular junction. *J. Physiol., Lond.*, *181*, 656–670.

Keatinge, W. R. & Evans, M. (1960) Effect of food, alcohol, and hyoscine on body temperature and reflex responses on men immersed in cold water. *Lancet*, *1*, 176–178.

Keatinge, W. R. (1969) *Survival in Cold Water*. Oxford: Blackwell.

Keatinge, W. R. (1970) Factors limiting exercise in the heat. In: *Physiological and Behavioural Temperature Regulation*, ed. J. D. Hardy, A. P. Gagge & J. A. J. Stolwijk, p. 250. Springfield, Ill: Charles C. Thomas.

Kelman, G. R. & Nunn, J. F. (1966) Nomograms for correction of blood PO_2, PCO_2, pH and base excess for time and temperature *J. appl. Physiol.*, *21*, 1484–1490.

Kornbluth, I & Siegel, R. A. (1977) cAMP in temperature- and ADH-regulating centres after thermal stress. *J. appl. Physiol.*, *42*, 257–261.

Lancet (1978) Hyperthermia and the neural tube. *Lancet*, *2*, 560–561.

Laufman, H. (1951) Profound accidental hypothermia. *J. Am. med. Ass.*, *147*, 1201–1212.

Macintosh, T. F. & Walker, C. H. M. (1973) Blood viscosity in the newborn. *Arch. Dis. Child.*, *48*, 547–553.

McKean, W. I., Dixon, S. R., Gwynne, J. F. & Irvine, R. O. H. (1970) Renal failure after accidental hypothermia *Br. med. J.*, *2*, 463–464.

Maclean, D. & Emslie-Smith, D. (1977) *Accidental Hypothermia*. Oxford: Blackwell Scientific.

Macmillan, A. L., Corbett, J. L., Johnson, R. H., Crampton-Smith, A., Spalding, J. M. K. & Wollner, L. (1967) Temperature regulation in survivors of accidental hypothermia in the elderly. *Lancet*, *2*, 165–169.

McNicol, M. W. & Smith, R. (1964) Accidental hypothermia. *Br. med. J.*, *1*, 19–21.

McNicol, M. W. (1967) Respiratory failure and acid-base status in hypothermia. *Postgrad. med. J.*, *43*, 674–676.

Masoro, E. J. (1966) The effect of cold on the metabolic use of lipid. *Physiol. Rev.*, *46*, 67–101.

Maxwell, B. E. (1967) Neonatal cold injury in the North West territories. *Can. med. Ass. J.*, *97*, 970–973.

McQueen, J. D. (1956) Effects of cold on the nervous system. In: *Physiology of Induced Hypothermia*, ed. R. D. Dripps, pp. 243–250. Washington: National Research Council.

Minard, D., Belding, H. S. & Kingston, J. R. (1957) Prevention of heat casualties. *J. Am. med. Ass.*, *165*, 1813–1818.

Monteith, J. L. (1974) Specification of the environment for thermal physiology. In: *Heat Loss from Animals and Man*, ed. J. L. Monteith & L. E. Mount, p. 3. London: Butterworth.

Morales, P., Carbery, W., Morello, A. & Morales, G. (1957) Alterations in renal function during hypothermia in man. *Ann. Surg.*, *145*, 488–499.

Myhre, L. G. & Robinson, S. (1977) Fluid shifts during thermal stress with and without fluid replacement. *J. appl. Physiol.*, *42*, 252–256.

Natalino, M. R., Zwillich, C. W. & Weil, J. V. (1977) Effects of hyperthermia on hypoxic ventilatory response in thermal man. *J. Lab. clin. Med.*, *89*, 564–572.

Nisbet, H. I. A (1964) Acid–base disturbance in hypothermia. *Int. Anesth. Clin.*, *2*, 829–855.

Opie, L. H. (1974) FFA lipolysis in acute myocardial infarction. *Lancet*, *1*, 621

Peterson, E. S. & Vejby-Christensen, H. (1977) Effects of body temperature on ventilatory response to hypoxia and breathing pattern in man. *J. appl. Physiol.*, *42*, 492–500.

Pettigrew, R. T. Galt, J. M., Ludgate, C. M. & Smith, A. N. (1974) Clinical effects of whole body hyperthermia in advanced malignancy. *Br. med. J.*, *4*, 679–682.

Pickering, B. G., Bristow, G. K. & Craig, D. B. (1977) Core rewarming by peritoneal irrigation in accidental hypothermia with cardiac arrest. *Anesth. Analg. (Cleve.)*, *56*, 574–557.

Popovic, V. & Popovic, P. (1974) *Hypothermia in Biology and Medicine*. New York: Grune and Stratton.

Price, H. V., Whelpton, D., & McCarthy, J. (1971) Newborn-infant heater. *Lancet*, *2*, 1294.

Rand, P. W., Lancombe, E., Hunt, H. E. & Austin, W. H. (1964) Viscosity of normal human blood under normothermic and hypothermic conditions. *J. appl. Physiol.*, *19*, 117–122.

Renold, A. E. & Cahill, G. F. (eds) (1965) *Handbook of Physiology*, p. 617. Washington, D.C.: American Physiological Society.

Rosenfeld, E. (1963) Acid–base and electrolyte disturbances in hypothermia. *Am. J. Cardiol.*, *12*, 678–682.

Rosenthal, T. B. (1948) The effect of temperature on pH of blood and plasma in vitro. *J. biol. Chem., 173*, 25.

Severinghaus, J. W. & Stupfel, M. (1955) Respiratory dead space increase following atropine in man, and atropine, vagal or ganglionic blockade and hypothermia in dogs. *J. appl. Physiol.*, *8*, 81–87.

Severinghaus, J. W., Stupfel, M. & Bradley, A. F. (1956) Variations of serum carbonic acid pK with pH and temperature. *J. appl. Physiol.*, *9*, 197–200.

Silverman, J. J. & Wilson, J. E. (1950) An unusual complication following thyroidectomy: heatstroke with permanent cerebellar damage. *Ann. int. Med.*, *33*, 1036–1041.

Sinclair, J. C. (1972) Thermal control of premature infants. *A. Rev. Med.*, *23*, 129–148.

Slotkoff, L. M., Eisner, G. M. & Lilienfield, L. S. (1963) Sodium and water reabsorption in the cold kidney. *Circulation*, *28*, 806–807.

Smith, R. E. & Horwitz, B. A. (1969) Brown fat and thermogenesis. *Physiol. Rev.*, *49*, 330–414.

Swan, H., Jenkins, D. & Helmreich, M. L. (1957) The adrenal cortical response to surgery. III: Changes in plasma and urinary corticosteroid levels during hypothermia in man. *Surgery, St. Louis*, *42*, 202–207.

Taggart, P., Parkinson, P. & Carruthers, M. (1972) Cardiac responses to thermal, physical and emotional stress. *Br. med. J.*, *3*, 71–76.

Thomas, D. J. & Green, I. D. (1973) Periodic hypothermia. *Br. med. J.*, *2*, 696–697.

Vandam, L. D. & Burnap, T. K. (1959) Hypothermia. *New Engl. J. Med.*, *261*, 546–595.

Vejby-Christensen, H. & Peterson, E. S. (1973) Effect of body temperature and hypoxia on the ventilatory CO_2 response in man. *Resp. Physiol.*, *19*, 322–332.

Wakim, K. G. (1964) Bodily reactions to high temperature. *Anesthesiology*, *25*, 532–548.

Wilkinson, R. T., Fox, R. H., Goldsmith, R., Hampton, I. F. G. & Lewis, H. E. (1964) Psychological and physiological responses to raised body temperature. *J. appl. Physiol.*, *19*, 287–291.

Wilson, O., Hedner, P., Laurell, S., Nosslin, B., Rerup, C. & Rosengren, E. (1970) Thyroid and adrenal response to acute cold exposure in man. *J. appl. Physiol.*, *28*, 543–549.

Wyndham, C. H., Strydom, N. B., Morrison, J. F., Williams, C. G., Bredell, G. A. G., Maritz, J. S. & Monro, A. (1965) Criteria for physiological limits for work in heat. *J. appl. Physiol.*, *20*, 37–45.

Yu, Y. S. & Jackson, R. (1974) Neonatal hypothermia in Australia. *Practitioner*, *213*, 790–794.

Methods of measuring body temperature   2

A sensation of warmth or cold is obtained when we touch an object which has a temperature different from that of our own skin. Temperature sensitivity in the hand varies according to the thickness of the skin: it may give accuracy to within ±1°C, but this is not accurate enough for clinical use.

It was John Hunter in 1776 who began the practice of measuring body temperature by means of a mercury-in-glass thermometer placed under the tongue. Where single recordings of normal body temperature have to be made, mercury-in-glass thermometers are still most frequently used. Where multiple temperature recordings are required from different body sites, others physical principles have to be employed. In anaesthetic practice electrical temperature measuring systems are often encountered and although an instrument with a direct read-out of temperature may be used, where prolonged or minute-by-minute recordings are necessary a recording device which will plot temperature against time is desirable.

Temperature Range of Humans
The upper lethal limit of the body temperature is between 42 and 43°C. The lower limit has not been adequately defined. Large gradients in temperature may be set up in the body during accidental or induced hypothermia: multiple temperature measurement becomes mandatory in hypothermia and hyperthermia to obtain as accurate a picture as possible of the thermal condition of the patient.

The temperature range of the very young is more limited than that of adults and accuracy in measurement of the temperature of infants and their environment is correspondingly more important (Day et al. 1964).

TEMPERATURE SCALES
A thermometer scale usually involves the selection of two suitable fixed temperatures to which numbers can be assigned. Between these defined temperatures a system of increments is chosen, the divisions of which are proportional to the corresponding increments in the measured pro-

perty. The boiling points and freezing points of pure liquids are constant at a standard pressure and in the seventeenth and eighteenth centuries they were used as the two fixed points for the temperature scales. The centigrade scale, devised by Celsius in 1742, divides the interval between the lower fixed point (the melting point of ice, taken as 0°C) and the upper fixed point (the boiling point of water, taken as 100°C) into 100 divisions. On the Fahrenheit scale this range is divided into 180 points between 32°F and 212°F. The Réaumur scale divides the same range into 80 degrees, the melting point of ice being taken as zero.

According to the second law of thermodynamics the thermodynamic temperature has a lowest value below which it cannot fall, and which can be given the value zero: the 'absolute zero' of thermodynamics. Lord Kelvin (1824–1907) accordingly devised a temperature scale on which bodies at 0° would have no heat left in them.

The Gas Thermometer

In designing a thermometer, a property of matter has to be chosen which varies with temperature. A criticism of the original temperature scales has been that although for example the expansion of a liquid and the electrical resistance of a wire vary systematically with temperature, scales based on these phenomena cannot have identical increments because they are not closely related properties. There is an arbitrary international scale which defines temperature changes as being proportional to changes in pressure in a constant-volume hydrogen thermometer of special design with the pressure of the gas specified at the ice-point. All other thermometers are now calibrated against this instrument or a suitable substitute.

SI Units

The thirteenth General Conference on Weights and Measures in October 1967 defined the base unit of thermodynamic temperature as the Kelvin (K) which is 1/273·16 of the thermodynamic temperature of the triple point of water, i.e. the point at which the solid, liquid and gaseous phases of pure water are in equilibrium. The relations of the Celsius and Fahrenheit scales to the Kelvin scale are given in Table II.

Table II: Comparison of the Kelvin, Celsius (Centigrade) and Fahrenheit Scales

Unit	Symbol	Absolute zero	Temperature value at triple point of water
Degree Kelvin	°K	0	273·16
Degree Celsius	°C	−273·16	0·01
Degree Fahrenheit	°F	−459·67	32·02

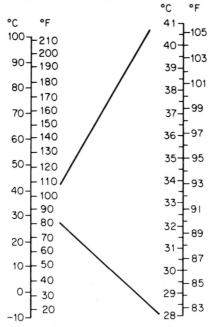

Fig. 14. A Comparison of Celsius and Fahrenheit Scales

Conversion of Temperature Units

$$1°K = 1°C = \tfrac{9}{5}°F$$

$$t°C = \tfrac{5}{9}(t°F - 32)$$

$$t°F = (t°C \times \tfrac{9}{5}) + 32$$

A nomogram for the conversion of temperatures from the Celsius to the Fahrenheit scale (and vice versa) is given in Figure 14.

Table III: Types of Thermometer

Type	Accuracy (°C)	Use	Cost	Comments
Glass thermometer	±0·2	Oral, rectal	Cheap	Fragile
Resistance coil	±0·1	Skin	Expensive	Large temperature range
Thermistor	±0·1	All sites	Cheap	Small, high sensitivity, fragile
Thermocouple	±0·1	All sites	Moderate	Versatile
Liquid crystals	±0·3	Skin	Cheap	Simple
Infra-red	±0·3	Oral, rectal	Very expensive	Complex

THERMOMETERS

The ideal thermometer should be convenient, accurate, harmless and unbreakable, have a fast response, be suitable for many sites and for remote recording and produce a permanent record. The various types of thermometers available are given in Table III. They are classified below according to the principles involved in their design.

Direct Measurement

Expansion	Mercury or liquid in glass
	Dial thermometer
Electrical	*Resistance thermometers*
	Resistance coil
	Thermistor
	Thermocouple
Chemical	Liquid crystal
Magnetic	

Indirect Measurement

Radiometer

Mercury or Liquid in Glass

Liquids expand with an increase in temperature. Mercury, pentane or alcohol have been used, sealed in a reservoir connected to a capillary tube of constant cross-sectional area. Mercury is commonly chosen in clinical practice, combining as it does the following characteristics: rapid heat conduction, low freezing and high boiling point (−40 and +357°C), a uniform large expansion with each unit rise in temperature, good visibility and cohesiveness in glass. Accurate mercury-in-glass thermometers are tested by the National Physical Laboratory, and are used to calibrate electrical thermometers.

Clinical thermometers are designed with a constriction between the reservoir and read-out scale. This and the surface tension prevent the mercury from returning to the reservoir and the addition of a 'lens' front further facilitates the reading. After use the liquid must be shaken down into the reservoir. Occasionally, if the constriction is not small enough, mercury returns to the bulb and the thermometer under-reads. If the constriction is too small the mercury column does not rise steadily, but in small jumps. The response time is about 90 sec in the body cavities since heat conduction is poor. The display is linear, but rapid recordings are impossible because of the relatively high thermal capacity of the materials. The extent of the display scale is limited by the length of the readout tube, and thermometers for clinical use are usually calibrated from 34 or 35°C at the lower reading to 41 or 42°C at the upper reading so that they cannot be used to diagnose hypothermia or hyperthermia.

Knapp (1966) found that ward thermometers may have inherent errors of up to 0·5°C at temperatures in the normal body temperature range and even greater errors at higher temperatures. Thus, the glass thermometer is least accurate when the patient is febrile. Using different thermometers compounds any error, so that the same thermometer should be used for the same patient (Robertson 1968). Other disadvantages of mercury-in-glass thermometers include fragility, unsuitability for remote reading or recording, and the limited number of body sites where it can be used. All liquid expansion thermometers should be cleaned using detergent or soap and then a cold sterilizing agent.

Dial Thermometer

Bimetallic Spring. Two dissimilar metals will expand by different amounts for the same increase in temperature. If they are welded together to form a spiral spring it will wind or unwind on heating: for example a brass and iron spring with brass on the inside will straighten on heating. One end of the spring is fixed and the other is attached to a pointer which moves on a dial graduated in degrees. This type of thermometer is not very accurate, but can be used to measure theatre temperatures, set off alarm systems or regulate the flow of gas through a vaporizer. Corrosion may be a problem.

Pressure Gauge (Bourdon Tube). This instrument measures pressure. It is made from a hollow tube of metal in the form of a spring which unwinds as the pressure inside it increases. A gas such as freon is used, or alternatively mercury in a steel tube or a volatile liquid in contact with its saturated vapour (Dornette 1965). The sensory element is large. The pressure changes produced by the active element have to be calibrated against their equivalent temperature units. Only moderate accuracy ($\pm 0\cdot3$°C) is obtained and the lower temperature range which can be measured is limited. However, a pressure gauge can be used for remote recording and there is a fairly rapid response (Hill 1959).

Resistance Coil

The resistance of a wire varies with temperature. Platinum, copper and nickel are used in resistance thermometry in the form of wires made into coils. The coils are wound non-inductively on a special former, sealed to stop contamination and supported in a strain-free condition. Their resistance decreases progressively as the temperature is lowered. Platinum is preferred because it resists corrosion at ordinary temperatures and has a large temperature coefficient of resistance—0·004 per degree centigrade—so that a 100 ohm resistance coil changes resistance by 0·4 ohm for a temperature change of 1°C. The resistance varies according to the formula:

$$R_t = R_0 (1 + \alpha t)$$

where

t = measured temperature

α = coefficient of resistance of the particular metal

R_0 = resistance at 0°C

R_t = resistance at t°C

R_0 and α are constants which are known for a particular coil. When R_t is measured, t can be calculated.

The resistance scale of temperature is linear over the clinical range but in the past the temperature probes used to be bulky, slow to respond, and difficult to mount in a needle. This has been overcome by using metal alloys. Multiple records can be made easily and the method is applicable over a wide range of temperature measurement (−200°C to 600°C).

In designing a suitable circuit (Figure 15), the constant resistances may be wound with a thermostable metal such as constantan, which has a negligible temperature coefficient of resistance. A dummy of the same material as the measuring coil is placed in the opposite arm of the bridge to the true leads, in order to cancel errors which may occur in the connecting leads to the coil. The current in the circuit is usually limited to avoid self-heating. This means that for a 100 ohm resistance coil, a current of 1 mA will produce a change in voltage of about 400 μV per °C. This cannot be measured easily in the bridge circuit shown and more complicated bridges are usually used. Occasionally stray thermocouple junctions develop within the circuit, but if the circuit current is large enough these will be negligible: a typical thermocouple output is only 40 μV per °C. The accuracy of the resistance coil thermometer can be as great as ±0·001°C.

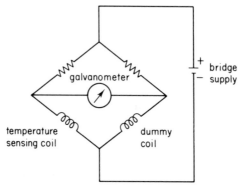

Fig. 15. Circuit Diagram of a Resistance Thermometer

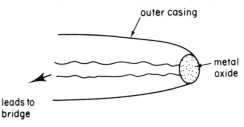

Fig. 16. A Thermistor Probe

Thermistor

A thermistor has a semiconducting element of a heavy metal oxide which has a large negative temperature coefficient of resistance. The oxide may be of cobalt, nickel, manganese, iron or zinc or a combination of these. The oxide is compressed to a bead and sintered at a high temperature to form a solid mass to which electrodes are attached. The measuring tip is very small (less than 0·1 mm) and may be sealed into a thin glass probe, stainless steel cover or cardiac catheter (Figure 16).

A thermistor probe undergoes a large change in resistance with changes in temperature. Its thermal capacity is very small and so its response to a temperature change is rapid – a fraction of a second. A probe cover can increase response time to about 30 sec. The oxide resistance falls as the temperature rises but the relation is non-linear: resistance varies exponentially and inversely with the absolute temperature, giving an equation of the form

$$\text{Resistance (ohms)} = A^{(B/\text{Absolute Temperature})}$$

where A and B are constants. In a suitable bridge circuit this non-linearity can be overcome (Cliffe 1962). Typical values of resistance are 1400 ohms at 40°C and 2000 ohms at 20°C. This large change in resistance with temperature makes the thermistor very sensitive. Temperatures may be recorded by this method throughout the range −80°C to +150°C but ranges are usually limited in order to improve the linearity of response. The resistance of the oxide increases with time (the precise cause is uncertain) and recalibration may be necessary if the instrument is subjected to abnormal temperatures. If kept at 40°C thermistors remain accurate to 0·5°C for many years (Trolander & Sterling, 1962). Multiple recording is not easy because it is difficult to reproduce probes exactly like each other. The probes can be used remote from the site of recording and can be made into transmitters.

Thermocouple

When a circuit is made up of two dissimilar metals and the two junctions are maintained at different temperatures, a current (I) is set up in the

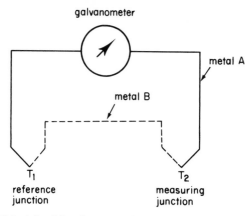

Fig. 17. *The Principle of the Thermocouple*

circuit and is proportional to the temperature difference between the two junctions (Figure 17):

$$I \propto T_1 - T_2$$

where I = current and T_1, T_2 are the temperatures of the junctions. This is the Seebeck effect, which was described in 1821. It is usually necessary to maintain one of the junctions, the *reference junction*, at a constant temperature so that the other can be used to measure a fluctuating temperature. This can be achieved in a number of ways.

1. The temperature of the reference junction can be maintained at 0°C in ice, but this is inconvenient.

2. The reference junction can be maintained at a constant ambient temperature using a thermostatically controlled oven.

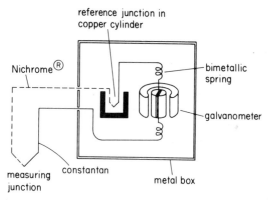

Fig. 18. *A Thermocouple Circuit Incorporating a Mechanically Compensated Reference Junction*

3. Mechanical compensation is obtained by using a bimetallic suspension for the galvanometer: a commonly used clinical thermometer using this principle is illustrated in Figure 18. The reference junction is maintained at ambient temperature in a small copper cylinder and is situated near a moving coil galvanometer. The instrument uses a reflected light beam as a pointer and the scale is calibrated directly in temperature. The galvanometer has to be clamped during transportation. Two bimetallic helical springs suspend the galvanometer and compensate for room temperature changes. The instrument is enclosed in a stout metal box. It has a temperature range of 0–50°C or 16–46°C.

Alternatively an electrical zero may be used. A bridge circuit is used in which three of the four resistances are made of resistance wire which undergoes only a small change of resistance with temperature. The fourth resistance has a high temperature resistance coefficient. This arrangement can be used in recording instruments.

When the other junction, the *measuring junction*, is exposed to a series of known temperatures, a calibration chart can be obtained.

Within the region of temperatures normally encountered in medicine the electromotive force generated in the circuit is linearly related to the temperature difference between the two junctions. The combination of copper and constantan (60% copper, 40% nickel) produces 40 μV/°C with one junction at 0°C and the other at 38°C. This is measured by a galvanometer or a potentiometer.

The choice of metals for the circuit depends on the cost and sensitivity of the instrument. Copper and constantan can be used to measure sub-zero temperatures. Iron and constantan are cheap and generate a larger electromotive force but iron rusts in moist atmospheres. Platinum and rhodium can be used for very precise work.

The measuring voltage may be affected by a number of factors. Any change in temperature of the wires away from the junction will alter the measured temperature (Krog 1962), so thermocouple wires must be insulated from the sheath of the probe. The law of intermediate metals states that provided the temperature remains unchanged over its length, a wire of any different metal may be placed in one part of the leads joining the two thermal junctions without changing the overall electromotive force. This requires zero variation in temperature at the galvanometer terminals. The design of the thermometer shown in Figure 19 illustrates this point. All connectors to the thermocouple should be thermally insulated.

The small voltage output per degree Celsius may also be affected by small changes in resistance in the outer circuit. In commercial instruments a balancing component, i.e. a variable resistor, may be incorporated but this makes the controls more complicated to operate.

Thermocouple junctions are small and versatile and give a rapid response because of a low thermal capacity. Highly reproducible temperature recordings can be produced but the length of the leads may be restrictive. The accuracy of most instruments is within ±0·1°C. This can be increased by careful selection of thermocouple materials and by heat treatment to bring them to their most stable condition.

Recording Instruments

Using the law of intermediate metals a recording circuit for a thermocouple can be developed (Figure 19) which can be connected to a potentiometric recorder. A potentiometer is an instrument for measuring electrical quantities by balancing an unknown potential difference against a known potential difference. A length of resistance wire or coil, AB, is supplied with a constant current from a large capacity dry cell with a known voltage. The unknown voltage to be measured, e.g. from the thermocouple, is applied between the sliding contact C and one end of the wire, A. In a self-balancing recorder a servo-mechanism balances the recorder automatically: any voltage difference between the voltage to be measured and the voltage at the sliding contact causes an electric motor to operate. The direction of the motor's rotation is dependent on the direction of current in the system and it will move until a balance is obtained and no current flows in the circuit. These instruments are used industrially and are reliable.

Liquid Crystal

Strips impregnated with micro-encapsulated chloresteric liquid crystals can be applied to any easily visible surface and their colour code

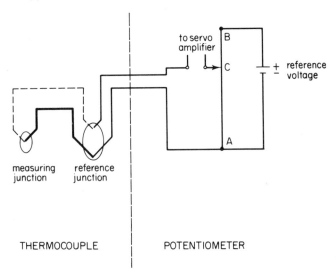

Fig. 19. A Recording Circuit for a Thermocouple

indicates the temperature. The minimum temperature change which can be detected is 0·3°C (Lees et al. 1978). They are used clinically as temperature-trend indicators that would indicate the need for more sophisticated monitoring, e.g. to detect hyperthermia or hypothermia. The range of a commercially produced indicator is 34·5–40·0°C in six equal divisions.

Magnetic

The magnetic flux density of certain ferrous alloys vary inversely to their temperature. To produce a thermometric probe the alloy is bonded to a disc of silver which makes contact with the skin. The method has been used clinically (Dornette 1965).

Indirect Methods

Indirect methods of measuring temperature are used when a thermometer cannot be brought into direct contact with an object. In industrial processes infrared pyrometers are used. Results may be affected by the pressure of gas or vapour between the heat source and the sensor.

Radiometer

The radiant heat emitted from a body can be measured indirectly by temperature-sensing methods or photon-sensing devices. Clinical thermography uses thermistors with a rapid response. The method is limited to the measurement of comparative and not absolute temperatures, in still air, of a body with a relatively static temperature. A photon-sensitive material such as indium antimonide is used in the thermographic scanning of tumours and vascular occlusions.

MEAN BODY TEMPERATURE

The temperature of a body is a measure of the kinetic energy it contains. It may be raised by the addition of heat or lowered by the loss of it. The unit of heat is the joule (J): 4·184 joules − 1 calorie. The joule is related to the SI base units by the formula

$$\text{joule (J)} = \text{newton (N)} \times \text{metre (m)}$$

i.e. the joule has the dimensions $m^2 \, kg \, s^{-2}$.

The human body contains many temperature gradients from the deep organs, where most of the basal metabolic heat is produced, to the more superficial tissues. Core temperature may be lowered even when the total quantity of body heat remains unchanged because of redistribution to the periphery (Holdcroft et al. 1979). A working model for assessing total body heat is needed which takes into account the temperatures of the central and peripheral tissues. Burton (1935) derived an equation for the mean body temperature using the mean skin

temperature and the rectal temperature as a measure of core body
temperature.

mean body temperature =
  (0·66 × rectal temperature) + (0·34 × mean skin temperature)   *Eq. 1*

The thermal environment will affect the measurement of mean skin
temperature. Gagge et al. (1941) assume an ambient temperature of
more than 21°C for thermal equations which have no corrections for air
temperature, wind velocity and type of clothing. The critical surface
factor for non-evaporative heat loss is the skin temperature, whether or
not the person is clothed. Skin temperature reflects blood flow to the
skin, but is also dependent on the blood temperature, the insulation
between the blood and the skin and the heat flow from the surface.
There is a large individual variation in tissue insulation which is
important when blood flow to the skin is reduced. Cannon and Keatinge
(1960) found that it is directly related to the percentage of fat in the
individual. Fat is not metabolically inert, however, and may itself
contribute to peripheral heat gain.

Burton calculated Equation 1 on a theoretical basis, excluding the
limbs. He gave a theoretical weighting of 0·8 to the core and 0·2 to the
surface temperature. When he included approximations for the arms
and legs he amended these figures to 0·66 and 0·34, respectively. The
resulting equation was tested experimentally using a calorimeter and
these weightings were found to be adequate.

Calorimetery is usually only applicable to situations in which body
heat exchange approaches a steady state. Body heat loss, by radiation
and convection, is measured by classical respiratory calorimetry using a
chamber around which water circulates. Any increase in the temperature
of this water can be related to the heat loss of the individual inside the
chamber. The main source of error in this method is heat loss from the
chamber to the surroundings and this is prevented by maintaining a
zero temperature gradient between the inner and outer walls of the
calorimeter. Insensible heat loss by evaporation is measured gravi-
metrically by absorption of water vapour in sulphuric acid. The oxygen
consumed and carbon dioxide produced by the subject are also
measured. A single calorimetric measurement takes a minimum of 20
minutes. Partition calorimetry and gradient calorimetry were designed
to overcome some of the slowness of this original method, but they are
still research tools (Houghton et al. 1929; Benzinger et al. 1958).

Traditionally, the core temperature has been the rectal temperature
but work by Benzinger and Taylor (1963) suggests that the oesophageal
(if the probe is correctly placed) and tympanic temperatures are more
accurate. Rectal temperature change is too slow to reflect rapid changes
in body heat content but it may have a role as a measure of the
temperature changes in poorly perfused tissues. The use of the tympanic

or oesophageal temperatures is open to criticism. Tympanic temperature can either lag behind oesophageal temperature or be equivalent to it and it may in certain circumstances merely be a measure of the temperature of the superficial tissues. The oesophageal temperature can be inaccurate if the measuring device is not correctly placed.

A formula has been proposed by Stolwijk and Hardy (1966) combining the tympanic membrane temperature with the mean skin temperature in a ratio of 9 : 1:

mean body temperature =
    (0·9 × tympanic temperature) + (0·1 × mean skin temperature)   *Eq. 2*

The weighting for the mean skin temperature is reduced because this equation is meant to apply to rapidly changing body temperatures. However this formula gives an underestimate of mean body temperature during heating and alterations in weighting factors do not change this inaccuracy. Minard (1970) suggests that in these circumstances the tympanic temperature would be less accurate than the correct oesophageal temperature because countercooling effects of venous blood returning to the head may affect the measurement.

The accuracy of Equation 1 lies in the individual temperature measurements. Skin temperature contributes approximately one-third to the total bodily heat (corresponding to the coefficient 0·34), but it has a greater range than the core temperature. The equation's coefficients are influenced by environmental and behavioural conditions and also by the weightings given to the various tissues, e.g. fat and muscle, but these factors may be less important if all that is required are the changes in the mean body temperature. This is an important concept in the derivation of the total body heat equation.

The other basic concept to consider is the site of production of heat. At rest the muscle mass contributes only 20% of the total heat production although it is a major part of the body mass in most individuals. When muscle heat production is increased, which can be tenfold, the source of heat is near to the surface of the body and heat loss is consequently increased.

No one formula therefore best suits all conditions of the human body and no equation is valid for such conditions as water immersion. Equation 1 (Burton 1935) still has the widest application but its assumptions must be borne in mind. Reliable estimates of mean body temperature outside the conditions necessary to this equation can only be made by total body calorimetry.

Total Body Heat

Changes in mean body temperature can be derived easily and accurately from the difference between heat produced and heat eliminated over a particular period of time.

$$\text{change in body temperature} = \frac{\text{heat produced} - \text{heat lost}}{\text{body weight} \times \text{specific heat}} \qquad Eq.\ 3$$

This formula can alternatively be used to calculate the specific heat of body tissues. Burton (1935) did not find a workable average value but a range from 0·7 to 0·9. Hardy and Du Bois (1938a) found values between 0·72 and 0·83. In practice the specific heat of a whole living human body is regarded as constant at a value of around 0·83. Colin et al. (1971) have confirmed the validity of this assumption and the total body heat can be calculated from the following equation:

$$\text{total body heat} = \text{mean body temp.} \times \text{specific heat of body} \times \text{mass}$$

$$\text{i.e. total body heat} = T°C \times 0·83 \times 4·18 \times \text{weight (kg)} \qquad Eq.\ 4$$

$$\text{where } T°C = \text{mean body temperature}$$

This indirect measurement can be verified by calorimetry, but this is time-consuming and the apparatus is not applicable to clinical measurements. Observation of the change in body temperatures requires the selection of sites of temperature measurement which best reflect the loss or gain in body heat content. The use of such measurements may help to elucidate changes in thermoregulatory control during anaesthesia and surgery and to provide an indication of the thermal 'stress' to which a patient is exposed.

BODY TEMPERATURE MEASURING SITES

Measurements should be taken at convenient points on the body where there is least risk to the patient and no structures which may interfere with good thermal contact. Measurements should not cause pain. Temperature at the site should not be influenced by local blood flow or by environmental temperature changes. Electrical safety is essential to avoid burns or electrocution (Schneider et al. 1977).

Prolonged recording of body temperature may be a necessity when a subject is exposed to an adverse environment, e.g. during space exploration, or is severely ill, in the case of burns for example. Rectal and oral sites have not proved satisfactory for prolonged measurements because of a number of factors. Temperature recording needs to be precisely reproducible at each site so that day-to-day variations are meaningful. This cannot be guaranteed when the gastrointestinal orifices are used. The passage of food and faeces will be an inconvenience at these sites. A dry, clean site will also be preferable to a moist, potentially infected one.

The first skin sensors were developed by Tepas and Vianello (1966). They were attached to the chest by a harness, but more recently with the development of liquid crystal thermography lightweight discs can be stuck semi-permanently onto a visible skin surface and the temperature monitored continuously (Lees et al. 1978). Continuous aural temperature monitoring can be used when a more accurate measure of body temperature is needed. Wilson et al. (1971) found this an acceptable method even in conscious children and Keatinge and Sloan (1973), using a probe which was incorporated into an ear pad and head harness, confirmed that this method was suitable for mobile patients and comfortable for long-term monitoring.

Oronasal

The mouth is the most easily located orifice. It is customary to position the measuring tip of the thermometer sublingually to achieve the closest possible contact with the mucous membranes. Oral temperatures depend on the mouth being closed both before and during the period of measurement. Temperature recording at this site is affected by mouth-breathing, the intake of food and the willingness of the patient to cooperate. The normal range is from 35·9 to 37·2°C (Robertson 1968). The method is not practical for an anaesthetized patient and oral temperature readings are misleading when taken in low or high ambient temperature conditions.

The nasopharyngeal temperature could be measured in the unconscious patient with a mercury-in-glass thermometer, but to avoid the danger of breakage electronic thermometers are used. The temperature at the back of the pharynx follows that of the brain, especially the hypothalamus. There is a danger of epistaxis and trauma to the mucosa.

Rectal

Rectal temperature recordings in a conscious individual are uncomfortable, but this site is preferable to the oral one in children. However, mercury-in-glass thermometers can cause injury to the rectum (bleeding and ulceration) and an electronic sensor is preferred. An adult electronic probe is 5·5 × 44 mm with a ball stop to prevent extrusion (Figure 20). A smaller probe should be used for infants and the probe should be well greased and not inserted with force. In the neonate, the possibility of rectal atresia should be excluded. The position required to achieve the best results can be difficult to find because the probe often curls round. Mead and Bonmarito (1949) found that there was a gradient of temperature in the anus and a long length of probe passed through the external anal sphincter often recorded a lower temperature than a shorter length. If the probe is inserted deep into the pelvis, cold blood returning from the lower extremities may give a misleadingly low temperature recording (Severinghaus 1962). The method cannot be used during pelvic operations for similar reasons. Faeces in the rectum can act as an insulator and produce a markedly delayed response. The normal range of readings obtained is from 36·9 to 37·7°C.

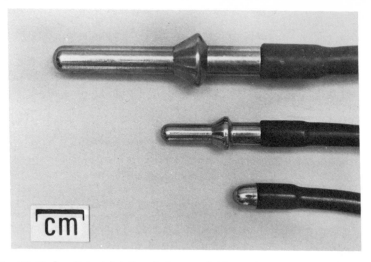

Fig. 20. Probes. Top, Adult Rectal. Centre, Child Rectal. Bottom, Oesophageal

Oesophageal

This site can be comfortably used only when the patient is unconscious. The probe is smaller in diameter than the rectal probe and has no protrusions. It can be introduced either orally or nasally, but before passing it an estimate of its required position in the oesophagus should be made. It should be inserted into the lower fourth of the oesophagus (Whitby & Dunkin 1968), i.e. at least 24 cm below the corniculate cartilages in adults and in the lower mediastinum, below the pulmonary veins. Lateral variation of temperature in the oesophagus can be a problem, but usually it is the longitudinal placement that gives the larger variation (up to 6°C). Incorrect temperature recordings are obtained higher in the oesophagus because of the proximity of the trachea which can be ventilated by cold or warm gases. Oesophageal temperature indicates myocardial or aortic temperature but its accuracy is affected by surgical procedures, e.g. thoracotomy (Cooper & Kenyon 1957) and it cannot be used in operations on the oesophagus, or when substances are passed into, through or round it. Probes may be displaced during intubation and extubation and if they pass into the stomach they may reflect the hepatic temperature, which is usually higher than true core temperature. The normal range of readings is from 36·9 to 37·7°C.

Skin

Any object in contact with the skin may alter its temperature. Skin probes may be in the form of loops or flat metal discs (Figure 21). They require close application but should not be applied with any material

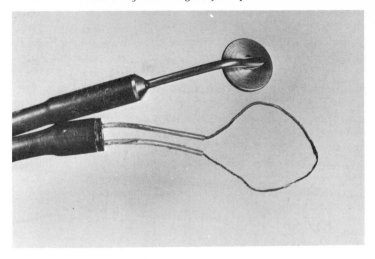

Fig. 21. Skin Probes. Solid Type (top) and Loop Type

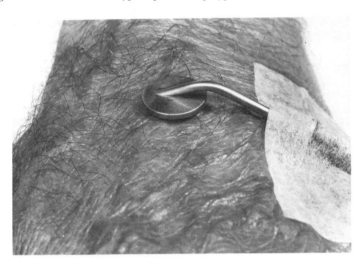

Fig. 22. Method of Application of a Skin Probe
Strapping attached to the temperature-sensing part of the probe can affect the reading. A suitable alternative is pictured here.

that will affect skin temperature (Figure 22). This is difficult to achieve in practice because adhesive tape provides insulation. Measurement of skin temperature with a radiometer or thermistor does not give a direct reading and can only compare a known surface temperature with an unknown one.

Skin thermometry is used in the diagnosis of peripheral vascular diseases, and in the evaluation of an effective sympathetic block. Different sites for measuring skin temperature are compared below.

Axilla

This site is the most stable for measurement of skin temperature. The arm needs to be abducted before the thermometer is positioned. The normal range of measurements obtained is from 35·3 to 36·7°C (Robertson 1968). The reading is usually 0·5°C lower than the oral temperature and 1°C lower than the rectal temperature (Kuzucu 1965). It is affected by pressure applied to the skin and by sweat production: a pressure of 4 g on the skin due to a thermometer can raise the temperature by 1°C. The groin as a skin temperature measuring site has similar features.

Abdominal

This position is used on premature infants and neonates and is a safe place to determine an infant's temperature. The temperature is 0·1–0·4°C below core temperature. It can be used to control radiation from an infra-red heater (Miller & Oliver 1966; Levison et al. 1966). The normal range of readings obtained is from 37·7 to 39·9°C.

Forehead

The introduction of liquid crystal thermometry has made available an inexpensive method of measuring intraoperative and postoperative hyperthermia. The coated plastic strip can be stuck to the skin of the forehead and in certain circumstances the reading obtained is linearly related to oesophageal temperature (Lees et al. 1978). The temperature of the forehead or some other suitable, visible, well perfused skin site may be monitored routinely in all patients to indicate the need to use other sites or other temperature monitoring techniques.

Great Toe

The temperature of the skin of the big toe is almost totally dependent on cutaneous blood flow because of the lack of tissue insulation or metabolism. Ambient conditions can be eliminated by covering the toe with a gauze pad and its temperature has been used as an additional index of cardiovascular status during trauma and major operations. Joly and Weil (1969) observed a correlation between cardiac output and the temperature of the toe in patients who presented with clinical signs of circulatory shock. In addition to assessing blood flow, big toe temperature appeared to be a guide to prognosis.

They also studied three other skin sites; the digital pad of the third finger, the deltoid region of the arm and the lateral portion of the thigh. The finger showed similar correlation with the cardiac output. This study is open to the criticism that a single skin temperature measurement such as that of the big toe is only a useful adjunct to other more vital monitors of tissue perfusion.

Eberhart and Trezek (1973) have described the temperature changes which occur in the first postoperative hours following rewarming from cardiac surgery. The patient is vasoconstricted and cool, but gradually rewarms centrally until the central temperature set point is reached. Then the thermoregulatory system begins to initiate mechanisms for the dissipation of heat and skin temperature rises. Failure of the skin temperature to rise, in the absence of drug administration, ambient temperature variations and peripheral vascular disease, indicates either cardiovascular or central thermoregulatory dysfunction. In the four postoperative cases which were studied, there was a large variation between different patients in the rewarming pattern of the digits. They found that rewarming was affected by thermoregulation, cardiac output and drug action: this confirms the limited usefulness of an isolated peripheral skin temperature measurement.

Mean Skin Temperature

The mean skin temperature is the average temperature of the skin over the whole body. This cannot be measured precisely. Mitchell and Wyndham (1969) used the mean value of fifteen measurements which were recorded from the following sites: forehead, nipple, outer upper arm, waist, outer lower arm, dorsum hand, anterior thigh, outer calf, top of the foot, back of the neck, scapula, posterior iliac crest, posterior thigh, posterior calf and inner thigh.

The accuracy of this calculation can be increased by weighting the various skin temperatures by factors which are supposedly equivalent to the fraction of the total surface area which that particular temperature represents. In 1936 Winslow et al. described a 15-site weighted formula which was subsequently used as a reference formula by Shanks (1975) to compare various methods of measuring the mean skin temperature. Shanks found that the unweighted mean of skin temperatures at 15 sites was within 0·2°C of the reference formula in 93% of patients, who were anaesthetized and ventilated mechanically. When he used formulae for which the number of measuring sites was less than 15 – the 12-site formula from Hardy and Du Bois 1938b; the 10-site formula from Colin and Houdas 1965; the four-site formula

$$T = 0·3 \, (\text{nipple} + \text{arm}) + 0·2 \, (\text{thigh} + \text{calf})$$

(Ramanathan 1964) – he found that, despite appropriate weighting factors, the accuracy of mean skin temperature measurement was compromised. The maximum correlation with the reference formula was obtained when changes in mean skin temperatures rather than absolute values were compared. The four-site formula then gave results as accurate as those of the 10-site formula. The use of a large number of skin temperature probes during anaesthesia reduces access to the patient for surgery and is technically difficult to manage: a reduction in the number of probes may be necessary for these reasons.

The comparative work by Shanks (1975) examined only one technique of anaesthesia and may not have allowed for rapid redistribution of the body's heat during the circulatory changes which occur during recovery from anaesthesia. Different types of anaesthetics were used in the study by Holdcroft and Hall (1978) and patients were studied preoperatively, intraoperatively and postoperatively. It was found that the four-site formula of Ramanathan (1964) is only likely to differ by 0.2°C from the mean skin temperature of 15 unweighted sites at 33°C, which is the normal mean skin temperature. This degree of agreement reflects the accuracy of the weightings which are applied to the four temperature measurements.

Clinically, the choice of a mean-skin-temperature formula should be made with three questions in mind. How many skin temperature probes are available? How much access will there be to various skin measuring sites? Will absolute values of temperature be required or will changes in mean temperature be adequate? When maximum accuracy is required and access to all parts of the body is available the 15-site formulae should be used but if conditions are not ideal the formula of Ramanathan (1964) is a suitable alternative for both anaesthetized and non-anaesthetized patients.

Muscle Probe

This probe is especially useful in a patient prone to or suffering from malignant hyperthermia. In design it is similar to an 18G needle but it is solid and is provided with a removable sheath. Its use would be painful to a conscious patient.

Ear Probe

The temperature of the ear can be measured either by positioning the measuring tip of the thermometer directly on the eardrum (this is termed the 'tympanic' temperature) or by allowing the probe to rest somewhere in the external auditory meatus (this is the 'aural' temperature).

Tympanic Temperature

The blood supply to the tympanic membrane comes from the external carotid artery and Benzinger and Taylor (1963) found that tympanic temperature was related to thermoregulatory responses to heat or cold and presumed that it closely reflected hypothalamic temperature. Rawson and Hammel (1963) demonstrated that rapid fluctuations in hypothalamic temperatures in monkeys closely paralleled tympanic membrane temperatures. Thermoregulation is controlled mainly in the hypothalamus, so a knowledge of this temperature is important both physiologically and clinically. For the purposes of clinical physiological research it would be helpful to have an easily accessible route to measure intracranial temperature in humans rather than to resort to direct measurements in animals. In practical terms, the two sites differ: the hypothalamus is an area of high metabolic activity which is cooled by the blood which supplies it and the tympanic membrane, with low metabolic heat production, is most probably warmed by arterial blood. Randall et al. (1963) occluded the carotid artery bilaterally in cats and observed that the anterior and posterior hypothalamic temperatures increased, whereas that of the tympanic membrane decreased. This does not mean that measurement of the tympanic membrane temperature is not a useful clinical tool, and attention has been focused on comparing this site with the oesophageal, rectal and oral sites. The temperature of the tympanic membrane can be assumed to reflect the temperature of the arterial blood flowing into the head (Benzinger 1969).

There are a number of problems associated with direct measurement of tympanic membrane temperature. It can be an uncomfortable procedure and may cause unnecessary structural damage and bleeding. Wallace et al. (1974) report perforation of the tympanic membrane following the positioning of a probe during anaesthesia. Any patient who has a history of ear problems should have an otoscopic examination prior to inserting the probe. Webb (1973) found that cerumen acts as an insulator and should be removed if accurate measurements are required. The temperature of the external auditory canal (aural temperature) may therefore be chosen in preference to traumatizing the tympanic membrane. However, measurements here will also be affected by cerumen and will also be contraindicated in situations where there is ear infection or previous middle ear surgery.

Aural Temperature

The external acoustic meatus extends from the concha to the tympanic membrane, a distance of about 2·5 cm. The medial two-thirds of the canal is enclosed in bone, the remainder in cartilage. In cross-section it is oval and because the tympanic membrane is positioned obliquely, the floor of the canal is longer than the roof: it forms an S-shaped curve. The skin of the canal is supplied by branches from the external carotid artery. Ceruminous glands secrete ear wax or cerumen which has a protective function. The warm, humid atmosphere within the external auditory meatus is essential for the mechanics of the tympanic membrane. The construction of the external auditory meatus allows a temperature gradient from the concha to the tympanic membrane. Thus the more distally the probe is positioned in the external auditory meatus, the less accurate is the measure of core body temperature.

In children the canal is almost the same diameter as in the adult but it represents only the fibrocartilagenous portion of the adult external auditory meatus. There is no bony meatus and this makes the tympanic membrane very superficial. Trauma is therefore more likely to follow misuse of an aural probe than it is with adults, but there have been no reports of such damage in children. The length of the canal in a neonate is no more than 10 mm and an aural probe can be inserted only half this distance with safety. Given that the probe is so superficial, draughts are more likely to affect the measurement of core body temperature by this route. Reports of misuse of the aural probe in children, where trauma is likely to be more common than in adults, have not occurred.

Cooper et al. (1964) evaluated the use of the external auditory meatal probe as a measure of central (core) temperature changes. They measured temperatures at four different positions in the external auditory meatus in an ear that was well protected from draughts. The maximum temperature difference between the most proximal and distal sites was 0·8°C. Despite a gradient of temperature, all the probes responded rapidly (in less than two minutes) and by the same amount to a change in body temperature induced by warming a limb. When warm saline was infused into the carotid artery there was a temperature rise in the ear on the side of the infusion only. Retrograde flow to the junction of the internal and external carotid artery may account for this finding. These workers concluded that temperature measurement at this site is an adequate substitute for more central methods.

Types of Probe

The adult tympanic or aural probe (Figure 23) is fitted with small stiff hairs 15 mm from its tip (some manufacturers allow for adjustment of the distance). These assist in its positioning in the external auditory meatus and allow the sensor to reset spontaneously after minor alterations in position. Its distal end may be prevented from traumatizing the tympanic membrane by a cotton wool tip: this type of probe is disposable. It is comfortable for prolonged temperature recordings in the conscious patient and unnecessary trauma is unlikely because of the discomfort it would cause to the patient. The auditory canal temperature can be used even in cold surroundings if adequate covering is used to protect the outer ear from draughts (Keatinge & Sloan 1973), but it is not enough to pad the ear with cotton wool. A portable commercial thermometer is available with a servo-controlled heating pad around the ear (Figure 24). The pad is heated electrically to within 0·2°C of the aural temperature and prevents local cooling. Keatinge and Sloan measured the aural temperature of ambulant

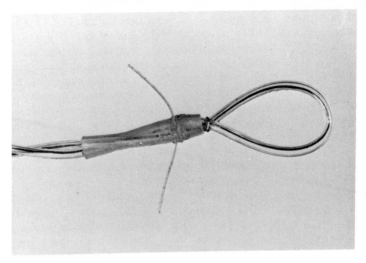

Fig. 23. *Aural Probe*

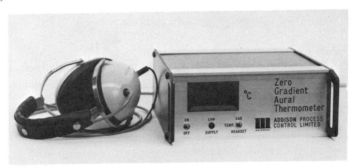

Fig. 24. *Aural Temperature Sensor with Local Heated Protection of the Outer Ear*

patients in ambient temperatures of 10–45°C and compared them with their oesophageal temperatures. The two temperatures, once the ear had warmed, were within 0·2°C of each other and there was less lag than when rectal temperatures were compared with oesophageal.

Urine
The temperature of freshly voided urine is about 0·2°C lower than the rectal temperature (Fox et al. 1973).

CHOICE OF TEMPERATURE-MEASURING DEVICE
In clinical practice we may need to know the temperature of apparatus, of patients and of their environment. 'Dial' thermometers are frequently

o measure the temperature of equipment but not to the exclusion
1er methods. The various types of thermometers available all have
ument error and even the most accurate can measure only at the site
at which it is positioned. The choice of temperature measuring device
should be appropriate to the site and type of use. For example, a highly
accurate and fast recording instrument is needed for the constantly
changing temperatures which occur in induced hypothermia, but will be
unnecessarily expensive for ward use. The errors inherent in any method
of measuring body temperature are compounded by the limitations of
the various sites of measurement. If measurements are to be comparable
and consistent there should be one standard site which can be used
preoperatively, intraoperatively and during the recovery period.

Cross-infection may be prevented by the use of disposable thermometer covers. Probes are double-covered, so that a contaminated
inner cover can be hygenically sheathed before disposal. Some have
aluminium foil tips to facilitate heat transfer and others are pre-
lubricated. Covers are used for liquid-in-glass or electronic thermometers but they increase the time for equilibration. Internal probes
(aural, rectal or oesophageal) that are not disposable should have a
suitable covering that allows repeated cleaning.

Ward Use

Mercury-in-glass thermometers are commonly used but their inac-
curacies have been described. Breakage of these thermometers is a
constant hazard when they are used for children and uncooperative
patients; also they require cleansing, sterilizing and shaking down, and
the degree marks can wear off.

Electrical thermometers, although initially accurate, can deteriorate
with age, and there are many built-in errors. Consideration should be
given to replacement cost, life expectancy, cumulative error,
sterilization, calibration procedures, the ease and cost of repairs and the
training needed by operators. Many electronic thermometers for clinical
use do not record temperatures less than 33°C. There is a need for a
low-reading thermometer on most wards and especially in the casualty
department. Where patients can move about or continuous monitoring
is necessary (in the recovery room and during intensive care) a
thermometer with a long lead is desirable.

Theatre Use

Temperature monitoring equipment should be available for every
neonate and for any patient who is undergoing a lengthy or major
surgical operation, i.e. it should be available in every theatre. In fact
there are some anaesthetists who advocate body temperature monitoring of all patients both intraoperatively and postoperatively. The
patients most at risk are described later.

In theatres it is important to monitor not only the patient's body temperature but the ambient temperature and that of the equipment. Wall thermometers in theatres may be innaccurate or insensitive and will not necessarily indicate the temperature of the air surrounding the patient. The temperature of sterilizing equipment can be assessed easily and accurately by both chemical methods and paper records, and anaesthetists, nurses and surgeons should be aware of the need for checking these records.

MEASUREMENT OF RELATIVE HUMIDITY: HYGROMETERS

The relative humidity of the inspired gas and surrounding air is important in the maintenance of normal body temperature. It is a measure of the actual amount of water vapour present in the gas expressed as a percentage of the amount that the same volume of gas

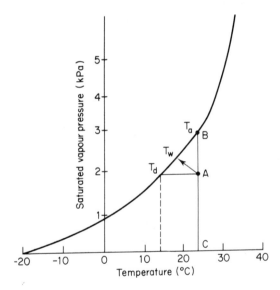

Fig. 25. *Relative Humidity*

Point A represents air conditions in a room where:

T_a = dry bulb temperature
T_w = wet bulb temperature
T_d = temperature of dew point
AB = saturation deficit

Relative Humidity (%) = $100 \times \dfrac{AC}{BC}$

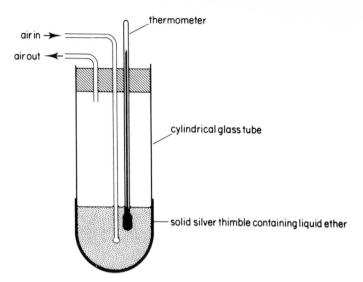

Fig. 26. A Regnault Hygrometer

would contain if it were fully saturated, temperature and pressure remaining constant (Figure 25).

The dew-point hygrometer (Figure 26) is the classical method of measuring relative humidity. Regnault's instrument consists of a glass tube ending with a very thin highly polished silver thimble. Ether is poured into it and the temperature of the liquid is measured by a thermometer. There are two inlets into the tube, one to pass air in and the other to let out air. Air is bubbled through the ether until condensation is seen on the outside of the silver surface. Readings of the thermometer are taken when the first deposit of condensation is seen on cooling and when it disappears as the ether returns to ambient temperature. Adequate thermal contact must be available between the ether and the ambient air: it is not sufficient to have the silver outside a glass surface. The mean of the two temperatures is the dew point and from this the relative humidity can be calculated.

Alternatively, relative humidity can be measured by using a hygroscopic material, e.g. human hair. One end of the hair is fixed and the other is attached to a lever system. When the humidity rises the hair increases in length. Readings over the range of 15–85% relative humidity are obtained with moderate accuracy ($\pm$2%). Some theatre monitoring equipment utilizes this principle.

The wet-and-dry-bulb hygrometer is the most convenient measure of relative humidity in ambient air (Figure 27). Two identical mercury-in-glass thermometers with adequate graduations are positioned side by

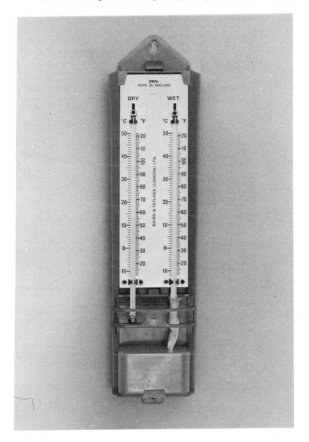

Fig. 27. A Wet and Dry Bulb Thermometer

side with the bulb of one exposed to air and the bulb of the other surrounded by a clean wick which is wet from a reservoir of distilled water. Evaporation of water from around the wet bulb will occur and cool the mercury reservoir and hence lower the temperature recorded. The evaporation rate of the water around the bulb is related to the relative humidity. When there is a high relative humidity there will be only a small difference in temperature between the two bulbs, but when the relative humidity is low a large temperature difference will occur. The relative humidity can be calculated mathematically but is more easily looked up in tables (Table IV). The dry bulb temperature and the temperature difference between the two bulbs are the two relevant measurements. The wet bulb should be covered with a single thickness of closely fitting muslin such that the length of cotton exposed to the air

Table IV: Wet and Dry Bulb Hygrometer

Dry Bulb	Depression of wet bulb (°C)																								
(°C)	0·5	1·0	1·5	2·0	2·5	3·0	3·5	4·0	4·5	5·0	5·5	6·0	6·5	7·0	7·5	8·0	8·5	9·0	9·5	10	11	12	13	14	15
10	93	87	81	74	68	62	56	50	44	38	33	27	21	16	10	5									
11	94	87	81	75	69	63	58	52	46	41	35	30	24	19	14	9	4								
12	94	88	82	76	70	65	59	54	48	43	37	32	27	22	17	12	7								
13	94	88	83	77	71	66	60	55	50	45	40	35	30	25	20	15	11	2							
14	94	89	83	78	72	67	62	57	52	47	42	37	32	27	23	18	14	6	1						
15	94	89	84	78	73	68	63	58	53	48	42	39	34	30	25	21	17	9	6	4					
16	95	89	84	79	74	69	64	59	55	50	43	40	37	32	28	24	19	12	8	7					
17	95	90	85	80	75	70	65	61	56	52	47	43	39	34	30	26	22	15	11	10	3				
18	95	90	85	80	76	71	66	62	57	53	49	45	40	36	32	28	24	18	14	13	6				
19	95	90	86	81	76	72	67	63	59	54	50	46	42	38	34	30	27	21	17	16	9	2			
20	95	91	86	81	77	73	68	64	60	56	52	48	44	40	36	32	29	23	22	18	11	5			
21	95	91	86	82	78	73	69	65	61	57	53	49	45	42	38	34	31	25	24	20	14	7	1		
22	95	91	87	82	78	74	70	66	62	58	54	50	47	43	40	36	33	27	26	23	16	10	4		
23	96	91	87	83	79	75	71	67	63	59	55	52	48	45	41	38	34	29	28	25	18	12	6	1	
24	96	91	87	83	79	75	71	68	64	60	57	53	49	46	43	40	36	31	30	27	20	15	9	3	
25	96	92	88	84	80	76	72	68	65	61	58	54	51	47	45	41	38	33	31	28	22	17	11	6	1
26	96	92	88	84	80	76	73	69	66	62	59	55	52	49	47	43	39	36	33	30	24	19	13	8	3
27	96	92	88	84	81	77	73	70	66	63	59	56	53	50	48	44	41	38	35	32	26	21	15	10	5
28	96	92	88	85	81	77	74	70	67	64	60	57	54	51	49	45	42	39	36	33	28	23	17	12	8
29	96	92	89	85	81	78	74	71	68	64	61	58	55	52	50	47	43	40	37	35	29	24	19	14	10
30	96	93	89	85	82	78	75	73	68	65	62	59	56	53	52	48	44	42	39	36	31	26	21	16	12
32	96	93	89	86	82	79	76	74	70	67	64	61	58	55	54	49	46	44	41	39	34	29	24	20	15
34	96	93	89	86	83	80	77	75	71	68	65	62	59	56	55	51	48	46	43	41	36	32	27	23	19
36	96	93	90	87	84	81	78	76	72	69	66	63	61	58	56	53	50	48	45	43	38	34	30	26	22

To determine humidity, locate the reading of the dry bulb thermometer and then the depression of the wet bulb thermometer. At the intersection of the column and the row the percentage relative humidity can be read off. When values fall between those on the table the mean value should be calculated, e.g. dry bulb 22·5°C and wet bulb depression 4·75°C: the value required would be the mean of

62	58
63	59

This gives a relative humidity of 60·5%.

is about 8 cm. Prolonged exposure without replacement of the muslin increases the concentration of salt in the material so that the saturation vapour pressure at the wet bulb is reduced and readings become inaccurate. For accuracy the thermometers should be shielded from radiation.

This method is slow: quick accurate readings require a psychrometer, which is a wet-and-dry-bulb thermometer artificially ventilated at a standard rate. Thermocouples and thermistors can be used in the measurement of relative humidity instead of mercury-in-glass thermometers (Penman 1958).

Another method involves electronic measuring of the change in electrical resistance or capacitance which occurs when a substance absorbs water. This is a sensitive method and is used in air-conditioning systems.

The mass spectrometer has also been used to measure the humidification of inspired gas (Hayes & Robinson 1970) and it is becoming a useful clinical tool in operating theatres because of its wide application (Severinghaus & Ozanne 1978).

Measurement of Gas Temperatures

It is essential to measure the temperature of inspired gases near the patient's mouth to prevent accidental burns when a hot water humidifier is used during intermittent positive pressure ventilation. Any type of simple thermometer can be used.

For accurate research purposes the temperature of the expired air should be known when lung volumes are measured. A thermometer standardized by the National Physical Laboratory should be used.

BRITISH STANDARDS FOR CLINICAL MAXIMUM THERMOMETERS (BS 691: 1966)

Range
 Ordinary 35–42°C (both long and stubby bulbs are available)
 Subnormal 25–40°C (only stubby bulbs available)

The subnormal thermometer is used to diagnose hypothermia. Rectal thermometers have a bulb of blue glass.

Dimensions
Overall length	10 cm
Stem diameter	> 4 mm
Bulb length	long: 12–18 mm
	stubby: < 9 mm
Minimum scale size	ordinary: 5 mm/°C
	subnormal: 2 mm/°C

Maximum Error Permissible
    Ordinary   ±0·1°C from 35 to 41°C
                  ±0·2°C above 41°C
    Subnormal   ±0·3°C over the entire range

Scale
    Ordinary   0·1°C increments with distinguishing mark at 37°C
    Subnormal   0·2°C increments throughout the range

Markings
Markings must be permanent and able to withstand the chemicals used for sterilization. There must be no indication, such as '1 minute', of the time required for an accurate reading to be obtained.

Design
A lens front is mandatory, with an enamel back for easy reading. A constriction should occur in the bore below the lowest graduation line so that, when the thermometer is held in the vertical position with the bulb downwards at room temperature after exposure to a temperature of at least 40°C, the thermometer shall indicate the temperature to which it was exposed to within the limits of error specified above.

References

Benzinger, M. (1969) Tympanic thermometry in surgery and anesthesia. *J. Am. med. Ass.*, *209*, 1207–1211.

Benzinger, T. H., Huebscher, R. G., Minard, D. & Kitzinger, C. (1958) Human calorimetry by means of the gradient principle. *J. appl. Physiol.*, *12*, S1–S24.

Benzinger, T. H. & Taylor, G. W. (1963) Cranial measurements of internal temperature in man. In: *Temperature: its measurement and Control in Science and Industry*, pp. 111–120. New York: Reinhold.

Burton, A. C. (1935) The average temperature of the tissues of the body. *J. Nutr.*, *9*, 264–280.

Cannon, P. & Keatinge, W. R. (1960) The metabolic rate and heat loss of fat and thin men in heat balance in cold and warm water. *J. Physiol. Lond.*, *154*, 329–344.

Cliffe, P. (1962) The measurement of temperature. *Anaesthesia*, *17*, 215–237.

Colin, J. & Houdas, Y. (1965) Initiation of sweating in man after abrupt rise in environmental temperatures. *J. appl. Physiol.*, *20*, 984–990.

Colin, J., Timbal, J., Houdas, Y., Boutelier, C. & Guieu, J. D. (1971) Computation of mean body temperature from rectal and skin temperatures. *J. appl. Physiol.*, *31*, 484–489.

Cooper, K. E., Cranston, W. I. & Snell, E. S. (1964) Temperature in the external auditory meatus as an index of central temperature changes. *J. appl. Physiol.*, *19*, 1032–1035.

Cooper, K. E. & Kenyon, J. R. (1957) A comparison of temperatures measured in the rectum, oesophagus, and on the surface of the aorta during hypothermia in man. *Br. J. Surg.*, *44*, 616–619.

Day, R. L., Caliguiri, L., Kamenski, C. & Ehrlich, F. (1964) Body temperature and survival of premature infants. *Pediatrics, Springfield*, *34*, 171–181.

Dornette, W. L. (1965) Thermometry in clinical practice *Int. Anesth. Clin.*, *3*, 437–488.

Eberhart, R. C. & Trezek, G. J. (1973) Central and peripheral rewarming patterns in postoperative cardiac patients. *Crit. Care Med.*, *1*, 239–251.

Fox, R. H., Woodward, P. M., Exton-Smith, A. N., Green, M. F., Donnison, D. V. & Wicks, M. H. (1973) Body temperatures in the elderly: a national study of physiological social and environmental conditions. *Brit. med. J.*, *1*, 200–206.

Gagge, A. P., Burton, A. C. & Bazett, H. C. (1941) A practical system of units for the description of the heat exchange of man with his environment. *Science, N.Y.*, *94*, 428–430.

Hardy, J. D. & Du Bois, E. F. (1938a) Basal metabolism, radiation, convection and vaporisation at temperatures of 22 to 35°C. *J. Nutr.*, *15*, 477–492.

Hardy, J. D. & Du Bois, E. F. (1938b) The technique of measuring radiation and convection. *J. Nutr.*, *15*, 461–475.

Hayes, B. & Robinson, J. S. (1970) An assessment of methods of humidification of inspired gas. *Br. J. Anaesth.*, *42*, 94–104.

Hill, D. W. (1959) The measurement and recording of temperatures during hypothermia. *Br. J. Anaesth.*, *31*, 22–25.

Holdcroft, A. & Hall, G. M. (1978) Heat loss during anaesthesia. *Br. J. Anaesth.*, *50*, 157–164.

Holdcroft, A., Hall, G. M. & Cooper, G. M. (1979) Redistribution of body heat during anaesthesia. *Anaesthesia*, *34*, 758–764.

Houghton, F. C., Teague, W. W., Miller, W. E. & Yant, W. P. (1929) Thermal exchanges between the human body and its atmospheric environment. *Am. J. Physiol.*, *88*, 386–406.

Joly, H. R. & Weil, M. H. (1969) Temperature of the great toe as an indication of the severity of shock. *Circulation*, *39*, 131–138.

Keatinge, W. R. & Sloan, R. E. G. (1973) Measurement of deep body temperature from external auditory canal with servo-controlled heating around ear. *J. Physiol., Lond.*, *234*, 8–9P.

Knapp, H. A. (1966) Accuracy of glass clinical thermometers compared to electronic thermometers. *Am. J. Surg.*, *112*, 139–141.

Krog, J. (1962) Electrical measurement of body temperature. *Acta anaesth. scand.*, Suppl. XI, 99–113.

Kuzucu, E. Y. (1965) Measurement of temperature. *Int. Anesth. Clin.*, *3*, 435–449.

Lees, D. E., Schuette, W., Bull, J. M., Whang-Peng, J., Atkinson, E. R. & Macnamara, T. (1978) An evaluation of liquid-crystal thermometry as a screening device for intraoperative hyperthermia. *Anesth. Analg. (Cleve.)*, *57*, 669–674.

Levison, H., Linsao, L. & Swyer, P. R. (1966) A comparison of infra-red and convective heating for newborn infants. *Lancet*, *2*, 1346–1347.

Mead, J. & Bonmarito, C. L. (1949) Reliability of rectal temperatures as an index of internal body temperature. *J. appl. Physiol.*, *2*, 97–109.

Miller, D. L. & Oliver, T. K. (1966) Body temperature in the immediate neonatal period: the effect of reducing thermal losses. *Am. J. Obstet. Gynec.*, *94*, 964–969.

Minard, D. (1970) Body heat content. In: *Physiological and Behavioural Temperature Regulation*, ed. J. D. Hardy, A. P. Gagge & J. A. J. Stolwijk. pp. 345–357. Springfield, Ill.: Charles C. Thomas.

Mitchell, D. & Wyndham, C. H. (1969) Comparison of weighting formulas for calculating mean skin temperature. *J. appl. Physiol.*, *26*, 616–622.

Penman, H. L. (1958) *Humidity.* London: Chapman and Hall.

Ramanathan, N. L. (1964) A new weighting system for mean surface temperature of the human body. *J. appl. Physiol.*, *19*, 531–533.

Randall, W. C., Rawson, R. O., McCook, R. D. & Peiss, C. N. (1963) Central and peripheral factors in dynamic thermoregulation. *J. appl. Physiol.*, *18*, 61–64.

Rawson, R. O. & Hammel, H. T. (1963) Hypothalamic and tympanic temperature in rhesus monkeys. *Fedn Proc. Fedn Am. Socs exp. Biol.*, *22*, 283.

Robertson, T. L. (1968) Clinical temperature measurement—survey. *Biomed. Sci. Instrum.*, *4*, 303–309.

Schneider, A. J. L., Apple, H. P. & Braun, R. T. (1977) Electrosurgical burns at skin temperature probes. *Anesthesiology*, *47*, 72–74.

Severinghaus, J. W. (1962) Temperature gradients during hypothermia. *Ann. N.Y. Acad. Sci., U.S.A..*, *80*, 515–521.

Severinghaus, J. W. & Ozanne, G. (1978) Multi operating room monitoring with one mass spectrometer. *Acta anaesth. scand.*, Suppl. *70*, 186–187.

Shanks, C. A. (1975) Mean skin temperature during anaesthesia: an assessment of formulae in the supine surgical patient. *Br. J. Anaesth., 47*, 871–875.

Stolwijk, J. A. J. & Hardy, J. D. (1966) Partition calorimetric studies of responses of man to thermal transients. *J. appl. Physiol., 21*, 967–977.

Tepas, D. I. & Vianello, M. A. B. (1966) Method of recording body temperature for prolonged time *Aerospace Med, 37*, 488–491.

Trolander, H. W. & Sterling, J. J. (1962) Behaviour of thermistors at biological temperatures. *I.R.E. Trans. biomed. Electronics, 9*, 142–144.

Wallace, C. T., Marks, W. E., Adkins, W. Y. & Mahaffey, J. E. (1974) Perforation of the tympanic membrane, a complication of tympanic thermometry during anaesthesia. *Anesthesiology, 41*, 290–291.

Webb, G. E. (1973) Comparison of oesophageal and tympanic temperature monitoring during cardiopulmonary bypass. *Anesth. Analg. (Cleve.), 52*, 729–733.

Whitby, J. D. & Dunkin, L. J. (1968) Temperature differences in the oesophagus. *Br. J. Anaesth., 40*, 991–995.

Wilson, R. D., Knapp, C., Traber, D. L. & Priano, L. L. (1971) Tympanic thermography: a clinical and research evaluation of a new technic. *Sth. med. J., Nashville, 64*, 1452–1455.

Winslow, C.-E. A., Herrington, L. P. & Gagge, A. P. (1936) A new method of partition calorimetry. *Am. J. Physiol., 116*, 641–655.

Drugs and body temperature   3

The interaction of drugs and body temperature may take the form either of the drug interfering with the central or peripheral physiological mechanisms which control body temperature, or an abnormality in body temperature influencing the effect of the drug. A chemical agent which alters body temperature may, indirectly, affect the action of another drug.

THE EFFECT OF DRUGS ON THERMOREGULATION

The physiological mechanisms by which man maintains homeothermia have been described in Chapter 1. The balance between heat gain and heat loss can be altered either deliberately or accidentally by the action of certain chemical agents. The dose of a drug and the duration of its action at existing body temperature are clearly important.

The specific thermal conditions under which a drug is used influences its effect. Johnson et al. (1963) have demonstrated that chlorpromazine does not affect the body temperature of rats at an environmental temperature of 30°C, but when they are exposed to lower temperatures there is a drastic fall in body temperature. However rats that have been acclimatized to cold show a gradual return to control values after the initial fall in body temperature.

Heat is gained by the body from its metabolic activities and from the environment. In a suitable environment, where the air temperature exceeds that of the skin, drugs which increase cutaneous blood flow can allow the body to take up more heat. The basal metabolic rate is affected by the availability of substrates, by their use in the tissues and central nervous system, and by the circulating concentrations of hormones such as adrenaline, noradrenaline and thyroxine.

Drug interactions with thermoregulatory mechanisms may be complex and depend on both ambient conditions and the physiological state of the individual. For example, studies on rats have shown that in a thermally neutral environment adrenaline has a marked hypermetabolic effect, but administered in high doses in a cold environment, it is hypometabolic and causes body temperature to fall (Andjus 1963): local vasoconstriction reduces limb blood flow leading to ischaemia and local cooling. Where generalized vasoconstriction occurs, for example after the administration of adrenaline, the skin temperature is reduced, but the core temperature may rise.

Chemical agents which affect the transfer of energy inside the cell and uncouple oxidative phosphorylation, or affect the concentration of ions within the cellular organelles, may cause a fatal rise of body temperature. The syndrome of malignant hyperthermia and the chemical agents associated with it are described in Chapter 4. When the basal metabolic rate is increased by the administration of excess thermogenic hormones, body temperature will rise unless compensatory mechanisms for heat loss come into effect. Since the central nervous system is involved in the control of the other metabolic activities of the body, such as shivering and muscular exercise, cerebral stimulants are also liable to increase body temperature. Chlorpromazine has both central and peripheral effects in man, inhibiting shivering, probably by an effect on the central thermoregulation, and peripherally causing vaso-dilatation. In rats exposed to cold, the administration of chlor-promazine causes the excretion of large amounts of catecholamines and this centrally mediated response means that lethal hypothermia can occur at higher environmental temperatures as the dose of chlorpromazine is increased because increased heat loss occurs from stimulated thermogenesis and vasodilatation.

Drugs affecting catecholamine metabolism can also affect the toxicity of other chemical agents: the availability of catecholamines can significantly influence the toxicity of reserpine (Lettau et al. 1964) and pretreatment of mice with dihydrophenylalanine also decreased the toxicity of reserpine, in a cold environment, presumably by a central stimulatory mechanism increasing motor activity (Airaksinen & Mattila 1962).

The physiological state of the patient has to be considered in predicting the effects of drugs on thermoregulation. For instance, when there is a rise in endogenous prostaglandins of the E series, a fever is produced which can be modified by prostaglandin inhibitors such as paracetamol, indomethacin and aspirin (Feldberg et al. 1973). These drugs in therapeutic doses have no effect on temperature regulation at normothermia.

Many nerve terminals in the hypothalamus contain noradrenaline or 5-hydroxytryptamine and they play a part in the thermoregulatory pathways. Administration of monoamine oxidase inhibitors (MAOI) which interfere with their enzymatic breakdown can be expected to cause some abnormality of temperature regulation and febrile illnesses may be modified in some patients receiving MAOI drugs. In rabbits, pargyline given with a large (but not lethal) dose of leucocyte pyrogen, resulted in a prolongation of fever and in some animals fatal hyperthermia (Cooper & Cranston 1966).

In man, the tranquillizer meprobamate impairs thermal balance in hot and cold environments. Iampietro et al. (1965) consider that it exerts a direct effect on the temperature-regulating centres and inhibits the normal responses to thermal stress such as shivering and vasoconstriction, in a similar manner to chlorpromazine.

Radiation losses from the skin are increased by the vasodilatation following the administration of alcohol, chlorpromazine and alpha-adrenergic blocking agents. Heat loss by evaporation, such as might occur in overventilation following an overdose of salicylates, usually causes no clinical problem. However, where evaporative heat loss is suppressed, for example during the administration of the belladonna alkaloids, a rise in core body temperature may occur. This rise in body temperature is usually only significant after large doses of atropine or hyoscine. Eger (1962) reports considerable individual variation in sensitivity which may be due to the environmental temperature. Moderate doses in infants can produce a high fever; suppression of sweating is a contributory factor but other more central mechanisms may also play a part (Goodman & Gilman, 1975). Magbagbeola (1973) found that in the tropics, atropine in clinical doses does not cause a dangerous rise in body temperature prior to anaesthesia. Unfortunately the study did not continue during surgery or into the recovery period, nor were the effect of the anaesthetic agents used or concurrent infection considered.

Patients at the two extremes of age and those with cardiovascular disease are less able to respond to alterations in environmental temperature and may be more susceptable to the effect of certain drugs. Elderly people and patients with cardiac disease often have their threshold to heat injury lowered even further by drugs such as reserpine, natiuretic diuretics, antihypertensive agents, atropine, meprobamate and anaesthesia (Burch & Miller 1969), and they should be protected not only from heat loss in a cold environment but also, by air conditioning, from warm weather (Burch & De Pasquale, 1959).

The neonate's ability to maintain normothermia and to respond to cold stress depends on non-shivering thermogenesis (Smith & Horwitz 1969). This is mediated by noradrenaline, and the alpha-adrenergic blocking action of drugs such as the phenothiazines can hasten the onset of hypothermia (Cohen & Olson 1970). Benzodiazepines administered during labour have a similar effect on the newborn infant. Cree et al. (1973) observed that infants become hypothermic and were unable to respond to cold stress after the administration of more than 30 mg of diazepam to a woman during her labour. Speight (1977) reports a similar effect following the use of nitrazepam for night sedation in pregnant women.

Where a patient is suffering from a disease of the thermoregulatory system, such as myxoedema, the cooling effect of the phenothiazines and the barbiturates may be potentiated and precipitate hypothermic coma (McGrath & Paley 1960). The interaction of two drugs may occasionally alter the temperature response of one of the drugs: for instance the use of cocaine with chlorpromazine can lead to a precipitous fall in the body temperature of rabbits (Wislicki 1961). The mechanism of this enhanced reaction can only be speculated upon: it may be due to the inhibition of the myotonic effect of cocaine.

THE USE OF DRUGS TO AFFECT BODY TEMPERATURE

To Induce Hypothermia

General anaesthetic agents and depressants of the central nervous system, such as barbiturates, phenothiazines, opiates, and benzo-diazepines, may have central and peripheral effects on temperature regulation. Lotti et al. (1965) observed a fall in body temperature following an analgesic dose of morphine. Whether this is primarily a central effect caused by direct action on the thermoregulatory neurones or whether the hypothermic effects of morphine are secondary to its action of depleting mono-aminergic neurones in the central nervous system is not yet clear (Lomax 1967). In 1965 Lomax found that the fall in temperature after systemic administration of a barbiturate is due to a combination of decreased heat production and increased heat loss through the skin. The rate of fall in temperature depends on the difference between the ambient temperature and the temperature of the animal. The dose, the duration of exposure to the drug and the physiological state of the recipient are also relevant. The techniques of inducing hypothermia are described specifically in Chapter 6, accidental hypothermia and its causes in Chapter 5.

To Induce Hyperthermia

Pyrogens are of mainly historical and experimental interest. They have been used as non-specific shock therapy in a variety of conditions, e.g. uveitis and syphilis. 'Pyrogen' is a term applied to any substance, whether exogenous or endogenous, which causes a fever when intro-duced into or released in the body (Bligh & Johnson 1973). An endogenous pyrogen is a heat-labile substance formed in body tissues which causes fever by its action on the central nervous system when released, e.g. leucocyte pyrogen. Leucocyte pyrogen entering the brain causes a release of prostaglandin E in the hypothalamus which results in a fever (Pickes 1972).

To Maintain Normothermia

Antipyretics

These are agents which lower the temperature of febrile patients but have no effect when the body temperature is normal. Acetylsalicylic acid is the drug *par excellence* in this respect. It produces its effect by inhibiting the synthesis of the endoperoxides which when converted to prostaglandins mediate the hyperthermic response. Heat loss is increased by an increase in peripheral blood flow and sweating. The analgesic and antipyretic effects of the salicylates are not equipotent: in animals, diflurophenyl salicylic acid is approximately ten times more active than acetylsalicylic acid as an analgesic, but is only one and a half times as effective as an antipyretic agent (Stone et al. 1977). Phenacetin and acetaminophen are equipotent with acetylsalicylic acid as antipyretic agents (Beaver 1965, 1966). Phenylbutazone is associated with serious toxic effects if used in a dose large enough to reduce a fever (Goodman & Gilman 1975).

Prevention of Hypothermia

The survival of people who have been immersed in water, as occurs during a shipwreck, may depend on the rate at which the deep body temperature is lowered. Drugs which affect skin blood flow may interfere with heat loss. Nausea and vomiting may have a detrimental effect due to increased blood flow to the muscles. Keatinge (1968) advocates the use of hyoscine (0·6 mg orally) as a rapidly acting and effective sea-sickness remedy. It is effective for up to six hours and may help to prevent heat loss in cold water.

TEMPERATURE CHANGES IN DRUG POISONING

Uncouplers of Oxidative Phosphorylation

When oxidative phosphorylation is 'uncoupled' electron transport still occurs but no phosphorylation of adenosine diphosphate takes place. In the intact mitochondria, electron transport and oxidative phosphorylation are closely associated; when they are uncoupled, the transport of electrons may speed up, indicating that the phosphorylation was a rate-limiting process. The energy used to incorporate inorganic phosphate into the high-energy compound, adenosine triphosphate, is dissipated as heat and the metabolic rate increases.

Commercial Products

Dinitro-ortho-cresol and 2,4-dinitrophenol were at one time prescribed for the treatment of obesity, but their use for this purpose was abandoned on account of their serious toxic effects. Dinitro-ortho-cresol is now used as a crop spray and poisoning can still occur if it is absorbed through the skin or alimentary tract. These two uncouplers increase cellular metabolism to a level which may lead to fatal hyperpyrexia (Bidstrup et al. 1952; Pollard & Filbee 1951). Other uncouplers include valinomycin and granicicidin (a circular polypeptide antibiotic), the salicylanilides (Conn & Stumpf 1976), dicoumarol, substituted phenyl hydrazones, and other substituted phenols (Mahler & Cordes 1969).

Salicylates

Brody (1956) and Miyahara and Karler (1965) showed that the action of sodium salicylate and related compounds had an effect on tissue metabolism that was similar to 2,4-dinitrophenol. The increase in heat, gained by uncoupling oxidative phosphorylation, is not offset by an increase in the heat loss produced by hyperventilation, and fever develops with sweating (Cranston et al. 1970).

Central Nervous System Stimulants

Amphetamine (Goodman & Gilman 1975) and cocaine (Wislicki 1961) cause hyperactivity and restlessness, leading to a rise in body temperature when given in toxic doses.

Antidepressants

The toxic effects of the monoamine oxidase inhibitors and the tricylic antidepressant drugs, such as imipramine and amytriptyline, include fever (Noble & Matthew 1969; Cooper & Guenter, 1977).

Table V: Temperature Changes in Drug Poisoning

Drug	Effect
Lysergic acid diethylamine Cocaine Antihistamines Amphetamine — *Speed*!!. Salicylates Methaqualone Belladonna alkaloids Tricyclic antidepressants	Temperature may be increased
Opiates Marihuana Phenothiazines Butyrophenones Barbiturates Benzodiazepines	Temperature may be reduced
Anticholinesterases	Temperature may be reduced or increased.

Anticholinesterases

Anticholinesterases are used therapeutically to reversibly inactivate cholinesterase for a few hours. Organophosphates, e.g. di-isopropyl fluorophosphate (used as an insecticide and nerve gas for warfare), produce irreversible inhibition. Meeter et al. (1971) describe the effect of these agents on body temperature as 'labile'; sometimes they produce hypothermia, but in most cases there is a rise in body temperature and a low-grade fever which can persist for up to a week.

THE EFFECT OF TEMPERATURE ON THE ACTION OF DRUGS

The action of drugs can be altered by local or general abnormalities of body temperature. The local temperature of an injection site is important and, in general, all drugs given to patients should be administered intravenously to avoid overdosage. The mode of action, rate of absorption, metabolism and excretion of drugs can also be modified by the body temperature. The fraction of a drug bound to proteins tends to increase as the body temperature falls, although the relative distribution of drugs through the body appears to be unchanged (Popovic & Popovic 1974).

The dose of the drug administered is obviously important. Its effectiveness may be reduced by decreased absorption from the gut. In the case of atropine, the half-time for its uptake by the liver is reduced three-fold in profound hypothermia (Kalser et al. 1965a) and the toxicity of the drug altered. The effect of deep hypothermia is much greater on renal excretion of atropine than on its hepatic excretion (Kalser et al. 1965b). When Kalser et al. (1965c) perfused rat livers at 17°C, they found that decreased hydrolysis of procaine accounts for its increased toxicity in hypothermia, despite a reduced uptake into the liver. Where there is reduced excretion, especially through the kidney, toxic effects may occur. Decreased metabolism of drugs, especially the hepatotoxic or nephrotoxic agents, increases the duration of their effects (Popovic & Popovic, 1974). The maximum rate of tubular excretion of a drug drops by 10% for each 0·6°C fall in body temperature. Pentobarbitone is detoxified prior to its excretion and its action is therefore prolonged at low body temperatures; while its parent compound, barbital, is not detoxified and its duration of action may not be influenced by low body temperatures (Fuhrman 1946). Arvela and Sotaniemi (1968) found that pretreatment of rats with phenobarbitone increased the rate that subsequently administered pentobarbitone was removed from the tissues and reduced the fall in body temperature that occurred during hypothermia. The effect of similar enzyme induction mechanisms during hypothermia may alter the metabolism of other drugs and their effects.

Where tubular absorption is responsible for maintaining the blood levels of a drug, depression of reabsorption by hypothermia may aid elimination. Acetylation by the liver is reduced exponentially (Kalser et al. 1968) so that for every 10°C fall in temperature there is a reduction in the rate of the reaction of between two and three times. This is important in anaesthesia where patients may be subjected to accidental or deliberate hypothermia.

Hypothermia can protect against the toxicity of drugs (Shingleton et al. 1961), but, during rewarming, accumulated drugs could have a potentially harmful effect. For example, the average lethal dose of digitalis in dogs at 29°C is double that at normothermia (Beyda et al. 1961; Akhtar et al. 1971). This effect can be used to provide valuable time to correct and treat digitalis toxicity. Hypothermia may have its beneficial effect by direct myocardial depression. In febrile states, digoxin has been known for many years to have an enhanced toxicity (Beyda et al. 1961). It should be apparent that if a patient who is hypothermic requires digoxin for therapeutic reasons a larger than normal dose will be required. Cellular thresholds of myocardial irritability to adrenaline and calcium may also be reduced (Blair 1964), but this effect is offset by reduced enzymatic detoxification. Cardiac arrest occurs at a lower body temperature after alcohol administration (Webb et al. 1968) but the toxicity and lethal concentration of potassium in the serum at 28°C is decreased (Hoff et al. 1961). Hypothermia can protect rats from the hepatotoxic effect of carbon tetrachloride.

In the rat, a combination of phenobarbitone and hypothermia to 23°C results in a more pronounced reduction in the cerebral metabolic rate for oxygen than can be achieved either by administration of barbiturates to normothermic animals or by reducing the body temperature to 15°C (Nordström & Rehncrona 1978). Other workers have confirmed this during moderate hypothermia (Lafferty et al. 1978; Hägerdal et al. 1978). This finding requires validation in the human, where the reduction in cerebral metabolic rate with the barbiturates and hypothermia is by different mechanisms (Michenfelder 1978), and the nature and extent of cerebral hypoxia may limit the additive effects. If synergism did occur it could be used to reduce the degree of cerebral hypoxia that may occur in situations such as partial interruption of cerebral blood supply. The central nervous system stimulants, strychnine, coramine and lobeline, exhibit increased toxicity at 30°C (Fuhrman 1946).

Endogenous production of hormones is depressed during hypothermia and the utilization of exogenous hormones is reduced. Antibiotic activity is not reduced until a temperature of 25°C is reached (Blach et al. 1955).

Table VI: Summary of Effect of Hypothermia on Drug Action

Reduced Toxicity	Increased Toxicity
Digitalis	Strychnine
Caffeine	Coramine
Insulin	Lobeline
Thyroxine	Potassium
Steroids	Calcium
Histamine	Procaine
Phenobarbitone	
Ethyl alcohol	
Carbon tetrachloride	

THE EFFECT OF TEMPERATURE ON SPECIFIC DRUGS

Neuromuscular Blocking Drugs

The synaptic delay at the neuromuscular junction is markedly lengthened in hypothermia. Katz and Miledi (1965) postulate that the delay is due to a delayed release of acetylcholine rather than slowness of diffusion or delay in receptor reaction. Hypothermia has minimal effect on acetylcholinesterase activity or post-junctional membrane sensitivity (Hubbard et al. 1971).

Depolarizing Agents

The effects of depolarizing agents on the neuromuscular junction may be modified by an alteration in blood flow to the muscle and in the rate of hydrolysis of the drug in the plasma. Lowering of body temperature is accompanied by a bradycardia and a reduction in blood pressure. A reduction in blood flow contributes to a more gradual onset of the depolarizing block. Brigland et al. (1958) demonstrated, in the cat, that the 50% recovery time following the administration of dexamethonium and suxamethonium increased by up to four times when the core temperature was changed from 36 to 31°C; on rewarming these effects were reversed. The nature of the blockade was not affected by temperature. Wislicki (1961) found that in cats a rise in body temperature reduced the duration of the depolarizing blockade. Plasma cholinesterase in vitro has an optimum activity between 40 and 42·5°C and may be partly responsible for shortening the duration of action of suxamethonium in a pyrexial patient (Wislicki 1960).

Non-Depolarizing Agents

Holmes et al. (1951) postulate that tubocurarine becomes less effective as a neuromuscular blocking agent when the temperature of the muscle is lowered. Brigland et al. (1958) conclude that cooling reduces the magnitude of the neuromuscular blockade but not its duration, and that the changes in neuromuscular function appear to be independent of blood flow to the muscle.

These findings are questioned by Miller and Roderick (1977) who postulate that hypothermia may initially facilitate neuromuscular transmission by increasing the number of quanta of acetylcholine released (Zaimis et al. 1958) but that after some minutes this antagonism disappears and the block becomes augmented, presumably because there is a reduction of the rate at which of choline taken up again into readily available stores. As the duration of hypothermia is lengthened, the blocking effect becomes more dominant.

When Miller and Roderick infused pancuronium bromide into cats, the time to its peak effect was prolonged. They suggest that the greater potency of this non-depolarizing agent may be related to delayed renal excretion (Agoston et al. 1973). Combined biliary and renal excretion is delayed at temperatures less than 28°C and, during induced hypotension at this temperature, the interval between repeated doses of tubocurarine and pancuronium should be lengthened (Ham et al. 1978; Miller 1979). The breakdown of pancuronium into inactive metabolites is also prolonged because of decreased metabolism during hypothermia, but, because tubocurarine is usually excreted unchanged (Cohen et al. 1967), there may be a difference at low body temperatures in the effect of doses of tubocurarine and pancuronium which are equipotent at normothermia.

Volatile Anaesthetic Agents

The solubility of a gas in an aqueous medium increases with decreasing temperature of the medium (Eger & Larson 1964), and halothane in whole blood also demonstrates this effect (Han & Helrich 1966a). When body temperature is lowered, the concentration of anaesthetic required to maintain anaesthesia can be reduced (Herbert et al. 1957). This may be due in part to cold narcosis and in part to the significant increase in the solubility. Han and Helrich (1966b) suggest that at 28°C the inspired concentration of halothane may be reduced to 60% of that at normothermia. In terms of the minimum alveolar concentration (MAC) in the dog, there is a reduction of 50% in the halothane concentration for a 10°C fall in temperature (Regan & Eger 1967). With other agents, where there is a smaller change of solubility with temperature, for example cyclopropane, there is a smaller reduction in MAC with a similar fall of temperature.

The theoretical system as it applies to anaesthesia has been considered by White and Halsey (1974). There are three phases: gas, blood and brain lipid. The gas phase represents the inhaled anaesthetic mixture containing halothane. Blood transports the halothane to the brain where the site of action of the anaesthetic is assumed to be of lipid nature. The Ostwald solubility coefficient describes the volume of gas, measured at the temperature and pressure at which the gas dissolves, taken up by unit volume of the liquid. When the gas phase contains 1% halothane and the system is in equilibrium at 37°C, halothane has Ostwald solubility coefficients of 0·8 for the aqueous (blood) phase and 220 for the lipid phase (Allot et al. 1973). A fall in temperature of 5°C will not affect the concentration of halothane delivered to the blood if the vaporizer is adequately temperature compensated. The solubility of halothane in the blood will increase and, provided blood flow to the brain is maintained, a new equilibrium with brain lipid will be achieved. An increase of 22% in the solubility of halothane in the lipid phase will occur and anaesthesia should deepen.

The solubility of halothane in blood and plasma depends partly on the concentration and composition of the proteins in these body fluids (Laasberg & Hedley-Whyte 1970). Alterations in these factors may occur in hypothermia, cardiopulmonary bypass and crystalloid haemo-dilution. The increase in the blood solubility of halothane during induced hypothermia has been shown to be initially antagonized by crystalloid haemodilution. Feingold (1977) postulates that this antagon-ism can also be anticipated for methoxyflurane, enflurane and iso-flurane, but not for nitrous oxide and diethyl ether. The change in the halothane blood/gas partititon coefficient during crystalloid haemodilution was similar to that associated with anaemia, and at normothermia would have minimal effect. During the rewarming from hypothermia, the reverse changes occur and the low blood/gas partition coefficient means that clearance of the anaesthetic agent is enhanced.

Anaesthesia requires the development of a critical partial pressure of anaesthetic agent in the brain. This is achieved as a result of a number of factors: alveolar ventilation, anaesthetic uptake by the lung, blood flow from the lung to the brain, and anaesthetic solubility. Hypothermia causes respiratory and cardiovascular disturbances unless cardiopul-monary bypass and intermittent posture pressure ventilation are instituted. The effect of hypothermia on anaesthetic solubility means that the rate at which the partial pressure of an anaesthetic agent in the brain reaches the critical pressure to induce anaesthesia is slowed down. However, the partial pressure required to produce anaesthesia decreases during hypothermia and so, although the level to which the partial pressure must rise is reduced, this is opposed by the slower rate at which anaesthetic concentration is built up during induction. In a mathematical model Munson and Eger (1970) predicted that, at inspired concentrations of anaesthetic agent in excess of the minimum alveolar concentration, induction of anaesthesia is delayed during hypothermia. What is important when hypothermia occurs insidiously during anaesthesia is that the combination of respiratory and cardiovascular depression compounds the delay in recovery with all agents, and particularly with the highly soluble anaesthetics. The time for induction of anaesthesia with volatile agents in the febrile patient is shortened.

White and Halsey (1974) and Halsey and Higgs (1976) considered the effects of temperature on the mechanisms of anaesthetic action. The term 'cold narcosis' has been used to describe the observed anaesthetic-like action of hypothermia in warm-blooded animals.

The 'cold narcosis' phenomenon may not be wholly due to a generalized depression of metabolism, but further work in this field is required to determine the effect of temperature on the site of action of anaesthetics.

Heparin

Plasma heparin activity in man during normothermia decays exponentially (Olsson et al. 1963). During cardiopulmonary bypass and moderate hypothermia (26–29°C), Cohen et al. (1977) found, using a thrombin clotting time, that heparin decay is relatively insignificant, which could mean that further administration of heparin at this temperature should be avoided. On rewarming a linear decay curve was found which may represent the beginning of an exponential curve, but decay rates were highly variable from patient to patient. They suggest that the effect of heparin can be reversed by an appropriate dose of protamine, the dosage being calculated on the basis of the concentration of heparin in circulation in order to avoid a subsequent excess of protamine. Adverse effects of protamine include myocardial depression and a reduced platelet count (Swedenborg 1974; Jastrzebski et al. 1974). Guffin et al. (1976) evaluated a low-dose protamine regimen and found reduced postoperative bleeding. There is controversy, however, over these findings. It is likely that the metabolism of heparin is reduced by an amount which depends on the body temperature. Bull et al. (1975) found a non-significant reduction in heparin metabolism at 30°C compared with 37°C but used the activating clotting time which is a semi-quantitative method. Wright et al. (1964) support Cohen's report. Ellison et al. (1974) used a low-dose protamine regimen but found anticoagulation and clinical bleeding postoperatively. Glass (1977) postulates that the diversity of clinical findings may be related to vasoconstriction, low cardiac output or undefined pharmacological agents.

References

Agoston, S., Vermeer, G. A., Kersten, U. W. & Meijer, D. K. F. (1973) The fate of pancuronium bromide in man. *Acta anaesth. scand.*, *17*, 267–275.

Airaksinen, M. M. & Mattila, M. (1962) The sedative and lethal actions of reserpine in mice, as modified by 5-hydroxytryptophan, 3,4-dihydroxyphenylalanine, methylphenidate and nikethamide in cold and warm environments. *Acta pharmac. toxicol.*, *19*, 199–204.

Akhtar, M., Chakravarti, R. N., Sarkar, A. K. & Wahi, P. L. (1971) Effect of hypothermia on digitalis toxicity: An experimental study. *Indian J. med. Res.*, *59*, 58–63.

Allott, P. R., Steward, A., Flook, V. & Mapleson, W. W. (1973) Variation with temperature of the solubilities of inhaled anaesthetics in water, oil and biological media. *Br. J. Anaesth.*, *45*, 294–300.

Andjus, R. K. (1963) Symposium on temperature acclimatisation. *Fedn Proc. Fedn Am. Socs exp. Biol.*, *22*, 748–749.

Arvela, P. & Sotaniemi, E. (1968) The influence of environmental temperature on the concentration of pentobarbitone in the liver and brain of rats. *Br. J. Pharmac.*, *34*, 210P

Beaver, W. T. (1965) Mild analgesics: a review of their clinical pharmacology. *Am. J. med. Sci.*, *250*, 577–604.

Beaver, W. T. (1966) Mild analgesics: a review of their clinical pharmacology. *Am. J. med. Sci.*, *251*, 576–599.

Beyda, E. J., Jung, M. & Bellet, S. (1961) Effect of hypothermia on the tolerance of dogs to digitalis. *Circulation Res.*, *9*, 129–135.

Bidstrup, P. L., Bonnell, J. A. L. & Harvey, D. G. (1952) Prevention of acute dinitro-ortho-cresol (DNOC) poisoning. *Lancet*, *262*, 794–795.

Blach, H. H., Noyes, H. E. & Hughes, C. W. (1955) The influence of hypothermia on experimental peritonitis. *Surgery, St. Louis*, *38*, 1036–1042.

Blair, E. (1964) *Clinical Hypothermia*, p. 74. London: McGraw-Hill.

Bligh, J. & Johnson, K. G. (1973) Glossary of terms for thermal physiology. *J. appl. Physiol.*, *35*, 941–961.

Brigland, B., Goetzee, B., Maclagan, J. & Zaimis, E. (1958) The effect of lowered temperature on the action of neuromuscular blocking drugs. *J. Physiol., Lond. 141*, 425–434.

Brody, T. M. (1956) Action of sodium salicylate and related compounds on tissue metabolism *in vitro. J. Pharmac. exp. Ther.*, *117*, 39–51.

Bull, B. S., Korpman, R. A., Huse, W. M. & Briggs, B. D. (1975) Heparin therapy during extracorporeal circulation. I. Problems inherent in existing heparin protocols. *J. thorac. cardiovasc. Surg.*, *69*, 674–684.

Burch, G. E. & Miller, G. C. (1969) Hot and humid environments and the cardiovascular system. In: *Modern Trends in Cardiology II*, ed. A. Morgan Jones, p. 250. London: Butterworths.

Burch, G. E. & De Pasquale, N. (1959) Influence of air conditioning on hospitalised patients. *J. Am. med. Ass.*, *170*, 98–101.

Cohen, E. N., Brewer, H. W. & Smith, D. (1967) The metabolism and excretion of d-tubocurarine H[3]. *Anesthesiology*, *28*, 309–317.

Cohen, J. A., Frederickson, E. L. & Kaplan, J. A. (1977) Plasma heparin activity and antagonism during cardiopulmonary bypass with hypothermia. *Anesth. Analg. (Cleve.)*, *56*, 564–570.

Cohen, S. N. & Olson, W. A. (1970) Drugs that depress the newborn infant. *Pediat Clins N. Am.*, *17*, 835–850.

Conn, E. E. & Stumpf, P. K. (1976) *Outlines of Biochemistry*, 4th ed. p. 391. New York: John Wiley.

Cooper, K. E. & Cranston, W. I. (1966) Pyrogens and monoamine oxidase inhibitors. *Nature, Lond.*, *210*, 203–204.

Cooper, K. E. & Guenter, C. A. (1977) The effect on pulmonary ventilation of drugs which influence body temperature. *Pharmac. Ther. B.*, *3*, 113–121.

Cranston, W. I., Hellon, R. F., Luff, R. H., Rawlins, M. D. & Rosendorff, C. (1970) Observations on the mechanism of salicylate—induced antipyresis. *J. Physiol, Lond.*, *210*, 593–600.

Cree, J. E., Meyer, J. & Hailey, D. M. (1973) Diazepam in labour; its metabolism and effect on the clinical condition and thermogenesis of the newborn. *Br. med. J.*, *4*, 251–255.

Eger, E. I. (1962) Atropine, scopolamine and related compounds. *Anesthesiology*, *23*, 365–383.

Eger, E. I. & Larson, C. P. (1964) Anaesthetic solubility in blood and tissues: values and significance. *Br. J. Anaesth.*, *36*, 140–149.

Ellison, N., Beatty, C. P., Blake, D. R., Werzel, H. & MacVagh, H. (1974) Heparin rebound, studies in patients and volunteers. *J. thorac. cardiovasc. Surg.*, *67*, 723–729.

Feingold, A. (1977) Crystalloid hemo-dilution, hypothermia and halothane blood solubility during cardiopulmonary bypass. *Anesth. Analg. (Cleve.)*, *56*, 622–626.

Feldberg, W., Gupta, K. P., Milton, A. S. & Wendlant, S. (1973) Effect of pyrogen and antipyretics on prostaglandin activity in cisternal c.s.f. of unanaesthetised cats. *J. Physiol., Lond.*, *234*, 279–303.

Fuhrman, F. A. (1946) The effect of body temperature on drug action. *Physiol. Rev.*, *26*, 247–274.

Glass, D. D. (1977). Plasma heparin activity. *Anesth. Analg. (Cleve.)*, *56*, 569–570.

Goodman, L. S. & Gilman, A. (1975) *Pharmacological Basis of Therapeutics*, 5th ed. New York: MacMillan.

Guffin, A. V., Dunbar, R. W., Kaplan, J. A. & Bland, J. W. (1976) Successful use of a reduced dose of protamine after cardiopulmonary bypass. *Anesth. Analg. (Cleve.)*, *55*, 110–113.

Hägerdal, M., Welsh, F. A., Keykhah, M. M., Perez, E. & Harp, J. R. (1978) Protective effects of combinations of hypothermia and barbiturates in cerebral hypoxia in the rat. *Anesthesiology*, *49*, 165–169.

Halsey, M. J. & Higgs, E. G. (1976) Temperature dependence of anaesthetic potencies at high pressure. *Br. J. Anaesth.*, *48*, 264–265.

Ham, J., Miller, R. D., Benet, L. Z., Matteo, R. S. & Roderick, L. L. (1978) Pharmacokinetics and pharmacodynamics of d-tubocurarine during hypothermia in the cat. *Anesthesiology*, *49*, 324–329.

Han, Y. H. & Helrich, M. (1966a) Effect of body temperature on anesthetic blood levels of halothane in man. *Anesthesiology*, *27*, 217–218.

Han, Y. H. & Helrich, M. (1966b) Effect of temperature on solubility of halothane in human blood and brain tissue homogenate. *Anesth. Analg. (Cleve.)*, *45*, 775–780.

Herbert, C. L., Severinghaus, J. W. & Radigan, L. R. (1957) Management of patients during hypothermia. *Anesth. Analg. (Cleve.)*, *36*, 24–31.

Hoff, H. E., Deavers, S. & Huggins, R. A. (1961) Potassium distribution and toxicity in hypothermia. *J. appl. Physiol.*, *16*, 250–252.

Holmes, P. E. B., Jenden, D. J. & Taylor, D. B. (1951) The analysis of the mode of action of curare on neuromuscular transmission: the effect of temperature changes. *J. Pharmac. exp. Ther.*, *103*, 382–402.

Hubbard, J. I., Jones, S. F. & Landau, E. M. (1971) The effect of temperature change on transmitter release, facilitation and post-tetanic potentiation. *J. Physiol., Lond.*, *216*, 591–609.

Iampietro, P. F., Fiorica, V., Dille, R., Higgins, E. A., Funkhouser, G. & Moses, R. (1965) Influence of a tranquilliser on temperature regulation in man. *J. appl. Physiol.*, *20*, 365–370.

Jastrzebski, J., Sykes, M. K. & Woods, D. G. (1974) Cardiorespiratory effects of protamine after cardiopulmonary bypass in man. *Thorax*, *29*, 534–538.

Johnson, G. E., Sellers, E. A. & Schönbaum, E. (1963) Interrelationship of temperature on action of drugs. *Fedn Proc. Fedn Am. Socs exp. Biol.*, *22*, 745–749.

Kalser, S. C., Kelvington, E. J., Kunig, R. & Randolph, M. M. (1965c) Drug metabolism in hypothermia, uptake, metabolism and excretion of C^{14}-procaine by the isolated perfused rat liver. *J. Pharmac. exp. Ther.*, *164*, 396–404.

Kalser, S. C., Kelvington, E. J. & Randolph, M. M. (1968) Drug metabolism in hypothermia, uptake, metabolism and excretion of S^{35}-sulphanilamide by the isolated perfused rat liver. *J. Pharmac. exp. Ther.*, *159*, 389–398.

Kalser, S. C., Kelvington, E. J., Randolph, M. M. & Santomenna, D. M. (1965a) Drug metabolism in hypothermia II C^{14}-atropine uptake, metabolism and excretion by the isolated perfused rat liver. *J. Pharmac. exp. Ther.*, *147*, 260–269.

Kalser, S. C., Kelvington, E. J., Randolph, M. M. & Santomenna, D. M. (1965b) Drug metabolism in hypothermia I Biliary excretion of C^{14}-atropine metabolites in the intact and nephrectomised rat. *J. Pharmac. exp. Ther.*, *147*, 252–259.

Katz, B. & Miledi, R. (1965) The effect of temperature on the synapatic delay at the neuromuscular junction. *J. Physiol., Lond.*, *181*, 656–670.

Keatinge, W. R. (1968) *Survival in Cold Water*, p. 58. Oxford: Blackwell Scientific.

Laasberg, L. H. & Hedley-Whyte, J. (1970) Halothane solubility in blood and solutions of plasma proteins: effect of temperature, protein composition and hemoglobin concentration. *Anesthesiology*, *32*, 351–356.

Lafferty, J. J., Keykhah, M. M., Shapiro, H. M., Van Horn, K. & Behar, M. G. (1978) Cerebral hypometabolism obtained with deep pentobarbital anaesthesia and hypothermia (30°C). *Anesthesiology*, *49*, 159–164.

Lettau, H. F., Sellers, E. A. & Schönbaum, E. (1964) Modification of drug-induced hypothermia. *Can. J. Physiol. Pharmac.*, *42*, 745–755.

Lomax, P. (1965) The hypothermic effect of pentobarbital in the rat: sites and mechanisms of action. *Brain Res.*, *1*, 296–302.

Lomax, P. (1967) Investigations on the central effects of morphine on body temperature. *Arch. Biol. Med. Exp.*, *4*, 119–124.

Lotti, V. J., Lomax, P. & George, R. (1965) Temperature responses in the rat following intracerebral microinjection of morphine. *J. Pharmac. exp. Ther.*, *150*, 135–139.

McGrath, M. D. & Paley, R. G. (1960) Hypothermia induced in a myxoedematous patient by imipramine hydrochloride. *Br. med. J.*, *2*, 1364.

Magbagbeola, J. A. O. (1973) The effect of atropine premedication on body temperature of children in the tropics. *Br. J. Anaesth.*, *45*, 1139–1142.

Mahler, H. R. & Cordes, E. H. (1969) *Basic Biological Chemistry*, p. 370. New York: Harper and Row.

Meeter, E., Wolthuis, O. L. & Van Benthem, M. J. (1971) The anticholinesterase hypothermia in the rat: its practical application in the study of the central effectiveness of oximes. *Bull. Wld Hlth Org.*, *44*, 251–257.

Michenfelder, J. D. (1978) Hypothermia plus barbiturates. *Anesthesiology*, *49*, 157–158.

Miller, R. D. (1979) Recent developments with muscle relaxants and their antagonists. *Can. Anaesth. Soc. J.*, *26*, 83–93.

Miller, R. D. & Roderick, L. L. (1977) Pancuronium-induced neuromuscular blockade and its antagonism by neostigmine at 29, 37 and 41°C. *Anesthesiology*, *46*, 333–335.

Miyahara, J. T. & Karler, R. (1965) Effect of salicylate on oxidative phosphorylation and respiration of mitochondrial fragments. *Biochem. J.*, *97*, 194–198.

Munson, E. S. & Eger, E. I. (1970) The effects of hyperthermia and hypothermia on the rate of induction of anaesthesia: calculations using a mathematical model. *Anesthesiology*, *33*, 515–519.

Noble, J. & Matthew, H. (1969) Acute poisoning by tricyclic antidepressants; Clincal features and management of 100 patients. *Clin. Toxicol.*, *2*, 403–421.

Nordström, C.-H. & Rehncrona, S. (1978) Reduction of cerebral blood flow and oxygen consumption with a combination of barbiturate anaesthesia and induced hypothermia in the rat. *Acta anaesth. scand.*, *22*, 7–12.

Olsson, P., Lagergren, H. & Stig, E. (1963) The elimination from plasma of intravenous heparin; an experimental study on dogs and humans. *Acta med. scand.*, *173*, 619–630.

Pickles, V. R. (1972) Prostaglandins and aspirin. *Nature, Lond.*, *239*, 33–34.

Pollard, A. B. & Filbee, J. F. (1951) Recovery after poisoning with di-nitro-ortho-cresol. *Lancet*, *2*, 618–619.

Popovic, V. & Popovic, P. (1974) *Hypothermia in Biology and in Medicine*, p. 215. New York: Grune and Stratton.

Regan, M. J. & Eger, E. I. (1967) Effect of hypothermia in dogs on anesthetizing and apneic doses of inhalational agents. *Anesthesiology*, *28*, 689–700.

Shingleton, W. W., Smith, A. G. & Durham, N. C. (1961) Hypothermia against lethal dose of mechlorethamine. *Archs Surg., Chicago*, *82*, 400–404.

Smith, R. E. & Horwitz, B. A. (1969) Brown fat and thermogenesis. *Physiol. Rev.*, *49*, 330–416.

Speight, A. N. P. (1977) Floppy infant syndrome and maternal diazepam and/or nitrazepam. *Lancet*, *4*, 878.

Stone, C. A., Van Arman, C. G., Lotti, V. J., Minsker, D. H., Risley, E. A., Bagdon, W. J., Bokelman, D. L., Jensen, R. D., Mendlowski, B., Tate, C. L., Peck, H. M., Zwickey, R. E. & McKinney S. E. (1977) Pharmacology and toxicology of diflunisal. *Br. J. clin. Pharmac.*, *4*, 19S–29S.

Swedenborg, J. (1974) Inhibitory effect of polyphloretin phosphate upon platelet aggregation and hemodynamic and respiratory changes caused by thrombin and protamine. *J. Pharmac. exp. Ther.*, *188*, 214–221.

Webb, W. R., Harrison, N., Dodds, R., Wax, S. D. & Sugg, W. L. (1968) Protective effect of ethyl alcohol in profound hypothermia. *Cryobiology*, *4*, 290–294.

White, D. C. & Halsey, M. J. (1974) Effects of changes in temperature and pressure during experimental anaesthesia. *Br. J. Anaesth.*, *46*, 196–201.

Wislicki, L. (1960) Effects of hypothermia and hyperthermia on the action of neuro-muscular blocking agents. *i* Suxa-methonium. *Arch. int. Pharmacodyn. Thér.*, *126*, 68–78.

Wislicki, L. (1961) Drugs and body temperature. *Georgetown med. Bull.*, *15*, 137–141.

Wright, J. S., Osborn, J. J., Perkins, H. A. & Gerbode, F. (1964) Heparin levels during and after hypothermic perfusion. *J. cardio-vasc. Surg.*, *5*, 244–250.

Zaimis, E., Cannard, T. H. & Price, H. L. (1958) Effects of lowered muscle temperature upon neuromuscular blockade in man. *Science, N.Y.*, *128*, 34–35.

Malignant hyperthermia 4

G. M. HALL, MB, BS, PhD, MIBiol, FFARCS
Senior Lecturer and Honorary Consultant
Hammersmith Hospital and Royal Postgraduate Medical
School, London

Hyperthermia in anaesthesia is not a new phenomenon (Gibson 1900), but typically arose from the inability of a febrile patient, premedicated with atropine and anaesthetized with diethyl ether, to lose heat in a hot, humid environment (Guedel 1951). In the last twenty years a new syndrome has been described called malignant hyperthermia or hyperpyrexia. It occurs as the result of an abnormal response to one or more of the anaesthetic agents administered and is characterized by an increase in muscle metabolism and thus in heat production.

The first case was described by Denborough and Lovell (1960) and occurred in a 21-year-old man who required an open reduction of a compound fracture of the tibia. A conventional anaesthetic technique of thiopentone–suxamethonium–nitrous oxide, oxygen and halothane was used, which produced an increase in the temperature of the patient to 42·5°C. The subject survived the hyperthermic episode.

Further isolated examples of malignant hyperthemia were reported during the following years. There is little doubt that cases of malignant hyperthermia occurred before 1960 but were unrecognized. Indeed ten of the relatives of the patient described by Denborough and Lovell had died during general anaesthesia but this was attributed to 'ether sensitivity'. It reflects little credit on anaesthetists, who pride themselves on their clinical acumen, that the syndrome was initially reported by two physicians.

Wilson et al. (1967) stated that the following factors enable malignant hyperthermia to be differentiated from other cases of hyperthermia.

1. The patients were usually afebrile and healthy at the start of anaesthesia.
2. A very rapid rise in body temperature occurred and levels in excess of 41°C were common.
3. Other obvious causes of hyperthermia could be eliminated.
4. The outcome was usually fatal.

Stephen (1967) reviewed twelve cases of malignant hyperthermia, ten of whom died, and noted that the two anaesthetic agents most commonly used were halothane and suxamethonium. As anaesthetists become more aware of this lethal syndrome the number of cases reported increased so rapidly that Britt and Kalow (1970a) were able to review 89 patients. The importance of this complication of anaesthesia was emphasized by the staging of International Symposia in 1971 and 1977.

It is not the purpose of this chapter to review extensively the clinical literature on malignant hyperthermia. Instead the more important clinical aspects of the syndrome will be discussed and recommendations made which are based upon the successful management of MH-susceptible patients. The experimental work in the related porcine syndrome will not be described except when it is directly relevant to the clinical syndrome.

Definition of Malignant Hyperthermia

One of the major problems associated with malignant hyperthermia is the lack of an adequate definition. Keaney and Ellis (1971) attempted to define the syndrome in terms of a body temperature rise greater than 2°C/hour. The practical application of this definition has caused considerable difficulties. But since malignant hyperthermia is defined in terms of a rate of temperature increase, the period of time over which the temperature is measured must be stated. For example, an increase in body temperature during anaesthesia of 0·4°C in 10 minutes (2·4°C/hour) is defined as malignant hyperthermia but may be due to many other factors. The definition fails to emphasize that the temperature rise is but one manifestation of an increase in muscle metabolism. Small increases in core temperature are not uncommon after the induction of anaesthesia and the urgent clinical decision has to be made of distinguishing the onset of malignant hyperthermia from other benign causes of thermogenesis. In this situation objective evidence of an increase in muscle metabolism such as a hypercarbia, metabolic acidosis and hyperkalaemia, as shown by analysis of an arterial blood sample, must be present before a diagnosis of malignant hyperthermia can be made.

These criticisms of the definition of Keaney and Ellis (1971) may seem unduly harsh but if the strict criteria described above for the diagnosis of malignant hyperthermia were universally adopted then much of the confusion surrounding the supposed incidence, triggering agents and therapeutic agents would not have arisen.

INCIDENCE

Malignant hyperthermia is most common in children, adolescents and young adults. Males are affected more often than females (Britt 1972). The frequency of malignant hyperthermia has been estimated at around

1 in 14 000 anaesthetics at the Hospital for Sick Children, Toronto (Britt & Kalow 1970*a*) but only 1 in 190 000 in the United Kingdom (Wilson & Ellis 1979).

Britt and Kalow (1970*a*), in an early review, observed that patients who developed malignant hyperthermia had an increased incidence of congenital musculoskeletal disorders such as idiopathic kyphoscoliosis, ptosis and strabismus, congenital hernia, pes excavatum, susceptibility to muscle cramps, etc. No satisfactory explanation has been offered for this statistical observation although it has been used to support the occurrence of a subclinical myopathy in malignant hyperthermia.

Inheritance

The familial incidence of malignant hyperthermia was first described by Denborough et al. (1962) who investigated the family of the first case reported. Other families with a high incidence were subsequently reported in Canada, South Africa and the United Kingdom. However, not all of the reported cases appear to be familial and the remainder are often referred to as 'sporadic'.

Until recently the pattern of inheritance was referred to as autosomal dominant with reduced penetrance and variable expressivity—an impressive phrase of dubious clinical value. Careful studies on susceptible families in both Canada and the United Kingdom have suggested recently that the inheritance of susceptibility to malignant hyperthermia may be multifactorial, involving more than one gene (Kalow et al. 1977; Ellis et al. 1978).

Aetiology

Some susceptible individuals have a subclinical or overt myopathy (Isaacs & Barlow 1970*a*; Denborough et al. 1970) and an increased serum creatine kinase (CK) concentration (Isaacs & Barlow 1970*b*). Thus, the primary defect appears to be in the muscle cell and Britt and Kalow (1970*b*) postulated that many of the biochemical features, such as the muscle rigor, heat production and glycogenolysis, could be explained by the presence of an abnormally raised calcium ion concentration within the cytoplasm. The anaesthetic agent responsible for triggering the episode either caused the release of excess calcium, or, less likely, interfered with the re-uptake mechanisms within the cell. The exact site of the defect in excitation–contraction coupling in the muscle cell has yet to be established: all three subcellular organelles involved in calcium ion modulation, the sarcolemma, sarcoplasmic reticulum and mitochondria have been implicated. Since many susceptible patients lead an otherwise normal and healthy life the defect is unlikely to be more than an exaggeration of a normal physiological process, e.g. alteration in calcium binding.

Identification of Susceptible Patients

The three main methods of identification of malignant hyperthermia-susceptible patients are family history, increased circulating creatine kinase (CK) concentrations and histological/pharmacological assessment of a muscle biopsy.

Family History

It is mandatory for an anaesthetist to question carefully all patients prior to general anaesthesia about possible hyperthermic episodes in relatives who have undergone surgery. It is unlikely that a clear pattern of familial deaths during anaesthesia will ever be elucidated, but failure to enquire about the family anaesthetic history will assume increasing medico legal importance in the event of the subsequent occurrence of malignant hyperthermia.

Increased Serum CK Concentrations

Isaacs and Barlow (1970*b*) identified susceptible members of a family by the elevated CK concentrations. Unfortunately CK values are increased in many muscle disorders and change on a day-to-day basis in any given patient. Furthermore, Ellis et al. (1978) have reported that the CK concentration was normal in over half the susceptible patients they investigated. The diagnostic value of this enzyme estimation is therefore very limited but it is reasonable to infer that an otherwise healthy patient with a family history of malignant hyperthermia and an elevated CK value is susceptible.

Histological and Pharmacological Assessment of a Muscle Biopsy

The presence of a specific histopathological abnormality in the muscle is doubtful. A wide variety of pathological changes have been described and in an effort to account for these differences Isaacs and Heffron (1975) concluded that malignant hyperthermia may be associated with a number of different myopathies and that these myopathies differ from family to family.

Kalow et al. (1970) observed that muscle biopsies obtained from susceptible patients had a greater than normal sensitivity to caffeine alone and halothane plus caffeine. Subsequently several centres developed their own in vitro tests with other pharmacological agents. For example the centre in Leeds, United Kingdom, has relied predominantly on halothane (Ellis et al. 1978) whereas in Melbourne, Australia, a wider pharmacological screen with caffeine, potassium chloride, suxamethonium and halothane has been used (Moulds & Denborough 1974). It is unfortunate that a standard test has not evolved but this is not surprising when there is no agreement about the best site for the biopsy (Kalow et al. 1977).

As there are several safe anaesthetic techniques available for the susceptible patient, there is no necessity for a person who is thought to be susceptible to undergo a muscle biopsy before surgery can be undertaken. The main use of the biopsy technique will probably be in the elucidation of the genetics of the syndrome. It is inevitable, although unfortunate, that the validity of this screening procedure can never be tested in man.

TRIGGERING AGENTS

Virtually every drug used in anaesthetic practice has at some time been implicated in causing malignant hyperthermia. However, most of these agents can be discounted. The position is best summarized by stating that all the potent inhaled anaesthetic agents, and suxamethonium, can induce malignant hyperthermia.

Ellis et al. (1974) suggested that nitrous oxide was a triggering agent although the clinical description of the syndrome was incomplete and there was no supporting biochemical data. Their report is incompatible with the successful administration of nitrous oxide to many survivors.

Britt et al. (1974) reported two cases in which tubocurarine was thought to be the causative factor. In both cases other agents known to induce malignant hyperthermia were given. Tubocurarine has been used successfully in several patients who had developed malignant hyperthermia during previous anaesthetics (author's unpublished results) and there is now little doubt that non-depolarizing neuromuscular blocking drugs are safe in susceptible patients.

CLINICAL SIGNS OF MH

The normal response to suxamethonium, i.e. muscle fasciculation followed by relaxation, does not occur in some susceptible patients. Instead they respond with vigorous fasciculations, but fail to relax. There is often marked spasm of the masseter muscles and endotracheal intubation is difficult. This abnormal response is the initial trigger to malignant hyperthermia and the correct procedure is to abandon the anaesthetic, if possible, and monitor the patient intensively for signs of MH.

Suxamethonium alone produces a mild and so far non-fatal hyperthermic response in man. The incorrect and probably fatal procedure is to carry on the anaesthetic with a potent volatile agent such as halothane.

The reliability of this abnormal response to suxamethonium as an indicator of the onset of malignant hyperthermia has yet to be established but it is one of the few gross signs available.

An unexplained tachycardia or dysrhythmia should alert the anaesthetist to the possibility of malignant hyperthermia since these are early signs of the syndrome, observed in nearly all the reported cases.

Overt muscle rigidity is not always present although this sign is not one which anaesthetists commonly look for except when it makes intubation or ventilation difficult.

An increase in carbon dioxide production from the muscle is responsible for the tachypnoea observed in the spontaneously breathing patient and the failure to synchronize with the ventilator sometimes found in the ventilated patient. The skin of the hyperthermic patient does not always feel warmer than usual because of the failure of the peripheral circulation which is shown by cyanosis of the extremities.

Clinical features found in the later stages include acute renal failure, disseminated intravascular coagulation and even decerebration if the brain temperature exceeds 43°C. Patients who have survived may require haemodialysis for acute, reversible tubular necrosis mainly caused by the excessive myoglobin release from damaged muscle.

The clinical features may be summarized (Ryan 1977):

Early Clinical Features of Malignant Hypothermia
1. Abnormal response to suxamethonium.
2. Unexplained tachycardia and dysrhythmias.
3. In some cases, muscle rigidity.
4. Tachypnoea.
5. Peripheral cyanosis.
6. In some cases, the patient's skin feels hot to the touch.
7. Increased use of soda-lime.

Late Clinical Features of Malignant Hypothermia
1. Acute renal failure.
2. Disseminated intravascular coagulation.
3. Decerebration

METABOLIC CHANGES

Although there is now an extensive literature on the metabolic and hormonal changes in the porcine syndrome, a detailed description of the biochemical changes in human malignant hyperthermia has not been obtained because of the unexpected and occasional nature of the syndrome. There is considerable inconsistency in the results of investigations of the clinical syndrome probably because of the variation in the severity of the cases and the adequacy of treatment given, e.g. correction of the acidosis and rehydration.

The most consistent finding is the presence of a severe acidosis with arterial pH values often below 7·0. As emphasized previously, a diagnosis cannot be made in the absence of a gross acidosis. The acidosis is due to hypercarbia and lactic acid from the increase in aerobic and anaerobic muscle metabolism respectively. Hyperkalaemia is usually present and potassium concentrations greater than 7·0 mmol/litre are common. It has been assumed that the excess potassium is derived from the damaged striated muscle but recent experiments on the porcine syndrome indicate that most of the potassium comes from the liver (Hall et al. 1980).

An early review (Britt & Kalow 1970a) indicated that arterial hypoxaemia was common but more recent work suggests that, although the mixed venous blood is profoundly desaturated, it is relatively easy to maintain normal arterial oxygenation. Gross haemoconcentration is observed in the established syndrome and may be due to a shift in water from the extracellular to the intracellular compartment as the 'leakiness' of the muscle membrane increases. Hyperphosphataemia has been reported (Britt et al. 1977a) and is caused by the breakdown of the muscle adenine nucleotides, in particular the conversion of adenosine triphosphate to the diphosphate with the release of heat and inorganic phosphate. The blood glucose concentration may be increased but this is not a consistent finding (Britt 1972). In the pig the hyperglycaemia is due mainly to hepatic glycogenolysis (Hall et al. 1980).

TREATMENT

The most important step in the treatment of malignant hyperthermia is to remove the triggering agent, e.g. discontinue the administration of halothane. The treatment is best considered in terms of general supportive therapy, cooling the patient and the administration of specific therapeutic agents.

General Supportive Therapy

Most treatment protocols recommend that once administration of the potent inhalational agent has been discontinued the patient should be hyperventilated with 100% oxygen to correct the hypercarbia and hypoxaemia. Since hypoxaemia is not a major problem in MH and nitrous oxide is not a triggering agent, the use of a 50% nitrous oxide/50% oxygen inspired gas mixture is perfectly adequate and does not rely on severe metabolic changes maintaining unconsciousness. Muscle rigidity can involve the muscles of the chest wall so that hyperventilation may not be possible with a pressure-cycled ventilator. The metabolic acidosis requires prompt and vigorous treatment with large quantities of intravenous sodium bicarbonate. Particularly severe cases have required a total of 1000 mmol of sodium bicarbonate to maintain normal acid–base balance, more than the total stock of some hospital pharmacy departments!

The hyperkalaemia is treated with an intravenous infusion of dextrose and insulin, 2·0–2·5 g of dextrose for each unit of soluble insulin. This regimen will need modification if hyperglycaemia is already present and this can be determined by the use of a Dextrostix. If the hyperkalaemia is so severe that ventricular fibrillation and cardiac arrest are considered imminent then calcium chloride is given intravenously, e.g. 5 ml of 10% calcium chloride, in spite of the raised calcium concentration within the muscle.

The haemoconcentration should be corrected by the rapid infusion of large volumes of crystalloid solutions. Although it is preferable that the infusion fluid is cold, rapid restoration of the circulating plasma volume is more important. Sodium chloride solution (0·9%) is the intravenous fluid of choice since Hartmann's solution contains lactate and potassium ions and 5% dextrose is inappropriate in patients with hyperglycaemia. Once adequate rehydration has been achieved a diuresis is induced with either frusemide or mannitol in an attempt to prevent renal failure.

The tachycardia and dysrhythmias are caused by a marked increase in sympathetic nervous system activity and, if troublesome, may be treated with a small intravenous dose of a β-adrenergic blocking drug.

Cooling the Patient

The undue emphasis on the increase in body temperature in malignant hyperthermia at the expense of prompt treatment of the associated metabolic changes has contributed to the high mortality rate of the syndrome, at present approximately 50%. All the reviews of the data collected from patients, for example Britt et al. (1977b), have shown that many patients die with a body temperature less than 42°C. The question must be asked; why have these patients died? It cannot be from the hyperthermia *per se*, since Pettigrew et al. (1974) have used induced hyperthermia to 42°C for four hours as a treatment for carcinomatosis without any ill effects. The lethal temperature for any animal is usually about 6°C more than the normal body temperature, so man can probably survive to at least 43°C. It is most likely that those patients who died at less than 42°C suffered from the lethal effects of a gross acidosis and hyperkalaemia. In the porcine model it is possible to control the temperature increase of the animal during the response but this has no effect on the fatal outcome despite the maintenance of normothermia.

The best method of cooling a patient is to use a specific therapeutic agent (see below) to restore normal muscle metabolism and thereby remove the cause of the increased thermogenesis. Many physical methods of cooling the patient have also been advocated. Surface cooling is quite useful in children but less so in adults and often ineffective when the peripheral circulation is inadequate. If an operation within the pleural or peritoneal cavity is in progress then these large surfaces may be utilized. Gjessing et al. (1976) have even suggested peritoneal dialysis with rapid exchanges of ice-cold dialysis solution.

The most effective method of cooling is to use cardiopulmonary bypass which can be instituted using cannulation of the femoral vessels (Ryan et al. 1974). Physical methods of cooling assume a low priority in the treatment of malignant hyperthermia, after the correction of the metabolic abnormalities and the use of a specific therapeutic agent.

Specific Therapeutic Agents
Three compounds have been considered as specific therapeutic agents: procaine or procainamide, corticosteroids and dantrolene.

Procaine
For several years procaine was advocated as the treatment for malignant hyperthermia. The interest in procaine stemmed from the observation by Harrison (1971) that large doses (30 mg procaine/kg body weight) reversed malignant hyperthermia in two of five pigs. It is important to note that many other investigators have failed in attempts to duplicate the beneficial effects of procaine in the porcine syndrome: Gronert et al. (1976b) also failed to prevent it when the procaine was given prophylactically. There is thus little evidence to support the use of this drug in porcine MH.

Several clinical case reports in the early 1970s advanced the claims for procaine but it was used in combination with many other agents. A more rational basis for its use was provided by Moulds and Denborough (1972) and Harriman et al. (1973) who demonstrated that procaine reduced a halothane-induced contracture in muscle biopsies obtained from susceptible patients. However, Hall and Lister (1974) pointed out that the concentrations used in vitro were at least ten-fold higher than those obtained in vivo. More recent case reports have found procaine to be ineffective and sometimes hazardous because of the myocardial depressant properties of the drug. Procaine can no longer be recommended for the treatment of human malignant hyperthermia.

Corticosteroids
Large doses of corticosteroids such as hydrocortisone (Ellis 1973) and dexamethasone (Ellis et al. 1974) have been advocated for the treatment of MH. No rationale for this therapy has been advanced other than the use of compounds with 'membrane-stabilizing properties' and it is impossible to see how they may have a direct and rapid effect in reducing the intracellular calcium ion concentration. Britt et al. (1977b), in a statistical evaluation of the treatment of 290 patients, found that the use of steroids was associated with a significantly increased mortality. Hall et al. (1977) also observed that the intravenous use of 30 mg methylprednisolone/kg body weight in pigs was totally ineffective. In conclusion: corticosteroids appear to be ineffective, although it is difficult to envisage how they may be harmful.

Dantrolene

Dantrolene is a phenytoin compound which was synthesized in 1967. In 1975, Harrison observed that dantrolene was effective in treating seven of eight pigs with malignant hypothermia and since then these results have been confirmed by other investigators using the porcine model. The lack of a suitable stable intravenous preparation has delayed the introduction of dantrolene for use in man, but the drug is at present on monitored release in the USA where it has been given successfully in a few cases. It is anticipated that a preparation of dantrolene for intravenous use will be marketed in the United Kingdom in 1980. When available, dantrolene will be the key therapeutic agent and should be given intravenously immediately after the removal of the triggering agent and the correction of the acidosis by hyperventilation and bicarbonate. The initial studies with porcine models suggested that 7·5 mg dantrolene/kg body weight was necessary to treat successfully the established syndrome but more recent work has found that 2–2·5 mg dantrolene/kg body weight is effective in the early stages of the response. As the response to dantrolene is so rapid it seems reasonable to suggest an initial dose of 2–2·5 mg/kg body weight in the clinical syndrome. More can be given if there are no beneficial effects within 10–15 minutes, for example reduction in the acidosis, tachycardia, muscle rigidity and body temperature. A major advantage of dantrolene compared with procaine is its lack of myocardial depressant properties at the dosage used.

Dantrolene acts on striated muscle by uncoupling the normal 'excitation–contraction' coupling mechanism. Depolarization of the sarcolemma and the invagination of the membrane, the T-tubular system, occur normally, but there is no release of calcium within the cell from the sarcoplasmic reticulum. If the exact site of action of dantrolene can be determined it may indicate the defect within the calcium-regulating mechanism responsible for malignant hyperthermia.

Monitoring in Established Malignant Hyperthermia

Once the initial therapeutic steps have been undertaken the following monitoring facilities are essential to provide guidance for further treatment (Ryan 1977):

1. Muscle temperature probe
2. Electrocardiograph (ECG)
3. Arterial cannulation
4. Central venous cannulation
5. Urinary catheter.

The temperature probe is preferably positioned in a large mass of skeletal muscle as this is the primary source of heat production: other sites of temperature measurement are less accurate. The ECG is used to show the dysrhythmias and the severity of the hyperkalaemia, and in monitoring the success or failure of therapy. Arterial and central venous cannulations are necessary to show changes in arterial pH, P_{CO_2} and potassium concentrations and also to assess the adequacy of fluid replacement.

ANAESTHESIA FOR SUSCEPTIBLE PATIENTS
The first case described by Denborough and Lovell in 1960 required a further anaesthetic a year later for the removal of a ureteric calculus. This was achieved successfully with a spinal anaesthetic. The use of local analgesic techniques is the most satisfactory method of anaesthetizing susceptible patients.

Local Analgesia
There is considerable confusion about the safety of some local analgesics in susceptible patients. This has arisen from the mis-application to the clinical situation of in vitro studies on isolated muscle strips with abnormally high concentrations of local analgesics (2–5 mmol/litre). It is known from such studies that the charged or protonated form of local analgesic lowers the intracellular calcium ion concentration, but the uncharged form increases the available calcium. On this basis it was concluded that local analgesics with a high dissociation constant (pK_a), such as procaine (8·9), existed largely in the protonated form at physiological pH and were not only safe but potentially beneficial (see specific therapeutic agents), but local analgesics with a low dissociation constant, e.g. lignocaine (7·9), had a significant number of uncharged molecules at physiological pH and may actually have exacerbated the development of malignant hyper-thermia. Thus for many years anaesthetists were advised that the local analagesic of choice was procaine and that lignocaine (pK_a 7·9) and bupivacaine (pK_a 8·1) were potentially dangerous. It is now realized that this extrapolation of the in vitro studies to the clinical situation is unjustified and all the local analgesic drugs are safe. For example, Willatts (1979) has recently reported the successful management of two susceptible patients in labour with extradural analgesia using bupivacaine.

General Anaesthesia
It is possible, with a knowledge of those agents responsible for triggering malignant hyperthermia, to devise a safe anaesthetic. Early techniques involved the use of neurolept anaesthesia or a nitrous oxide–oxygen–pethidine sequence (Relton 1971). Muscle relaxation can be achieved with either tubocuraine or, better still, pancuronium which has not been implicated as a possible triggering agent. All the common

intravenous induction agents and analgesics are safe. I use routinely a thiopentone, pancuronium, nitrous oxide, oxygen, fentanyl technique in malignant hyperthermia patients after heavy premedication. Adequate sedation before the induction of anaesthesia is essential because preoperative apprehension and undue muscle activity increase the likelihood of developing malignant hyperthermia.

Two controversial points associated with general anaesthesia for susceptible patients are the necessity for a vapour-free anaesthetic machine and the use of atropine. It is well known that the volatile agents dissolve in the circuit tubing and other parts of the anaesthetic machine and that a vaporizer set in the 'off' position may have a small leak (Robinson et al. 1977). The amount of volatile agent required to trigger malignant hyperthermia in man is not known but in the porcine model we have found that at least 1% halothane for five minutes is necessary to start the response in a previously anaesthetized animal. This is far in excess of the amount of anaesthetic agent that is likely to be present in the anaesthetic machine and circuits. I have found that the use of an anaesthetic machine from which the vaporizer has been removed, together with clean tubing, is satisfactory.

Britt and Kalow (1970a) observed in a statistical survey that the use of atropine for premedication was associated with a much increased incidence of rigidity. However, it is difficult to envisage how a small dose of atropine can increase muscle metabolism and atropine should be given if indicated on clinical grounds.

Harrison (1975) and Gronert et al. (1976a) found that pre-treatment with intravenous dantrolene protected pigs. Although dantrolene is not available clinically as an intravenous preparation it is used orally, as Dantrium, to treat muscle spasticity. It is logical, therefore, to treat susceptible patients with oral dantrolene preoperatively and several successful cases have been reported. As dantrolene achieves a peak blood value four hours after oral administration and has a half-life of just over eight hours, intensive treatment within the 12–24 hours before surgery is sufficient, e.g. 10 mg dantrolene/kg body weight in the 24 hours before surgery would be appropriate (Gronert et al. 1976a).

CONCLUSION

A knowledge of those anaesthetic agents which trigger malignant hyperthermia, together with the use of oral dantrolene, enables the anaesthetist to manage successfully a patient who is known preoperatively to be potentially susceptible. The problem still arises of the treatment of the hyperthermic episode which occurs unexpectedly during anaesthesia. When intravenous dantrolene is available there will be a dramatic reduction in mortality. It is important to remember that the successful use of dantrolene will depend not only on prompt diagnosis but also on treatment of the associated metabolic changes. Dantrolene will be of no value if given after a series of cardiac arrests due to profound hyperkalaemia and acidosis.

It is unwise to rely on the routine measurement of body temperature for the early recognition of malignant hyperthermia since severe biochemical changes can arise with only a small increase in body temperature. The patient's best protection, as always, is the presence of a well-informed and skilful anaesthetist.

In conclusion, the future for susceptible patients is improving. During the next few years the management of such cases will become routine and the syndrome which has caused so much interest and alarm in the last twenty years will be regarded as just another complication of anaesthesia.

References

Britt, B. A. (1972) Recent advances in malignant hyperthermia. *Anesth. Analg. curr. Res.*, *51*, 841–850.

Britt, B. A. & Kalow, W. (1970a) Malignant hyperthermia. A statistical review. *Can. Anaesth. Soc. J.*, *17*, 293–315.

Britt, B. A. & Kalow, W. (1970b) Malignant hyperthermia: Aetiology unknown! *Can. Anaesth. Soc. J.*, *17*, 316–330.

Britt, B. A., Kwong, F. H. F. & Endrenyi, L. (1977a) The clinical and laboratory features of malignant hyperthermia management— A review. In: *Malignant Hyperthermia: Current Concepts*, ed. E. O. Henschel, p. 9. New York: Appleton–Century–Crofts.

Britt, B. A., Kwong, F. H. F. & Endrenyi, L. (1977b) Management of malignant hyperthermia susceptible patients—a review. In: *Malignant Hyperthermia: Current Concepts*, ed. E. O. Henschel, p. 63. New York: Appleton–Century–Crofts.

Britt, B. A., Webb, G. E. & LeDuc, C. (1974) Malignant hyperthermia induced by curare. *Can. Anaesth. Soc. J.*, *21*, 371–375.

Denborough, M. A., Ebeling, P., King, P. O. & Zapf, P. W. (1970) Myopathy and malignant hyperthermia. *Lancet*, *1*, 1138–1140.

Denborough, M. A., Forster, J. F. A., Lovell, R. R. H., Maplestone, P. A. & Villiers, J. D. (1962) Anaesthetic deaths in a family. *Br. J. Anaesth.*, *34*, 395–396.

Denborough, M. A. & Lovell, R. R. H. (1960) Anaesthetic deaths in a family. *Lancet*, *2*, 45.

Ellis, F. R. (1973) Malignant hyperthermia. *Anaesthesia*, *28*, 245–252.

Ellis, R. F., Cain, P. A. & Harriman, D. G. F. (1978) Multifactorial inheritance of malignant hyperthermia susceptibility. In: *Malignant Hyperthermia* ed. J. A. Aldrete & B. A. Britt, p. 329. New York: Grune and Stratton.

Ellis, F. R., Clarke, I. M. C., Appleyard, T. N. & Dinsdale, R. C. W. (1974) Malignant hyperthermia induced with nitrous oxide and treated with dexamethasone. *Br. med. J.*, *4*, 270–271.

Gibson, C. L. (1900)) Heat stroke as a post-operative complication. *J., Am. med. Ass.*, *27*, 955.

Gjessing, J., Barsa, J. & Tomlin, P. J. (1976) A possible means of rapid cooling in the emergency treatment of malignant hyperthermia. *Br. J. Anaesth.*, *48*, 469–473.

Gronert, G. A., Milde, J. H. & Theye, R. A. (1976a) Dantrolene in porcine malignant hyperthermia. *Anaesthesiology*, *44*, 488–495.

Gronert, G. A., Milde, J. H. and Theye, R. A. (1976b) Porcine malignant hyperthermia induced by halothane and succinylcholine: Failure of treatment with procaine or procainamide. *Anaesthesiology*, *44*, 124–132.

Guedel, A. E. (1951) *Inhalational Anaesthesia*, 2nd ed., p. 110. New York: MacMillan.

Hall, G. M. & Lister, D. (1974) Procaine and malignant hyperthermia. *Lancet*, *1*, 208.

Hall, G. M., Lucke, J. N. & Lister, D. (1977) The failure of methyprednisolone treatment in porcine malignant hyperthermia. *Lancet*, *2*, 1359.

Hall, G. M., Lucke, J. N., Lovell, R. & Lister, D. (1980) Porcine malignant hyperthermia: VII Hepatic metabolism. *Br. J. Anaesth.*, *52*, 11–17.

Harriman, D. G. F., Sumner, D. W. & Ellis, F. R. (1973) Malignant hyperpyrexia myopathy. *Q. Jl. Med.*, *42*, 639–664.

Harrison, G. G. (1971) Anaesthetic-induced malignant hyperpyrexia: A suggested method of treatment. *Br. med. J.*, *3*, 454–456.

Harrison, G. G. (1975) Control of the malignant hyperpyrexic syndrome in MHS swine by dantrolene sodium. *Br. J. Anaesth.*, *47*, 62–65.

Issacs, H. & Barlow, M. B. (1970*a*) Malignant hyperpyrexia during anaesthesia: possible association with sub-clinical myopathy. *Br. med. J.*, *1*, 275–277.

Issacs, H. & Barlow, M. B. (1970*b*) The genetic background to malignant hyper-pyrexia revealed by serum creatine phosphokinase estimations in asymp-tomatic relatives. *Br. J. Anaesth.*, *42*, 1077–1084.

Issacs, H. & Heffron, J. J. A. (1975) Morphological and biochemical defects in muscles of human carriers of the malignant hyperthermia syndrome. *Br. J. Anaesth.*, *47*, 475–481.

Kalow, W., Britt, B. A. & Richter, A. (1977) The caffeine test of isolated human muscle in relation to malignant hyperthermia. *Can. Anaesth. Soc. J.*, *24*, 678–694.

Kalow, W., Britt, B. A., Terreau, M. E. & Haist, C. (1970) Metabolic error of muscle metabolism after recovery from malignant hyperthermia. *Lancet*, *2*, 895–898.

Keaney, N. P. & Ellis, F. R. (1971) Malignant hyperpyrexia. *Br. med. J.*, *4*, 49.

Moulds, R. F. W. & Denborough, M. A. (1972) Procaine in malignant hyperpyrexia. *Br. med. J.*, *4*, 526–528.

Moulds, R. F. W. & Denborough, M. A. (1974) Identification of susceptibility to malignant hyperpyrexia. *Br. med. J.*, *2*, 245–247.

Pettigrew, R. T., Galt, J. M., Ludgate, C. M., Horn, D. B. & Smith, A. N. (1974) Circulatory and biochemical effects of whole body hyperthermia. *Br. J. Surg.*, *61*, 727–730.

Relton, J. E. S. (1971) Malignant hyperthermia—Anaesthetic techniques and agents. In: *International Symposium on Malignant Hyperthermia*, ed. R. A. Gordon, B. A. Britt & W. Kalow, p. 425. Springfield, Ill.: Charles C Thomas.

Robinson, J. S., Thompson, J. M. & Barratt, R. S. (1977) Inadvertent contami-nation of anaesthetic circuits with halothane. *Br. J. Anaesth.*, *49*, 745–754.

Ryan, J. F. (1977) Treatment of malignant hyperthermia. In: *Malignant Hyperthermia: Current Concepts*, ed. E. O. Henschel, p. 47. New York: Appleton–Century–Crofts.

Ryan, J. F., Donlon, J. V., Malt, R. A., Bland, J. H. L., Buckley, M. J., Sreter, F. A. & Lowenstein, E. (1974) Cardiopulmonary bypass in the treatment of malignant hyperthermia. *New Engl. J. Med.*, *290*, 1121–1122.

Stephen, C. R. (1967) Fulminating hyperthermia during anaesthesia and surgery. *J. Am. med. Ass.*, *202*, 178–182.

Willatts, S. M. (1979) Malignant hyperthermia susceptibility. Management during pregnancy and labour. *Anaesthesia*, *34*, 41–46.

Wilson, M. E. & Ellis, F. R. (1979) Predicting malignant hyperpyrexia. *Br. J. Anaesth.*, *51*, 66P.

Wilson, R. D., Dent, T. E., Traber, D. L., McCoy, N. R. & Allen, C. R. (1967) Malignant hyperpyrexia with anaesthesia. *J. Am. med. Ass.*, *202*, 183–186.

Maintenance of body temperature   5

About forty years after the introduction of general anaesthesia, it was noticed that a fall in body temperature frequently occurred. The open technique of administering the volatile anaesthetic agents which were used at that time chills each inspired breath as it passes through the layers of gauze on which liquid is vapourizing. It was also recognized at about that time that an increase occurred in heat loss by radiation from exposed surfaces of the body and that there was a reduction in heat production as a result of the lowered tissue metabolism.

In the early part of this century, attempts were being made to reduce heat loss during surgery by warming the ether vapour, by maintaining operating room temperatures above 27°C and by the use of dry swabs in surgery instead of wet ones. However, the use of high ambient temperature and humidity was incriminated by Clarke et al. (1954) in the production of hyperpyrexia, convulsions and death which occurred in association with general anaesthesia in infants.

Air-conditioning of operating theatres can prevent heat accumulation during anaesthesia and allow a degree of control (depending on the type of air-conditioning unit) over environmental conditions in theatre. Air-conditioning is rarely installed in recovery areas, and not always in intensive care units.

Roe (1970) describes the anaesthetized patient as existing in a state of 'poikilothermy'. This is defined as a pattern of thermoregulation in which a species exhibits a large variation in core body temperature which is closely related to ambient temperature. An example of such an animal is a fish which conforms to the temperature of the water surrounding it. The application of the term poikilothermy to man should only be allowed to emphasize the importance of environmental conditions during operations and the effects of altered temperature regulation during anaesthesia: man remains a homeotherm even during anaesthesia and attempts to maintain his body temperature within limits despite large variations in ambient temperature.

The physiological effects of sleep should be understood when the effect of anaesthetics on thermoregulation are being considered. The diurnal variation of body temperature has already been described

(Chapter 1) and may have an influence on body temperature responses which have been attributed to anaesthesia. Kreider et al. (1958) measured the oxygen consumption and the rectal and mean skin temperatures (using a weighted formula of ten sites) in young, sleeping men in a comfortable ambient temperature of 26–27°C. Their rectal temperatures decreased by a mean of 1·2°C over the first six hours of sleep and the oxygen consumption fell significantly over the same period. A heat loss of 17–42 J/hour produced no discomfort or shivering on waking.

Anaesthesia affects the behavioural and the physiological heat-regulating mechanisms. The patient is deprived of his conscious feeling of heat or cold and is unable to respond by changing his clothes and environment. His autonomic nervous defenses can also be greatly impaired. The surroundings of the patient come under the control of the theatre staff, although the anaesthetist should have the responsibility of coordinating the activity of the technical, nursing and surgical staff in the patient's best interest.

Roe (1970) lists the various physiological effects of anaesthetic agents. There is a partial inactivation of the hypothalamic regulatory centres (no direct evidence for this is presented) and circulatory changes occur, especially in the peripheral vessels. Muscle tone is altered and oxygen consumption is reduced.

Factors producing an alteration in body temperature can usually be avoided or measures can be taken which reduce their effects. For this to be done, however, the anaesthetist must be aware of them and the efficiency of the methods which are available to counteract them. The selection of method depends on the preoperative condition of the patient, the type of operation and the recovery facilities available. Preoperatively the patient may present with a derangement of body temperature. Patients with infections are usually pyrexial, as are some patients with malignancies. Where there is an inadequate thermoregulatory response to an obvious infection, an abnormality of temperature regulation may already be present. Hypothermia may occur in neonates simply on transfer from the ward to the theatre and this must be diagnosed prior to induction of anaesthesia so that the effects of hypothermia will be avoided. The use of routine temperature monitoring has been advocated for all anaesthetized patients and Lees et al. (1978) recommend the use of a forehead liquid crystal thermometer.

Temperature Measuring Sites for use During Anaesthesia

The majority of temperature studies in anaesthesia before 1970 used the rectal temperature only as an indication of heat loss or gain. Not only is a record of a single temperature an inaccurate assessment of the situation, but rectal temperatures are notoriously inaccurate indicators of core temperature. Cooper and Kenyon (1957) compared rectal and oesophageal temperatures during induced hypothermia. Rectal temperatures deviated by up to 2°C from oesophageal temperatures during cooling and rewarming. Benzinger (1969) reflects that the anal area has no thermal significance because it is far removed from both the central nervous system and the heart. Hall (1978) states that rectal temperature measurements during anaesthesia should be used only when no other site is possible.

The placement of an oesophageal probe, although reflecting aortic temperatures (Cooper & Kenyon 1957), does require skill and attention to detail and the position should be checked (e.g. radiographically) wherever possible, particularly in studies which require accuracy. Whitby and Dunkin (1968) have shown that the probe should be placed in the lower quarter of the oesophagus in order to avoid the cooling effects of inspired gases into the trachea. In 1971 the same workers confirmed the reliability of the probe in this position, provided that the thorax was not open and there was no infusion of cold blood into the patient. They found that nasopharyngeal temperatures were unreliable because of the effect of leakage of gases from around the endotracheal tube and because there was insufficient insulation from external cold. Accidental displacement may also have occurred. There are anatomical differences between individuals with regard to the length of the oesophagus and in infants and children the formula of Whitby and Dunkin (1970) should be used to calculate the correct location for an oesophageal probe, d cm below the corniculate cartilages, where

$$d = 10 + \frac{2 \times \text{age in years}}{3}$$

It would be helpful if oesophageal probes were calibrated in centimetres, and Whitby and Dunkin (1970) stress that the tip of the probe should be moved about 2 cm up and down before taping in position, to confirm that the probe is below the area affected by ventilation.

The other site of measurement of core body temperature is the ear. The validity of tympanic thermometry has been discussed previously (see Chapter 2), but after reports of occasional trauma to the tympanic membrane the method has been modified. Keatinge and Sloan (1973) made use of the external auditory canal with a probe inserted 1 cm into it (using cotton wool as packing) and a servo-controlled heating pad around the ear and compared that site with the oesophageal temperature recordings from conscious subjects who were partially immersed in hot and cold water. Even in cold surroundings the method was reliable and it is convenient enough to be used in all cases except surgery on the head. Holdcroft and Hall (1978), using a similar method, found that the aural canal temperature had a correlation of 0·93 with the oesophageal temperature but only 0·75 with the rectal temperature for the periods before, during and after operation.

Calculation of Heat Loss

Redistribution of body heat during anaesthesia is to be expected from a theoretical consideration of the peripheral circulatory changes which occur. These can vary not only from one anaesthetic agent to another but also from one technique to another with the same agent. A single core temperature will not indicate the occurrence of this phenomenon (Figures 28 and 29). House and Vale (1972) designed nomograms for the calculation of body heat loss in order to make the calculation easier and thereby facilitate its more widespread use. Their mean skin temperature is derived from a weighted formula using the forearm, calf and abdominal skin temperatures. The three-site formula has not been evaluated during anaesthesia or in the recovery phase, but its simplicity is to be recommended. A four-site formula for mean skin temperature has been evaluated by Holdcroft and Hall (1978) and found to be reliable for calculations of heat loss or gain in anaesthetized patients. The sites themselves, like those chosen by House and Vale (1972), are readily accessible and do not require a large number of leads to be connected to the patient. Total heat content can be calculated rapidly with a simple pocket calculator using these equations, whose characteristics and deficits have been described in a previous section:

Mean skin temperature $= 0{\cdot}3$ (nipple + arm) $+ 0{\cdot}2$ (thigh + calf)

Mean body temperature $= (0{\cdot}66 \times$ core temperature) $+ (0{\cdot}34 \times$ mean skin temperature)

Body heat content (J) $=$ mean body temperature (°C) $\times 0{\cdot}83$ (specific heat of the tissues) $\times$ weight (kg) $\times 4{\cdot}18$

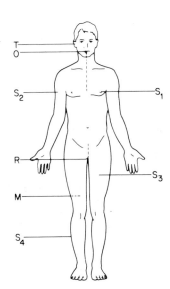

Fig. 28. Position of Temperature Probes

T = aural (external auditory meatus)
O = oesophageal
R = rectal
M = muscle
S = skin: 1, nipple; 2, upper outer arm; 3, anterior mid thigh; 4, lateral mid calf

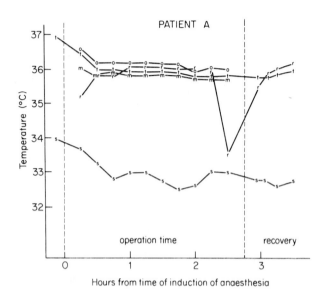

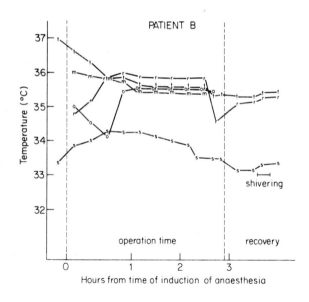

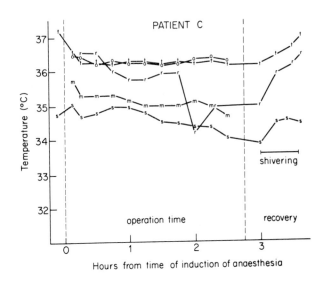

Fig. 29. Variation in Temperature at Different Sites in Three Patients Undergoing Similar Operations

Patient A. This woman had a surface area of 1·9 m², weighed 75 kg and was anaesthetized with 1% halothane and nitrous oxide in oxygen (with IPPV) in ambient conditions of 23°C and 41% relative humidity. A marked fall in rectal temperature occurred at the end of the operation in response to pelvic irrigation. The other temperatures were not affected. No shivering occurred during recovery.

Patient B. This woman had a surface area of 1·6 m², weighed 58 kg and was anaesthetized with fentanyl (10 μg/kg) and nitrous oxide in oxygen (with IPPV) in ambient condition of 24°C and 49% relative humidity. Poor correlation was obtained between oesophageal, rectal and tympanic temperatures at the beginning and end of anaesthesia. Shivering occured for a short period during recovery but was not associated with a marked rise in core temperature.

Patient C. This woman had a surface area of 1·4 m², weighed 48 kg and was anaesthetized with 0·5% halothane and nitrous oxide in oxygen (with IPPV) in ambient condition of 25°C and 44% relative humidity. A marked fall in rectal temperature occurred at the end of the operation due to irrigation with cold fluids and postoperative shivering caused a significant rise in deep body temperature in the recovery period. This was despite the maintenance of satisfactory core temperatures during the operation. (*after Holdcroft & Hall 1978*)

PREOPERATIVE FACTORS WHICH INFLUENCE ANAESTHETIC MANAGEMENT

Preoperative assessment of a patient by an anaesthetist is essential if complications due to abnormal heat loss or gain are to be prevented. The anaesthetist must consider the age of the patient and his physical status and diagnosis.

Age

Roe (1970) reports that the average fall in temperature in an unselected group of patients undergoing general anaesthesia was 0·3°C/hour at 20 years of age and 1·1°C/hour at 80 years of age. Thermoregulatory failure is common in old age (Fox et al. 1973) and mechanisms for conserving body heat are impaired. Heat production is limited because of a loss of muscle mass by atrophy and a decrease in resting muscle tone which will be further reduced by the administration of anaesthetic agents and muscle relaxants. The average body's heat production as measured by oxygen consumption is 155 kJ/m^2/hour in a 20–40-year age group and 128 kJ/m^2/hour in a group aged 60 years and older (Roe 1970). Wagner et al. (1974) found that in a thermoneutral environment the mean rectal temperature, the mean skin temperature and the metabolic rate varied inversely with age. Younger subjects reacted rapidly to a cold environment (16–17°C), increasing metabolism and reducing heat loss by cutaneous vasoconstriction. Men who were above 45 years of age showed minimal increase in metabolism and their body heat stores became depleted more quickly.

The elderly patient has a limited cardiovascular reserve. Myocardial blood flow may be reduced by coronary artery atheroma and it can be assumed that other major arterial systems may be similarly affected. The stress of hypothermia with the initial rise in catecholamine secretion and secondary rise in blood pressure and cardiac output should be avoided. The concept that mild hypothermia is beneficial because oxygen demands are reduced is fallacious unless mild hypothermia is purposefully used: during recovery from hypothermia oxygen consumption increases at a time when the body is least able to satisfy tissue oxygen requirements. Heymann (1977) cautions that an increasing number of elderly patient are being presented for surgery and precautions must be taken to maintain body temperature. There is obviously no dividing line to indicate who is and who is not at risk from hypothermia. Physiological studies indicate detectable thermoregulatory impairment even in the mid-forties age group, but certainly most patients in their sixties will be at risk and all patients over 80 fall into a high-risk category as regards hypothermia occurring during anaesthesia.

At the other extreme of age the newborn child is at risk of losing heat not only during surgical operations but also during transport, recovery and intensive care. Infants of low birth weight require more care in the maintenance of core temperature than normal weight babies (Day et al. 1964; Buetow et al. 1964). Hackel (1975) considers that a core temperature of more than 35·5°C increases the likelihood of survival if a baby has to travel. For a premature baby, the core temperature should be higher (Jolly et al. 1962). The neonate usually has to travel to and from the theatre or intensive care unit in an incubator and heat loss may occur on this journey. Often the anaesthetist is only aware of the air temperature within the incubator which arrives, but other thermal conditions in the incubator can affect the baby's temperature. Air currents may alter conductive loss in different incubators and variations in wall temperature may lead to different radiant losses from the baby's skin.

Factors which contribute to the fall in body temperature are the infant's large surface area relative to its mass, its limited capacity to maintain body temperature because of its low basal metabolism and the effects of illness and drugs (including anaesthetic agents) on these mechanisms. The possibility of hyperpyrexia should also be considered if the patient is exposed to excessive heat: the neonate has poor tolerance of heat and imperfect sweat mechanisms.

Elimination of heat loss in infants requires not only prevention and insulation but also a supply of heat. Where high gas flows and a non-rebreathing technique are used, heat loss from the lungs may be more significant than it is in the adult, although when other methods of supplying warmth are used Vivori and Bush (1977) claim that humidification and heating of the anaesthetic gases are not required in children. Insulation can be provided by blankets, cotton wool, gamgee and surgical and plastic drapes. Heat cannot be supplied by convective heating, but the use of overhead infra-red lamps may be considered (Levison et al. 1966) especially where large abdominal exposures are required. Other forms of heat include warm intravenous fluid, when the length of tube between the blood warmer and the patient should be kept to a minimum because relatively small volumes of blood are usually required; warming blankets, which should if possible be positioned all round the patient; and high ambient operating theatre temperatures. Particular details to note are to cover the head with suitable insulating material and to use warm skin-sterilizing solutions. It is not only during the operation that these measures are necessary, for, apart from travelling, the other times of possible major heat loss due to careless exposure are at induction and at the end of operation. Access to limbs should be allowed only when absolutely necessary and induction should preferably be performed in the warm theatre with the baby on a warmed mattress.

If intensive nursing is required during the recovery period, an infra-red heater should be used (Figure 30) rather than a poorly controlled incubator. It is only when an infant is in thermally neutral

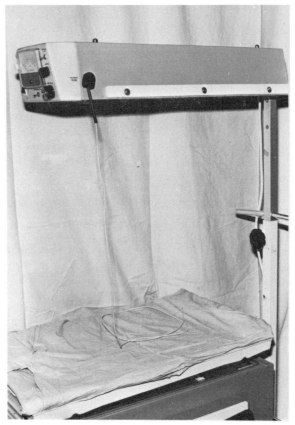

Fig. 30. A Radiant Heater which Allows Easy Access for the Intensive Nursing Care of Neonates

conditions that thermal instability becomes a reliable early sign of pathological conditions such as infections and hypoglycaemia (Miller & Oliver 1966). A neonate who is hypothermic may delay in establishing a feeding routine, but adequate feeding is essential in the postoperative period after the starvation of the preoperative and operative period.

Physical Status
The possibility, small though it is, of hyperpyrexia, is a factor to be considered in anaesthetizing a pregnant woman, especially in early pregnancy. It has been suggested (*British Medical Journal*, 1978*b*) that fetal malformations may be associated with maternal hyperthermia.

Disorders of the central nervous system, in particular the hypothalamic regulating centre, may affect the temperature response of an individual. Hydrocephalic neonates react with high temperatures to intercurrent infections, presumably because the raised intracranial pressure or a defect in the development of the hypothalamus further disorientates the immature temperature regulation. Calvert (1962) found that a fall in rectal temperature in hydrocephalic infants occurred despite adequate ambient temperatures and a warming mattress which maintained normothermia in normal neonates.

Cannon and Keatinge (1960) in immersion experiments in human subjects found that fat men were particularly well insulated from ambient cold. The percentage of fat in relation to body weight can be calculated using skinfold thickness over selected sites: Durnin and Rahaman (1967) used skinfold calipers to measure the thickness of tissues over the mid-point of the biceps and triceps muscles and positions just below the tip of the inferior angle of the scapula and just above the iliac crest in the mid-axillary line. Holdcroft and Hall (1978) attempted to correlate the percentage of fat in various patients to the amount of heat loss which occurred during abdominal operations. Their patients were, however, selected preoperatively for their physical size in that the majority of the patients only had 20 to 35% fat in relation to weight. They found no correlation between the core temperature, mean skin temperature and heat loss in relation to the percentage of fat. Body fat has clasically been thought of as an insulating layer protecting the central core temperature from the environment, but it is also metabolically active and may have importance in maintaining body temperature.

Patients who have received third-degree burns (full thickness) are greatly at risk from heat loss during anaesthesia. Burn eschar loses the normal property of the skin to limit the passage of water vapour. Incessant evaporation occurs from the body surface and burned skin is unable to participate in peripheral temperature regulatory mechanisms. These patients require a large energy input and adequate fluid therapy to maintain circulating blood volume. Control of environmental temperature is important in order to reduce the metabolic rate.

OPERATIVE FACTORS AFFECTING MAINTENANCE OF BODY TEMPERATURE

The site and extent of exposure of a surgical wound influences the amount of heat loss which can occur during an operation. Patients with large surface areas exposed lose more heat than those undergoing procedures requiring less exposure. The same applies to patients with larger surface areas relative to body mass, such as infants, the cachectic and the elderly. Operations within the pleural and peritoneal cavities require exposure of both visceral and parietal surfaces which have a large surface area from which heat can be lost by evaporation and radiation. Irrigations of cold saline can lead to further heat loss and should not be used unless cooling is required. Dyde and Lunn (1970) found that operations involving the pleural cavity are often associated with large heat losses. They could obviously not relate core temperature to oesophageal, but measured nasopharyngeal and rectal temperatures. Roe (1970) reports a 70% increase in heat loss in patients in whom the peritoneal cavity was opened, but Morris and Wilkey (1970), who assessed the influence of environmental temperature on oesophageal temperature, found no difference between patients undergoing intra-abdominal surgery and those having surgery not involving body cavities. They used light anaesthesia and neuromuscular paralysis for all their operations. Smith (1962) did not find any significant differences in the reduction of oesophageal and muscle temperatures between paralysed and spontaneously respiring patients under light general anaesthesia. It is therefore unlikely that muscular paralysis has been responsible for the difference reported between intra- and extra-abdominal operations and heat loss.

Accidental hypothermia may complicate neurosurgery, particularly because of the duration of neurosurgical operations. It can lead to acute arterial hypertension immediately after surgery. The maintenance of oesophageal temperature in neurosurgical patients has been discussed by Radford and Thurlow (1979) and they recommend active warming during neurosurgical operations, especially during induction. Although oesophageal temperature gives a reliable indication of core body temperature in these circumstances they waited 25 minutes from the induction of anaesthesia before making the first temperature recording. At that time the oesophageal temperature was only a fraction of a degree above 36°C.

Vascular surgery is another area where large areas of the abdomen and legs may be exposed during an operation. Newman (1971) records falls in oesophageal temperature of as much as 4·5°C during this type of procedure. As in the previous study of neurosurgical patients, the first temperature recorded was low: almost half the patients had temperatures before surgery of less than 36°C. If surgery commences when body temperature has reached this level, hypothermia is highly likely to occur if adequate warming measures are not instituted. Shanks (1975*b*) concluded that the temperature response in this type of surgery was normal.

Occasional problems in the maintenance of body temperature may be encountered when cold bladder irrigations are used in urological surgery (Roland 1956). All irrigations should have been kept warm in a cupboard at 40°C until immediately before use. This applies also to gastric washouts. Postoperative hypothermia has even been attributed to the heat loss which occurred during the drying of a large plaster jacket (Vale 1969).

Skin preparation for operations involves the use of volatile antiseptics as well as allowing exposure of a large skin surface area before the drapes are positioned. The evaporation of these skin preparation solutions results in the loss of heat from the body. Paradoxically these solutions are generally warmed by the nursing staff if the patient is awake (with full thermoregulatory reflexes) but not if the patient is anaesthetized and vulnerable to cold. Any period of exposure of the patient at this stage should be minimized and in the case of a delay in the start of the operation the patient should be covered by more than his gown and a sheet.

The use of surgical drapes prevents the formation of convection currents, traps moist air around the patient and provides an insulating layer in the same way as clothes do. The radiant energy of the operating lights is converted to heat on contact with dark drapes and evaporative heat loss is reduced. When drapes used by the surgeon become saturated with blood or fluid these insulative properties are reduced and occasionally it may be necessary to redrape the patient.

The skill of the surgeon is another important factor in the maintenance of body temperature during anaesthesia, because the length of the operation will influence the total heat balance of the patient. Morris (1971) found that the oesophageal temperature in paralysed patients fell by an average of $1.3°C$ in the first hour but over the next two hours this rate of fall was reduced to more acceptable levels: during the third hour the temperature change was only $0.1°C$. Morris and Wilkey (1970) studied patients in cool operating theatres and observed a mean fall of $0.3°C$ in oesophageal temperature during each hour of anaesthesia up to three hours. Radford and Thurlow (1979) found a similar fall in oesophageal temperature in neurosurgical cases: about $1° \pm 0.6°C$ over three hours. Holdcroft and Hall (1978) confirmed the results of Morris (1971) but a lesser effect was observed. The fall in core body temperature was greatest during the first hour of anaesthesia and then a steady state was reached. However, the changes in mean skin temperature showed that redistribution of body heat was occurring, because in the first hour of anaesthesia an increase in mean skin temperature occured in most patients. This redistribution of body heat has been described in a subsequent study (Holdcroft et al. 1979) and the quantity of heat lost, rather than the fall in core body temperature, was related to time.

EFFECTS OF ANAESTHETIC AGENTS ON MAINTENANCE OF BODY TEMPERATURE

Eger (1962), in a review of the pharmacology of parasympathetic drugs, warns that hyperpyrexia with subsequent convulsions can result from the administration of atropine to children when exposed to high ambient temperatures and relative humidity. The suppression of sweating by atropine which is manifest by a dry, warm skin, is thought to be a major causative factor in the increase of body temperature. However, Magbagbeola (1973) examined the effect of premedication with atropine on the rectal temperatures of children under tropical conditions and did not observe a significant rise after atropine administration, but the study did not continue into the operative period. Simpson (1970), working in a similar environment, observed increased sensitivity to premedicant drugs and changes in body temperature which he concluded were related to the lowering of the metabolic rate in the hot climate, rather than to race or ambient temperature. This means that the effect of acclimatization must be considered and studies on patients who are unacclimatized to high ambient temperatures may show different results.

The normal thermoregulatory mechanisms for the control of body heat can be affected by anaesthetics at a number of different sites, both central and peripheral. Indirect effects are due to the action of anaesthetics on muscle tone, sensitivity to catecholamines and the peripheral circulation, notably the vasodilatation produced by epidural and spinal anaesthesia and the inhaled agent halothane. Smith (1962) found that alterations in body temperature were related to the depth of anaesthesia. Patients who were lightly anaesthetized had less of a fall in oesophageal temperature than those who were deeply anaesthetized. He also showed that there was no difference in the pattern of temperature change during light general anaesthesia when muscle relaxants were used and when they were not. It has been postulated that neuro-muscular blocking drugs may potentiate agents which tend to increase heat loss by reducing muscular heat production. Goldberg and Roe (1966) observed a fall in body temperature during operations when curare was used that was almost twice as great as when no muscle relaxants were necessary. Muscle relaxants are certainly of use in inducing hypothermia deliberately, because they prevent shivering. However, if the reversal of induced hypothermia has been incomplete, or for some other reason a patient has a lower than normal body temperature in the postoperative period, the length of action of the non-depolarizing muscle relaxants may be prolonged. The most important effect of this will be to reduce the tone in the respiratory muscles, which may contribute to respiratory failure. Another effect is that the rate at which heat is gained by muscle activity will be reduced by residual curarization so that hypothermia may persist unless actively treated.

Anaesthetic induction agents are not usually incriminated in alter-ations of body temperature except when barbiturates in large doses are administered deliberately. However, Boggild-Madsen and Cargnelli (1978) report an accidental overdose of Althesin which when used both for induction and maintenance of anaesthesia resulted in hypothermia. A rectal temperature of 31°C was recorded which returned to normal over a period of seven hours.

Inhaled anaesthetics have been studied more closely. Cyclopropane can theoretically cause retention of heat by inducing peripheral vasoconstriction, an increase in muscle tone and an increased sensitivity to catecholamines. Ether anaesthesia has been thought to predispose to hyperpyrexia: Naito et al. (1974) found that rectal temperatures increased in infants anaesthetized with diethyl ether, but not in those anaesthetized with halothane. Harrison et al. (1960), in an early study of heat loss in infants and children, measured rectal temperatures and found that the mean reduction was 1°C in the halothane group and 0·5°C in a group anaesthetized mainly with ether. These heat losses could be lessened by an increase in ambient temperature and warmed blood replacement. In this case an insignificant change in body temperature occurred when ether was used, but a significant reduction in rectal temperature still occurred with halothane. Engelman and Lockhart (1972) observed the effect of a halothane or ketamine anaesthetic on the rectal temperatures of children. Halothane was again associated with a greater fall in rectal temperature than ketamine, but ambient temperatures were not well controlled. Ketamine is associated with an increase in muscle tone and arterial vasoconstriction. This is likely to affect its actions on the temperature regulating mechanisms, but no clinical data are available.

When ambient and surgical conditions were kept constant, Holdcroft and Hall (1978) found no significant difference at first between the effects of halothane (0·5% and 1%) and those of moderate doses of fentanyl with regard to mean skin and aural temperatures in adults for lower abdominal gynaecological surgery. It was only in the third hour of anaesthesia that there was significant difference ($P < 0·01$) between halothane and fentanyl, when the 1% halothane group of patients showed a significant reduction in the rate of fall of core temperature. The major heat loss occurred on transferring the patient from the theatre to the recovery ward, but no differences between the groups were apparent at this time. This is the time when active heating ceases, insulating drapes are removed from the patient, there is exposure to draughts and alterations in peripheral vascular control.

The concept of body heat rather than a single isolated temperature change is physiologically more meaningful in determining the effects of heat loss or gain from an individual during anaesthesia, unless the temperature of a specific organ is being considered. Holdcroft et al. (1979) compared the heat loss associated with anaesthetics that were known to prevent the rise in blood glucose concentration associated with surgery (Hall et al. 1978). An epidural anaesthetic (0·5% bupivacaine without adrenaline extending caudally from the eighth

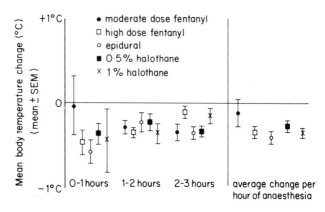

Fig. 31. Body Heat Changes Compared for Different Anaesthetic Agents
Total body heat change during each hour of anaesthesia and the average change
per hour in patients anaesthetized with fentanyl (10 μg/kg and 50 μg/kg), epidural
anaesthesia and halothane (0·5% and 1%).

thoracic dermatome), or intravenous high dose fentanyl (50 μg/kg), was
used to supplement nitrous oxide and oxygen anaesthesia and muscular
relaxation for a standard lower abdominal operation. The mean fall in
aural temperature was 0·46°C/hour and 0·6°C/hour respectively.
These figures are significantly different from the mean values of 0·14°C
and 0·2°C/hour which occurred with moderate dose fentanyl (10 μg/kg)
and halothane respectively (Figure 31). The fall in core body temperature with the first two groups would appear to be excessive in
prolonged operations, but when total body heat was calculated, that is
when the mean body temperature and weight of the patient was
considered, there was no difference between the four groups. When a
redistribution of body heat from the core to the periphery is an
acknowledged consequence of a specific anaesthetic technique, the
anaesthetist must pay particular attention to the prevention of heat loss
from the surface of the patient.

METHODS OF MAINTAINING BODY TEMPERATURE DURING ANAESTHESIA

Apart from the choice of anaesthetic technique (anaesthetic agents/local
or general/gas flow rates and ventilation), the following methods are
available to maintain body temperature during anaesthesia:

1. Protection of the body with surface insulation and warming of
   exposed viscera with warmed saline pads
2. Warmed infusions
3. Control of ambient temperature

4. Humidification
5. Heating/cooling mattress
6. Insulating overblankets

The choice of one or more of these methods is available to the anaesthetist in most cases. A combination of surface insulation, warmed intravenous fluids and humidification of the inspired gases has been shown by Shanks (1975*a,b*) to increase body heat in operations involving the body cavities and in vascular surgery.

Infusions

Blood is stored at 4°C and Roe (1970) maintains that an infusion of 1 litre of blood at this temperature can reduce body temperature during anaesthesia by 1°C. This is a much greater fall than that reported by Boyan (1964) during a massive transfusion of cold blood. He found that after more than 25 units of blood at 4°C the core temperature was about 29°C, which is the level at which ventricular arrhythmias are known to occur. The incidence of cardiac arrest in patients who receive more than three litres of cold blood at a rate exceeding 50 ml/min is 58%. Whenever more than four units (2 litres) of blood are to be transfused during an operation, Miller (1973) recommends that the blood should be warmed. The quantity of blood transfused is less significant than the rate and the site at which the blood is given. For example, a rapid transfusion of even a small quantity of blood into a central vein such as the internal jugular puts the patient at risk of developing cardiac arrhythmias from the local effect of a stream of cold blood reaching the myocardium. In any case warming facilities rapid transfusion of blood because it reduces its viscosity and causes vasodilatation.

Fluids other than blood are stored at room temperature, so that non-blood infusions will result in a temperature gradient not of 4°C to 37°C but of 20°C to 37°C. This is usually acceptable in clinical practice, but if hypothermia is developing despite precautions to prevent it then suitable warming measures should be instituted.

Blood may be warmed before or during infusion. In the latter case the blood can pass through plastic coils exposed to dry heat or in a water bath which is thermostatically heated and constantly stirred. The temperature of the water bath needs to be measured, because there is a danger of overheating the blood and haemolysing it. The temperature of the bath can be maintained at up to 45°C (Chalmers & Russell 1973): the generally recommended temperature is 40°C, but at high flow rates this may mean that the blood is only warmed to about 30°C before it is delivered to the patient. Russell (1974) reviews the efficiency of various blood warmers. He recommends that the apparatus must be able to provide the patient with blood at a temperature above 32°C at rates of up to 150 ml/min.

Unfortunately, the preparation of water immersion coils is time-consuming and most types have a dead space of 50–75 ml. Microwave blood warmers are designed to heat a whole unit of blood prior to transfusing it but Staples and Griner (1971) warn that there is a danger of overheating with subsequent haemolysis. The main disadvantage with this technique is that blood cools as it passes down the giving set.

An electronic in-line blood warmer for paediatric surgery has been developed and assessed by Jackson (1974). It holds a loop of 6 mm diameter tubing from a transfusion giving set and the temperature of the warming plate can be adjusted from 37°C to 40°C. The advantage with this type of heater is that it can be positioned close to the intravenous cannula, but because of the short length of tube which is being heated the temperature of the blood reaching the patient is only about 32°C at flow rates of approximately 560 ml/hour. However, this is adequate for patients up to 14 kg.

Ambient Temperature

Environmental temperature plays an important role in the maintenance of body temperature during anaesthesia. Humidity also affects the evaporative heat losses which occur during surgery, but no single ambient temperature or humidity is suitable for all patients. The anaesthetist therefore has to decide on the best conditions for the patient consistent with the needs of the nursing and surgical staff. In most studies the position of the theatre thermometer for measuring ambient conditions is not stated, but clearly the temperature which is important for the patient's thermoregulation is that of the air surrounding him and not the air half-way up the wall on the opposite side of the theatre.

Clark et al. (1954) have shown that if ambient temperatures exceed 24°C there is a danger of heat retention which may lead to hyperpyrexia. The majority of operating theatres are air-conditioned to some extent and the ambient temperature is usually maintained at about 20°C (Vale 1973). Occasionally the air-conditioning plants fail to work, or cannot be easily controlled and in these situations air temperature and humidity should be closely monitored. The temperature of 20°C was selected because heat stroke was a hazard when rooms were overheated and poorly ventilated, and it is the most comfortable temperature for the operating staff, who are well insulated in gowns, caps, masks and gloves and who work in close proximity to a heat-producing lamp. Wallace et al. (1978) found that at operating theatre temperatures in excess of 26°C, the sweating of operating room personnel increased the operation time and was a possible cause of bacterial contamination of the surgical site.

Morris and Wilkey (1970) studied the effects of ambient temperature on patients who had operations which did not involve the body cavities and who were infused with intravenous fluids and transfusions at room temperature. Measurements were made at oesophageal and nasopharyngeal sites in individuals who were exposed to environmental temperatures of less than 21°C. Body temperatures were below 36°C 45 minutes after the induction of anaesthesia and they declined progressively by 0.3°C/hour. Morris and Wilkey found no relation between the extent of the temperature reduction and the age of the patient, but the numbers of subjects involved was small. The ambient temperature of 21°C appeared to be critical in maintaining a normal body temperature in patients in this study. This critical temperature will be higher where a larger heat loss occurs, such as in operations at the extremes of age and those involving the exposure of a large wet surface area to ambient temperature and humidity. Vale (1973) comments that females can tolerate lower ambient temperatures than males but this has not been substantiated in anaesthetized patients.

A recent recommendation by Bennett et al (1977), who have been presented with sick neonates for prolonged major operations is that the less active the newborn infant the higher the ambient temperature should be. Small-for-date premature babies, they suggest, require theatre temperatures of 32°C, whereas large active babies can cope with ambient temperatures of 26°C. Providing that these temperatures are maintained, the operation time is not important. They emphasize that for emergency procedures, such as diaphragmatic hernias, there may not be adequate time for the theatre to attain this temperature and other warming measures should be used. The theatre temperature is not the only significant temperature; in babies of up to four weeks they observed that only 12% had normal (37°C) tympanic temperatures prior to the operation and the temperature of the majority of babies was rising spontaneously during the operation (providing that the theatre temperature was 29°C). This demonstrates clearly that to have the theatre temperature as high as this is not enough: the same temperature is required in the induction and recovery rooms where intravenous procedures and monitoring may necessitate partially unwrapping the neonate. If ancillary rooms are cold, all procedures should be carried out in the warmed theatre.

Humidification

Respiratory heat exchange is affected by the quantity of dry gas with which the lungs are ventilated. Intermittent positive pressure ventilation with high gas flows and a large minute volume may increase respiratory heat loss but reduce the arterial carbon dioxide tension, thus causing vasoconstriction that will reduce radiant heat loss from the skin. Shanks (1974) observed a heat loss of approximately 40 kJ/hour in adults ventilated with dry gases at 10 litres/min. This was reduced to almost zero by a heated hot water humidifier in the inspiratory limb of a circle absorber system. Each litre of inspired air requires 63J to raise its temperature from 20°C (room temperature) to 37°C and to saturate it with water vapour. Walker and Bethune (1976) tested the ability of currently available condenser humidifiers to reduce respiratory water loss and found that it could be almost halved. The use of the to-and-fro carbon dioxide absorption technique is another simple method of promoting heat gain because of the proximity of the cannister. A to-and-fro carbon dioxide absorber is shown in Figure 32 and a Bennett humidifier in Figure 33.

Humidification of the patient's inspired gases has two major beneficial effects: prevention of lung damage and conservation of heat by preventing the evaporative water loss from the respiratory tract. The inhalation of dry gases through a tracheal or tracheostomy tube causes ciliary paralysis and drying of the mucosa resulting in the inspissation of mucus and encrustation of the trachea. Further complications include pulmonary infection, microatelectasis and a decrease in functional residual capacity. Pflug et al. (1978) compared two groups of patients for elective surgery, one group receiving humidification of the inspired gases with a temperature of 42–47°C at the Y-connector of the anaesthetic tubing and the other group dry gases. No postoperative shivering occurred in the humidified group and the mean tympanic temperature in the recovery period was 37°C compared with 35·6°C in the unhumidified group. These temperatures are very significantly different $(P < 0.001)$ and the authors conclude that shivering was abolished and body temperature maintained by adequate humidification.

The hazardous effects of saturating and warming inspired gases should, however, be considered. If the patient inhales air preheated above body temperature and saturated with water vapour, air will be cooled in the tracheobronchial system and water vapour may condense

Fig. 32. A 'To-and-Fro' Carbon Dioxide Absorber (Water's Cannister) which can be Connected to a Mask or Endotracheal Tube

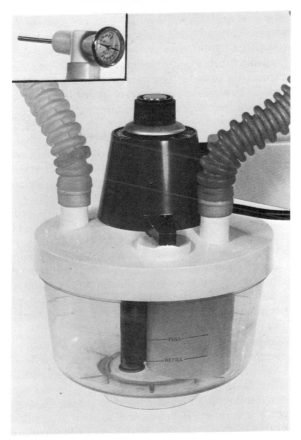

Fig. 33. A Bennett Humidifier
An efficient heated humidifier which can be used in a ventilator circuit.
Inset. A temperature probe to record the inspired gas temperature. It should
be positioned as close as possible to the patient.

and mechanically obstruct the small airways. Bacterial infection may be
transmitted by the water droplets and water and electrolyte imbalance
can occur, causing water intoxication, especially when water vapour is
supersaturated by ultrasonic humidifiers. An increase in airway
resistance can develop because of bronchoconstriction and the swelling
of secretions.

The most popular form of humidification is heated water vapour.
Saturation of the inspired air is unlikely to occur but condensation can
be a problem, with water-logging of the tubing if a large temperature
drop occurs between the humidifier and the patient: this can limit the
effectiveness of the humidifier. The average relative humidity in the

tracheal tube is about 60–80%. Hayes (1979) outlines the problems of deciding whether or not humidification would be beneficial to a patient during anaesthesia. He supposes that the relative humidity of the inspired gas is kept below 100%, although it is assumed that the body usually saturates the air in the respiratory tract (Déry 1973). Tsuda et al. (1977) prevented epithelial desquamation in dogs by using inspired gas with 100% relative humidity at temperatures ranging from 25 to 30°C, that is, with a water vapour content which is less than the saturation level at body temperature. Noguchi et al. (1973) found that significant pulmonary dysfunction, as measured by a fall in arterial oxygen tension and functional residual capacity and an increase in intrapulmonary shunt, may follow the use of dry gases at 15°C and fully saturated gas (100% relative humidity) at 40°C.

Humidification should therefore be used for a specific purpose and it is most likely to be of use in patients who are at risk of losing body heat, but care should be taken to select the method of humidification most advantageous to the patient. Wallace et al. (1978) report that they were unable to prevent heat loss in infants with ambient temperatures of 24°C, a warming mattress and warmed blood, but with the addition of a heated humidifier most of their young patients could be maintained at normothermia.

Thermal Mattresses

The idea of a thermostatically controlled water mattress developed from the use of hot water bottles to maintain body temperature (Harrison et al. 1960). Thermal mattresses prevent heat loss by increasing conduction of heat from the surroundings to a patient. They are convenient to use provided they are in place before the patient is positioned on the operating table. Calvert (1962) describes an early version of a heated mattress which was developed for keeping infants warm. The temperature of water from the mains taps was measured by a dial thermometer after a predetermined mix had been achieved by a simple thermostatic mixing valve. The mattress was placed under the patient and any other necessary equipment (X-ray plate or diathermy plate) was inserted between the mattress and the patient. There was no risk of electric shock or power failure and no report of burns due to overheating. Harrison et al. found that although the skin temperature was maintained warm and well perfused this did not affect the haemodynamic state of the patient.

Vale (1973) describes a heat-retaining mattress filled with methylcellulose gel. This has the high thermal capacity of water without its difficult physical properties and, provided that the initial temperature is not too high, it cannot produce burns. A liquid transport garment has recently been described by Goldblat and Miller (1972) and electric blankets have been used for years: Bering and Matson were using an

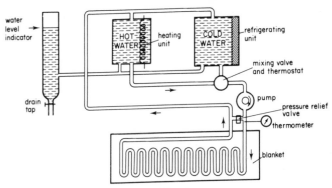

Fig. 34. A Warming/Cooling Mattress Circuit

electric blanket with infants in 1953. It was designed to be fastened by snap buttons and to fold and cover the patient. Newman (1971) describes the use of an electric blanket in vascular surgery, but the electrical safety of blankets is open to doubt and a water mattress is usually preferred as being the most convenient and safe heat source.

Before a water mattress is used its operation should be checked. Commonly, the mattress is filled with water that circulates continually around a closed circuit at a controlled temperature of up to 40 or 41°C (Figure 34). The level of water in the reservoir should be observed and if necessary it should be topped up. Most machines operate a cut-out switch if the volume falls below a certain level. Leaks can easily occur and an algicide/fungicide should be added to the circulating water in case of inadvertent puncture. Any discoloration of the mattress should be checked. The circulating water does not reach a pasteurizing temperature and bacterial contamination may also be a problem. The thermostat and the pump for circulating the water should be checked preoperatively. An emergency connection to a domestic tap if the machine breaks down is a hazardous procedure because precise regulation of the temperature of the water is difficult without a thermostat. There is usually one thermometer connected to the inlet water supply to the blanket, and this temperature should be checked regularly. As an extra precaution against burns it would probably be wise also to measure the exit temperature of water coming from the blanket. The machine should be designed to have a safety cut-out switch that comes into operation when the temperature of the circulating water exceeds 41°C and electrical safety must also be ensured.

It is common to place one or two cotton sheets between the warming mattress and the patient in order to prevent direct pressure of the water cells on poorly perfused tissues. Pressure necrosis of the skin and subcutaneous tissues can occur (Scott 1967), thermal burns have been reported in two patients who were both diabetic and obese and required prolonged operations. The maximum blanket temperature was 40·5°C and the blanket was not malfunctioning (Crino & Nagel 1968). Temperature-controlled rippling mattresses are now available to ease the problem of pressure sores and their use may be desirable in prolonged operations on patients who have poor tissue perfusion.

Radiolucent warming mattresses are now manufactured so that contact between the mattress and the patient is not interfered with by X-ray plates. Various sizes of mattress are available and so are machines which provide pumping and thermostatically controlled heating for more than one mattress. The correct length of mattress is one that fits from the shoulders to the feet. Depending on the operation side, if the machine can cope with two mattresses, one may be used as an overblanket.

Morris and Kumar (1972) estimate that only a third of a person's body surface area comes into contact with a single under-mattress and the cutaneous vessels in the parts of the body which are in contact with the mattress are compressed, which can reduce heat exchange. They found that covering the mattress with cotton sheets lowered the temperature of the surface in contact with the patient from 41°C to 38°C. Assuming a mean skin temperature of 33°C to 35°C, this meant that the temperature difference between the sheet and the patient was only 3–5°C, so it is not surprising that after an hour's anaesthesia, in operating theatre temperatures of 18–21°C, the patients' oesophageal temperature was no different from the temperatures of a control group who had no warming mattress underneath them. In rooms of 21°C and above, the warmed patient's oesophageal temperature remained above 36°C. They concluded that the warming mattress was no substitute for an adequate ambient temperature.

Following this study in adults, Goudsouzian et al. (1973) examined the effect of warming mattresses on the maintenance of body temperature in anaesthetised infants. They used a mattress set at 40°C covered with two cotton sheets in an ambient temperature of 23°C. Infants with surface areas less than 0·5 m² (about 10 kg and 14 months old) conserved heat better when the mattress was used, although the oesophageal temperature still fell by more than 1°C after induction of anaesthesia. Children with a larger surface area showed no effect on body temperature with the warming device, just as happened with the adults in the previous study. Harrison et al. (1960) have shown that patients weighing less than 10 kg cool significantly more than heavier patients because their surface area is large compared with their body mass. However, this also means that they have a proportionately larger surface area in contact with the warming mattress.

It can take up to twenty minutes for a mattress to warm. Rapid warming facilities would be useful, although some manufacturers recommend that their particular apparatus is always kept switched on ready for use. Many of the commercial mattresses have a wide range of temperature control. Medical blankets are usually used within the range 4–41°C. Temperatures below 4°C are not recommended because of the risk of cold injury to the tissues.

Overblankets

Metallized plastic sheeting has been used for many years to reflect infra-red radiation and thus prevent heat loss (Dyde & Lunn 1970); it is used in the design of space suits. Light blankets are made from a single layer with a metallized side. The heavy blankets are smaller (approximately 2 × 1·5 m) and more durable: they are made from two layers of metallized plastic sheeting separated by an artificial fibre layer (Figure 35). In a study by Dyde and Lunn (1970) of patients undergoing thoracic

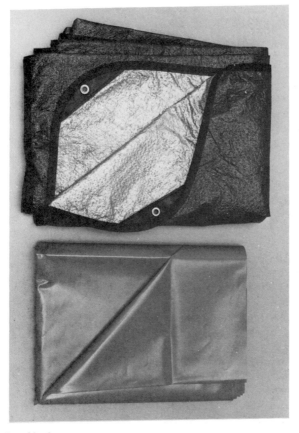

Fig. 35. Overblankets
Top. Heavy metallized plastic sheeting. *Bottom.* Polythene sheeting.

operations, nasopharyngeal and rectal temperatures were measured as an index of core temperature (the oesophageal route would be inaccurate in this situation). A fall in these two temperatures was prevented by using metallized plastic sheeting over the patient and this form of protection from radiant heat loss appeared to be satisfactory. However, Radford and Thurlow (1979) examined the use of these overblankets during neurosurgery and found that hypothermia, as measured by oesophageal temperature, was not prevented. After three hours the group of patients covered with the sheet achieved a mean core temperature of $35\cdot4 \pm 0\cdot6°C$ and those without the sheet $35\cdot4 \pm 0\cdot9°C$. Marcus et al. (1977) showed that in non-anaesthetized patients metallized plastic sheeting has no advantage over simple polythene in insulating the body in a cold environment, and of course polythene is cheaper and more robust.

RECOVERY

The effect of alterations in heat balance which have occurred during operations may not be seen until the patient is recovering. The desirability of the patient's core body temperature being continuously monitored at this time and the suitability of various access sites has already been discussed. Routine temperature monitoring of patients who have had prolonged operation, who have infections or central nervous system injury or are at the extremes of age should be mandatory.

Increased postoperative oxygen consumption will occur in patients who develop mild hypothermia during anaesthesia and surgery. Adequate minute ventilation can compensate for this but where there is preexisting respiratory or circulatory disease, or an obstructed airway, the increased demand for oxygen by the tissues may not be met. The pain associated with thoracic and abdominal incisions is usually accompanied by a reduction in vital capacity and hypoxaemia and these are the very patients who have had pleural or peritoneal cavities exposed to evaporative heat loss during surgery. Smith (1962) found that after a thoracotomy the local cooling of intercostal muscles impairs their contractile function and possibly prolongs the local action of curare. Where there is unreplaced blood loss, the circulation will be less able to deal with demands for increased tissue oxygenation.

Holdcroft et al. (1979) found that patients were slow to rewarm after epidural anaesthesia. However, this technique provided adequate analgesia for diaphragmatic movement without central depression of respiration and it was concluded that epidural anaesthesia may maximize tissue oxygenation.

Cooling which occurs during general anaesthesia may cause pro-

longed unconsciousness in the postoperative recovery period and prolongation of the action of muscle relaxants is also a hazard (Miller &
Roderick 1977). Drug overdosage may only be manifest when the
peripheral circulation is restored.

The recovery of neonates who have undergone prolonged major
surgery requires specialized intensive nursing and the anaesthetist would
be well advised to transfer such a patient personally to the intensive care
unit.

Postoperative oxygen therapy is essential in most patients and, in
patients at risk from reduced tissue oxygenation during rewarming from
mild intraoperative hypothermia, blood gases and acid base status
should be measured and corrected as necessary. Cullen and Cullen
(1975) recommend that in a hypothermic patient with fluid and
circulatory problems, poor respiratory function should be treated by
intermittent positive pressure ventilation. Of course, one has to assume
that the anaesthetist can identify the patient at risk, but this may not be
the case and coronary ischaemia may only be detected postoperatively.

Shivering can increase oxygen consumption and carbon dioxide
production to five times the resting values (Prys-Roberts 1968) at a time
when, due to residual respiratory depression, the patient is least able to
satisfy tissue requirements. Cardiac output is increased mainly by an
increase in heart rate (Prys-Roberts 1968) but this will necessitate
increased myocardial work and oxygen consumption, and when a
patient has coronary artery disease this added stress can lead to
myocardial infarction. Shivering in the recovery period may not be
associated with a fall in body temperature during surgery. Bay et al.
(1968) observed that minute ventilation volumes were significantly
higher in shivering patients and were associated with lower levels of
arterial carbon dioxide tensions, despite increased production of carbon
dioxide. There was a significantly greater base deficit in shivering
patients which was associated with non-respiratory acidosis, but this
could not be correlated with the degree of arterial hypoxaemia and is
probably related to the oxygen debt occurring during violent shivering.

A hypothermic patient in the recovery ward or postoperative intensive
care unit is often intensely vasoconstricted. This results in impaired
peripheral perfusion, metabolic acidosis, and often systemic hypertension. This may mask hypovolaemia which only becomes apparent on
rewarming, making monitoring of fluid balance and cardiovascular
status essential. Covering a vasoconstricted patient with blankets will
make the patient more comfortable but warming will be slow.

Curiously enough, when a patient is peripherally cold the core body
temperature may begin to rise to pyrexial levels and measures should
then be taken to treat the rise in temperature (Vale 1973). However, the
application of cold externally to the body surfaces by fans and ice packs
will affect the central core temperature to only a limited extent and may

enhance the vasoconstriction. Pharmacological vasodilatation can be used to increase cutaneous blood flow and allow a redistribution of heat from the core to the periphery, but if vasodilating drugs such as chlorpromazine are used, adequate fluid replacement is necessary.

Postoperative fever unrelated to a vasoconstricted peripheral circulation can occur very early in the postoperative period. Roe (1970) suggests that fevers of less than 48 hours duration may be an effect of anaesthetic agents continuing to act on the hypothalamus and reduce its sensitivity. A more likely explanation involves the mild wound respiratory or urinary infections and bacteraemia which can complicate poor anaesthetic or surgical techniques (Dominguez de Villota et al. 1974).

ACCIDENTAL HYPOTHERMIA

The main causes of accidental hypothermia are disease, drugs and exposure. The diseases responsible include cerebrovascular accident, myxoedema and hypopituitarism. The drug is commonly alcohol. Exposure may be semi-preventable, as occurs in shipwrecks or in the mountains, or wholly preventable, as in the use of cold fluids in the operating theatre or a low ambient temperature in a delivery room.

Although there are many factors which precipitate accidental hypothermia Lloyd (1979) describes the following three main clinical types which are distinguished by their case history:

1. Exposure or immersion hypothermia, where the cold stress is greater than the maximum heat production of the body.
2. Exhaustion hypothermia, where the major problem is a depletion of the body's energy stores.
3. Subclinical chronic hypothermia, which is the type usually found in the elderly, in whom chronic cold stress results in considerable intercompartmental fluid shifts and in whom the temperature may vary from normal to subnormal.

Exposure Hypothermia

Exposure hypothermia is the same clinical condition as the hypothermia induced in physiological research and for treating patients. Man can adjust to a wide range of atmospheric conditions of which not only the ambient temperature is important but also the humidity and air movement. Responses to thermal stress involve both behavioural and physiological adjustments, with alterations in heat production, in circulation and in evaporation from the skin surface. Evaporation will be decreased by warm water immersion. Craig and Dvorak (1966) found that there was a very narrow range of water temperature in which man can survive without becoming either hypothermic or hyperthermic: they suggested that for young men it was 35–35·5°C.

At water temperatures below 35°C vasomotor control of heat loss was evident and increased heat production occurred if the water temperature was below 30°C. The vasomotor responses of the subject immersed in water seemed to occur in the same range as when the subject was in air, but a subject in air at 35°C would experience significant heat stress. It is not always realized that the sea around Britain is cold enough even in summer to cause death by hypothermia.

The rate of heat loss will depend on the protection of the individual from exposure to both cold and wind. General measures of conservation of heat are important: survival drill must be taught to all people who are likely to enter an adversely cold environment and equipment should be provided for their protection. Graham and Keatinge (1978) outline the advice which should be given to all who venture on or near water:

1. A lifejacket should be worn in small boats in cold waters.
2. If a person enters the water, it is less energy-consuming to float rather than to swim about.
3. Warm clothing should be worn as well as a lifejacket in the water.
4. Not even small quantities of alcohol should be taken, especially in conjunction with exercise, unless a large meal is eaten at the same time (Haight & Keatinge 1973).

It has been recommended (*British Medical Journal* 1978*b*) that immersion suits should not allow a fall in core body temperature of more than 2°C after immersion in water of 5°C for two hours. Unprotected exposure leads to a rapid loss of body heat and death may ensue after relatively few minutes.

If a person is conscious at the time of being rescued, severe hypothermia is unlikely, but if there is a further loss of heat, consciousness may be lost after the rescue. This 'afterdrop' in body temperature, which may even occur after active rewarming has started, may be as much as 3°C and be alarming by the rapidity with which it occurs (Golden 1973). Severe shivering accompanies this type of hypothermia if the temperature is above 33°C but it may not be present continuously. As body temperature falls below 33°C shivering stops and is replaced by muscle rigidity which persists until the body temperature falls to about 27°C. In immersion or exposure hypothermia fluid and electrolyte balances are usually normal and the blood glucose concentration and plasma cortisol levels are often higher than normal.

Although much is known about the effects of induced hypothermia, data from cases of exposure hypothermia are fragmentary (*Lancet* 1978*a*). Measurement of core temperature is difficult: the oesophageal route is not tolerated and mouth temperature is useless. Rectal temperature measurements have practical difficulties and tend to lag behind aural and oesophageal recordings. The external auditory meatus has been used with a heating pad, but in very cold conditions equilibration has taken 30 minutes to achieve.

Exhaustion Hypothermia
Exhaustion hypothermia, for example in mountain walkers, is characterized by a slow onset, sometimes with mood changes, particularly aggression. The person walks more slowly and eventually falls, and shivering may not in fact occur. Hervey (1973) comments that, in exhaustion, body energy stores will not have been depleted by more than 10%, although heat production decreases. The exact nature of exhaustion is not fully understood but it has been suggested that the concentration of glycogen in active muscles may be of importance. Fluid and electrolyte imbalances are common and blood glucose and cortisol levels can be variable. Exhaustion hypothermia should be preventable: the victim can be taken to shelter, dressed in all the available clothing and put into a heavy-gauge polyethylene exposure bag to minimize heat loss by evaporation. If the person is conscious, glucose or other sugary food should be given (Andrew & Parker 1978).

As a simple guide to the management of patients suffering from exposure and exhaustion, the rectal temperature is of great value for immediate measurement. Patients who can shiver are probably in a better condition than those who have ceased to shiver. It may be difficult to be certain whether someone who is profoundly hypothermic is actually dead. At core temperatures above 30°C death is more easily detected. There have been remarkable case reports of hypothermic individuals who have seemed dead but have subsequently fully recovered. Bristow et al. (1977) report the recovery of a young man with an apparent cardiac arrest for ninety minutes at 25°C. The difference in mortality in drowning accidents in Norway and California suggest a protective effect of cold in the more northern climate (*British Medical Journal* 1977a). A child's relatively larger ratio of surface area to body mass predisposes to more rapid chilling than in an adult.

Drowning can complicate immersion hypothermia. Golden (1973) recommends that the drowned hypothermic patient who is conscious should have priority treatment for the drowning, whereas if the patient is unconscious, serious respiratory difficulties are unlikely to manifest themselves until the temperature is above 30°C and rewarming should be the first priority.

Treatment of Exposure and Exhaustion Hypothermia
This can be divided into immediate treatment, continuing treatment during transportation and hospital management. Initial treatment is aimed at preventing further heat loss and keeping the patient alive until he arrives in hospital. Golden (1973) suggests that if the journey from the scene of exposure to the hospital is to take more than half an hour

than treatment must be started before transfer. Shelter from the wind should be provided and wet clothing replaced by dry. Gentle handling is important, not only because of the risk of inducing vagal inhibition of the heart or ventricular standstill by a sudden return of cold blood back to the heart, but also because of possible injuries already sustained. If cardiopulmonary arrest is suspected, closed chest cardiac massage and mouth-to-mouth ventilation should be started and maintained at half normal rates to avoid hypocapnia (Hillman 1971, 1972). There is debate as to whether cardiac massage and intubation should precede rewarming. Certainly any movement may precipitate ventricular fibrillation. Davies (1975) reports successful resuscitations of apparently dead individuals when treated by rapid surface rewarming but Hillman (1972) stresses the opposite viewpoint, that hypothermia is not dangerous but hypoxia is. This would seem to be reasonable, but the circumstances, the physical state of the patient and the experience of the rescue team have to be considered.

Oxygen should be administered whenever possible. The head-down position should be adopted because of the likelihood of hypotension and aspiration. A record of the patient's blood pressure may be valuable. Electrocardiographic (ECG) equipment is not usually helpful because the absence of ECG activity does not exclude the possibility of recovery.

A patient who is shivering violently should be kept well insulated in a warm place and is likely to recover spontaneously from any biochemical or cardiac problems. Rewarming during shivering occurs at a rate of 1-2°C/hour. The patient who cannot shiver must be actively rewarmed and this can start at the time of rescue if the necessary equipment is available. Active surface rewarming (at more than 0·5°C/hour) can be hazardous. There are a number of problems to consider: peripheral vasodilatation can lower still further the victim's blood pressure, body temperature can continue to fall because blood flow through cold tissues increases, and there is a release of high concentrations of acidic metabolites from hypoxic tissues. The technique of choice is a hot water bath between 40 and 44°C. Other methods have been considered and found lacking (*Lancet* 1978*b*).

Internal rewarming with peritoneal dialysis, haemodialysis and cardiopulmonary bypass has been successfully used but experienced personnel and equipment are needed in these techniques. Soung et al. (1977) report the case of a young diabetic who was exposed to freezing temperatures after a heavy consumption of alcohol. His rectal temperature was 28°C. An hour's peritoneal dialysis with fluid at 38°C raised the rectal temperature by 5°C. There was a further rise of 4°C in the second hour. This rate of rewarming appears to be fast but may in fact reflect the particular site used for temperature monitoring. In uncontrolled conditions dialysis may encourage electrolyte imbalances. Where hypoventilation occurs, further impairment of diaphragmatic movement can lead to severe hypoxia unless respiration is managed actively by intermittent positive pressure respiration and an adequate inspired oxygen tension is maintained.

Less drastic methods of rewarming include warming the inspired air and heating by intragastric balloon, but this last method can precipitate cardiac arrhythmias. Shanks and Marsh (1973) consider that a heated humidifier to warm the inspired gases prevents heat loss from the respiratory tract and can account for a heat gain in the body of about 4 kJ-hour for each litre of respiratory minute volume. Lloyd (1973) used a modified Water's canister for resuscitation. He found that there was no afterdrop of core temperature and, as would be expected, the oesophageal temperature rose first, followed by the rectal. The rate of rise of temperature was faster when ventilation was assisted than when the patients breathed spontaneously. Theoretically, the lungs are efficient heat exchangers because the alveolar area of the lungs is twenty times the area of the skin, but in practice the temperature of the gases is moderated before they reach the alveoli because a countercurrent heat exchange occurs in the upper air passages and limits extremes of temperature. Moritz et al. (1945) found that when hot inspired gases were delivered to the intubated tracheas of dogs, the highest temperature in the trachea occurred at or near the end of inspiration. Dry gases lost most of their heat before reaching the lungs, whereas humidified gases lost their heat less rapidly. Another factor affecting the rewarming of a patient via the inspired gases is the alveolar ventilation. The two methods available (humidifier and Waters canister) have yet to be evaluated in terms of minute ventilation, pulmonary blood flow and the metabolic processes of the lungs. Wessel et al. (1966) found that with increasing alveolar ventilation, heat exchange in the large airways is diminished and part of the heat exchange occurs with the blood in the pulmonary vascular bed. This causes an increased temperature difference between the aorta and the pulmonary artery directly proportional to the minute ventilation and inversely related to pulmonary blood flow.

Inspired humidified air should not be warmed to more than 44°C especially in intermittent positive pressure ventilation, otherwise there is a risk of mucosal burning. Where slow (that is over more than 12 hours) exposure or exhaustion hypothermia has occurred and also in hypothermia complicating age or disease, rapid surface rewarming is not recommended because it can induce acute hypotension in cases where the blood volume is reduced. Davies (1975) suggests that rapid rewarming in patients with major injuries hinders resuscitation.

Craig and Dvorak (1966) and Golden (1973) found that a large amount of subcutaneous fat was protective in preventing immersion hypothermia. The differential diagnosis of 'near drowning' has to be considered in immersion hypothermia (Conn et al. 1978). The clinical picture can be similar: stupor, mild cyanosis and hypopnoea, unconsciousness and cardiac arrest. Pulmonary oedema is the commonest respiratory problem for the patient who is drowned. It may not manifest itself at the initial rescue but can develop rapidly after the initial resuscitation is complete.

Hospital Management

On the basis of treatment described by Ledingham and Mone (1978) the following basic management is recommended. Management of accompanying disease or injury will be additional.

1. Additional inspired oxygen to counteract any hypoxia and tissue acidosis which may have developed. The percentage of oxygen should be adjusted according to the results of blood gas and acid–base measurements.

2. Intermittent positive pressure ventilation (IPPV) is necessary if the patient is not breathing, but if spontaneous respiration is inadequate, IPPV should be started early so as to minimize tissue hypoxia. IPPV expands collapsed and oedematous alveoli and should be used in conjunction with a heated humidifier. The temperature of the inspired gas at the mouth should be maintained at 40°C to prevent heat loss.

3. A chest X-ray is always necessary to exclude trauma and accidental aspiration of stomach contents into the lung.

4. Base-line values and monitoring of the following are necessary: (a) Core body temperature. A variety of sites should be chosen according to the patient's state of consciousness and the type of rewarming method chosen. (b) Arterial blood pressure. An arterial cannula should be inserted to allow direct monitoring of blood pressure and the sampling of blood for blood gases, acid-base status, packed cell volume, coagulation defects, urea, glucose, and electrolyte levels, especially potassium. The frequency at which these measurements are made will depend on their initial values and the clinical state of the patient. (c) Central venous pressure. This measurement may indicate the need for fluid replacement and restoration of blood volume, especially in exhaustion hypothermia. The use of plasma and plasma substitutes should be considered. (d) Urine output. A urinary catheter should be passed aseptically and a fluid balance chart kept of fluid intake and output. The initial sample should receive routine urine testing and be cultured. (e) Electrocardiogram. An ECG tracing and monitor may detect cardiac irregularities and electrolyte disturbances before clinical deterioration occurs. A severe sinus bradycardia may be treated by intracardiac pacing or by an isoprenaline infusion. Most of the arrhythmias that occur during hypothermia (except ventricular fibrillation) disappear spontaneously and at low temperatures anti-arrhythmic drugs may be ineffective or dangerous. Maclean and

Emslie-Smith (1977) recommend that ECG monitoring should be continued for up to three days after recovery. (*f*) A monitor of EEG activity may be helpful.

5. External rewarming in a hot bath or warm environment should be organized to produce a rise in core temperature of 1°C per hour. Rewarming should cease when the temperature is above 33°C: the temperature will continue to rise spontaneously. Contraindications to this type of rewarming have been discussed. More invasive rewarming methods may be necessary if ventricular fibrillation occurs at temperatures less than 28°C or if rewarming by external methods is not adequate.

6. Infusion of warm fluids is necessary if the patient is hypotensive or has a high peripheral vascular resistance.

7. Drug therapy. Opinions vary as to whether antibiotics should be given prophylactically, or only on clinical grounds. Ledingham and Mone (1978) advocate caution in their use, but Maclean and Emslie-Smith (1977) recommend prophylactic broad-spectrum bactericidal drugs to try to prevent the common occurrence of respiratory infections. Where aspiration of stomach contents has occurred both antibiotics and corticosteroids are required.

8. A nasogastric tube should be inserted for aspiration of stomach contents and feeding if necessary.

Investigation of the Elderly Person with Hypothermia
  1. Radiology: Chest and abdominal pictures.
  2. Blood: Haemoglobin, white blood count, platelets
           Urea, electrolytes, creatine, calcium, magnesium
           Glucose
           Acid–base status
           Amylase, cortisol, T_3, T_4
           Drug levels (barbiturates, tricyclics)
  3. Cultures of blood, urine, sputum and CSF.
  4. Lumbar puncture.
  5. ECG.
  6. EEG (not routine).
  7. Thermoregulatory responses after recovery.

Diagnosis and Treatment of Chronic Hypothermia
Exton-Smith et al. (1964) highlighted the problem of hypothermia in the elderly in a Ministry of Health report following the severe winter of 1963. It is not generally the thin, seemingly undernourished person who is predisposed to this condition but the obese and inactive person. Hypothermia in the elderly is usually precipitated by factors other than cold and the signs of hypothermia may prevent the immediate diagnosis of the underlying disease. More than one factor may be present. A

typical example would be an unstable diabetic in poor housing who has a cerebrovascular accident (Gale & Tattersall 1978). Disorders which may predispose to hypothermia include:

1. Endocrine abnormalities: hypopituitarism and myxoedema, although in myxoedema only a minority of patients with hypothermia have reduced thyroid function.

2. Neurological disturbances: cerebrovascular accidents, heat injuries, carotid artery stenosis and drop attacks, mental impairment and confusional states.

3. Conditions causing vascular collapse: myocardial infarction.

4. Severe infections, especially pneumonia.

5. Drugs affecting temperature regulation. The precription of tranquilizing and antidepressive drugs for the elderly should be avoided, especially where there is mental confusion.

Suspicion of hypothermia should be aroused by a coarse muscle tremor, slurred speech, ataxia, pale or cyanosed puffy skin, bradycardia or slow atrial fibrillation and ECG changes which are typical of hypothermia. The patients do not usually complain that they feel cold.

A definition of hypothermia in the elderly is difficult: a consistent core body temperature of less than 35°C is the one usually accepted, but Fox et al. (1973) found that the deep body temperatures of 10% of elderly people living at home were below 35·5°C. They considered that these people were at risk from developing hypothermia because they were less successful than the others in conserving body heat and had a proportionately lower body heat content. Deep body temperatures reflected room temperature, which were minimal in the morning. The temperatures of individuals who were hypothermic in the morning fluctuated above and below 35°C depending on the time of day that it was measured.

Half the heat loss from a clothed adult is from the exposed areas, especially the head (*British Medical Journal* 1977*b*), and adequate insulation may go a long way towards preventing hypothermia in the elderly. Collins et al. (1977) made a study of forty-seven elderly people over a five-year period. They found that their environmental conditions had not changed but their ability to vasoconstrict cutaneous blood vessels had diminished, indicating progressive thermoregulatory impairment. Those with depressed core temperatures also seemed to have a higher incidence of orthostatic hypotension. Lloyd and Little (1979) have stressed the need for low-reading and normal-reading electronic thermometers to be available in accident and emergency departments.

Maclean and Emslie-Smith (1977) advocate the use of slow spontaneous rewarming in the elderly hypothermic patient, i.e. a temperature rise of less than 0·5°C per hour. However, spontaneous rewarming may simply not happen. The patient should receive treatment initially and during transportation to hospital to ensure maintenance of adequate cardiorespiratory function and to prevent further heat loss. Blankets and plastic sheets should be used for insulation. If possible, rewarming should be started in an ambient temperature of 25–32°C and normal humidity.

Intensive nursing care is required for all hypothermic patients. The airway must be unobstructed: intubation is required if this cannot be achieved or if intermittent positive pressure ventilation is needed. Arterial oxygen tensions are often low because of underlying broncho-pneumonia or pulmonary oedema. Controlled ventilation is required when hypoxia or hypercapnia occurs during rewarming: the values of the gas tensions should be corrected for the patient's body temperature. Shivering may have to be prevented because of the extra metabolic demand on an ischaemic myocardium, and if muscle relaxant drugs are used respiration must be assisted.

General management of the patient will include all the items listed in the previous section such as fluid balance, restoration of blood volume. As soon as it is safe to do so the underlying cause of the episode should be investigated. During spontaneous rewarming there is usually no need for specific cardiovascular management as the cardiac output and stroke volume rise and the peripheral resistance falls. All these cardiovascular effects may accelerate towards the end of rewarming. Occasionally, severe hypotension results from a sudden fall in peripheral resistance. This can be prevented by keeping close control over blood volume on the basis of careful monitoring of the central venous pressure. A warm solution of 5% dextrose or a plasma expander may be used, care should be taken to avoid overloading the circulation and producing pulmonary oedema. There is no evidence that the routine use of vasoactive drugs or steroids is helpful.

Even using this type of management mortality rates are high, about 40% of patients dying in the first three days. Overall, the recovery rate is only 50%, but many patients die from the precipitating illness rather than from the hypothermia. The prognosis is significantly worse for those patients whose temperatures fall below 32°C.

Complications of Accidental Hypothermia
The most lethal complication is common to all unconscious patients: inhalation of stomach contents. The circumstances of the exposure to cold may make aspiration of water or other fluid a factor to be considered.

Bronchopneumonia occurs frequently in the elderly, and may be a precipitating factor in the illness or develop as a result of aspiration of stomach contents or immobility or following the introduction of infection by an endotracheal tube and intermittent positive pressure ventilation.

Gastrointestinal bleeding has occurred. In any patient showing a sudden fall in blood pressure, this possibility should be considered, although the most likely cause of the pressure drop is a fall in circulating blood volume secondary to peripheral vasodilatation.

Acute pancreatitis is a later complication, and vascular thromboses in the limbs, coronary and visceral arteries can occur (Maclean et al. 1973).

References

British Medical Journal (1977b) The old in the cold. Br. med. J., 1, 336.

British Medical Journal (1978a) Is hyperthermia a teratogen? Br. med. J., 2, 1586–1587.

British Medical Journal (1978b) Preventing immersion hypothermia Br. med. J., 2, 1662–1663.

Andrew, P. J. & Parker, R. S. (1978) Treating accidental hypothermia. Br. med. J., 2, 1641.

Bay, J., Nunn, J. F. & Prys-Roberts, C. (1968) Factors influencing arterial P_{O_2} during recovery from anaesthesia. Br. J. Anaesth., 40, 398–407.

Bennett, E. J., Patel, K. P. & Grundy, E. M. (1977) Neonatal temperature and surgery. Anesthesiology, 46, 303–304.

Benzinger, M. (1969) Tympanic thermometry in surgery and anaesthesia. J. Am. med. Ass., 209, 1207–1211.

Bering, E. A. & Matson, D. D. (1953) A technic for the prevention of severe hypothermia during surgery on infants. Ann. Surg., 137, 407–409.

Boggild-Madsen, N. B. & Cargnelli, T. (1978) Accidental overdose of aifathesin under general anaesthesia: case report. Can. Anaesth. Soc. J., 25, 245–247.

Boyan, C. P. (1964) Cold or warmed blood for massive transfusions. Ann. Surg., 160, 282–286.

Bristow, G., Smith, R., Lee, J., Auty, A. & Tweed, W. A. (1977) Resuscitation from cardiopulmonary arrest during accidental hypothermia due to exhaustion and exposure. Can. med. Ass. J., 117, 247–249.

British Medical Journal (1977a) Immersion and drowning in children. Br. med. J., 2, 146–147.

Buetow, K. C., Klein, P. H. & Klein, S. W. (1964) Effect of maintenance of 'normal' skin temperature on survival of infants of low birth weight. Pediatrics, Springfield, 34, 163–170.

Calvert, D. G. (1962) Inadvertent hypothermia in pediatric surgery. Anaesthesia, 17, 29–45.

Cannon, P. & Keatinge, W. R. (1960) The metabolic rate and heat loss of fat and thin men in heat balance in cold and warm water. J. Physiol., Lond., 154, 329–344.

Chalmers, C. & Russell, W. J. (1973) When does blood haemolyse?: A temperature study. Br. J. Anaesth., 45, 1237–1238.

Clarke, R. E., Orkin, L. R. & Rovenstine, E. A. (1954) Body temperature studies in anaesthetised man: effect of environmental temperature humidity and anesthesia system. J. Am. med. Ass., 154, 311–319.

Collins, K. J., Dore, C., Exton-Smith, A. N., Fox, R. H., Macdonald, J. C. & Woodward, P. M. (1977) Accidental hypothermia and impaired temperature homeostasis in the elderly. Br. med. J., 1, 353–356.

Conn, A. W., Edmonds, J. F. & Barker, G. A. (1978) Near-drowning in cold fresh water: current treatment regimen. Can. Anaesth. Soc. J., 25, 259–265.

Cooper, K. E. & Kenyon, J. R. (1957) A comparison of temperatures measured in the rectum, oesophagus, and on the surface of the aorta during hypothermia in man. Br. J. Surg., 44, 616–619.

Craig, A. B. & Dvorak, M. (1966) Thermal regulation during water immersion. *J. appl. Physiol.*, *21*, 1577–1585.

Crino, M. H. & Nagel, E. L. (1968) Thermal burns caused by warming blankets in the operating room. *Anesthesiology*, *29*, 149–150.

Cullen, D. J. & Cullen, B. L. (1975) Post anaesthetic complications. *Surg. Clins N. Am.*, *55*, 995.

Davies, D. (1975) Treatment of hypothermia. *Lancet*, *2*, 656.

Day, R. L., Caliguiri, L., Kamenski, C. & Ehrlich, F. (1964) Body temperature and survival of premature infants. *Pediatrics, Springfield*, *34*, 171–181.

Déry, R. (1973) Water balance of the respiratory tract during ventilation with a gas mixture saturated at body temperature. *Can. Anaesth. Soc. J.*, *20*, 719–727.

Dominguez de Villota, E. Astorqui, B. F., Damaso, D. & Avello, F. (1974) Pyrexia following open heart surgery. *Anaesthesia*, *29*, 529–536.

Durnin, J. V. G. & Rahaman, M. M. (1967) The assessment of the amount of fat in the human body from measurement of skinfold thickness. *Br. J. Nutr.*, *21*, 681–689.

Dyde, L. A. & Lunn, H. F. (1970) Heat loss during thoracotomy. *Thorax*, *25*, 355–358.

Eger, E. I. (1962) Atropine, scopolamine and related compounds. *Anesthesiology*, *23*, 365–383.

Engelman, D. R. & Lockhart, C. H. (1972) Comparisons between temperature effects of ketamine and halothane anesthetics in children. *Anesth. Analg. (Cleve.)*, *51*, 98–101.

Exton-Smith, A. N., Agate, J., Crockett, G. S., Irvine, R. E. & Wallis, M. G. (1964) Accidental hypothermia in the elderly. *Br. med. J.*, *2*, 1255–1258.

Fox, R. H., Woodward, P. M., Exton-Smith, A. N., Green, M. F., Donnison, D. V. & Wicks, M. H. (1973) Body temperatures in the elderly: a national study of physiological social and environmental conditions. *Br. med. J.*, *1*, 200–206.

Gale, E. A. M. & Tattersall, R. B. (1978) Hypothermia: a complication of diabetic ketoacidosis. *Br. med. J.*, *2*, 1387–1389.

Goldberg, M. J. & Roe, C. F. (1966) Temperature changes during anaesthesia and operations. *Archs Surg., Chicago*, *93*, 365–369.

Goldblat, A. & Miller, R. (1972) Prevention of accidental hypothermia in neuro-surgical patients. *Anesth. Analg. (Cleve.)*, *51*, 536–543.

Golden, F. St. C. (1973) Recognition and treatment of immersion hypothermia. *Proc. R. Soc. Med.*, *66*, 1058–1061.

Goudsouzian, N. G., Morris, R. H. & Ryan, J. F. (1973) The effect of a warming blanket on the maintenance of body temperature in anesthetised infants and children. *Anesthesiology*, *39*, 351–353.

Graham, J. M. & Keatinge, W. R. (1978) Deaths in cold water. *Br. med. J.*, *2*, 18–19.

Hackel, A. (1975) A medical transport system for the neonate. *Anesthesiology*, *43*, 258–267.

Haight, J. S. J. & Keatinge, W. R. (1973) Failure of thermoregulation in the cold during hypoglycaemia induced by exercise and ethanol. *J. Physiol., Lond,*. *229*, 87.

Hall, G. M. (1978) Body temperature and anaesthesia. *Br. J. Anaesth.*, *50*, 39–44.

Hall, G. M., Young, C., Holdcroft, A. & Alaghband-Zadeh, J. (1978) Substrate mobilisation during surgery. *Anaesthesia*, *33*, 924–930.

Harrison, G. G., Bull, A. B. & Schmidt, H. J. (1960) Temperature changes in children during general anaesthesia. *Br. J. Anaesth.*, *32*, 60–68.

Hayes, B. (1979) Humidification in anaesthesia. *Br. J. Anaesth.*, *51*, 389–390.

Hervey, G. R. (1973) Physiological changes in hypothermia. *Proc. R. Soc. Med.*, *66*, 1053–1058.

Heymann, A. D. (1977) The effect of incidental hypothermia on elderly surgical patients. *J. Gerontol.*, *32*, 46–48.

Hillman, H. (1971) Treatment after exposure to cold. *Lancet*, *2*, 1257.

Hillman, H. (1972) Treatment after exposure to cold. *Lancet*, *1*, 140–141.

Holdcroft, A. & Hall, G. M. (1978) Heat loss during anaesthesia. *Br. J. Anaesth.*, *50*, 157–164.

Holdcroft, A., Hall, G. M. & Cooper, G. M. (1979) Redistribution of body heat during anaesthesia. *Anaesthesia*, *34*, 758–764.

House, F. & Vale, R. (1972) Nomograms for calculation of heat loss. *Br. med. J.*, *4*, 20–21.

Jackson, D. M. (1974) A new blood warmer. *Br. J. Anaesth.*, *46*, 692–696.

Jolly, H., Molyneux, P. & Newell, D. J. (1962) A controlled study of the effect of temperature on premature babies. *J. Pediat.*, *60*, 889–894.

Keatinge, W. R. & Sloan, R. E. G. (1973) Measurement of deep body temperature from external auditory canal with servo-controlled heating around the ear. *J. Physiol., Lond.*, *234*, 8P–9P.

Kreider, M. B., Buskirk, E. R. & Bass, D. E. (1958) Oxygen consumption and body temperatures during the night. *J. appl. Physiol.*, *12*, 361–366.

Lancet (1978a) Treating accidental hypothermia. *Lancet*, *1*, 701–702.

Lancet (1978b) Rewarming for accidental hypothermia. *Lancet*, *1*, 251–252.

Ledingham, I. McA. & Mone, J. G. (1978) Accidental hypothermia. *Lancet*, *1*, 391.

Lees, D. E., Schuette, W., Bull, J. M., Whang-Peng, J., Atkinson, E. R. & Macnamara, T. E. (1978) An evaluation of liquid crystal thermometry as a screening device for intraoperative hyperthermia. *Anesth. Analg. (Cleve.)*, *57*, 669–674.

Levison, H., Linsao, L. & Swyer, P. R. (1966) A comparison of infra-red and convective heating for newborn infants. *Lancet*, *2*, 1346–1348.

Lloyd, E. L. (1973) Accidental hypothermia treated by central rewarming through the airway. *Br. J. Anaesth.*, *45*, 41–48.

Lloyd, E. L. (1979) Treatment of accidental hypothermia. *Br. med. J.*, *1*, 413–414.

Lloyd, E. L. & Little, K. (1979) Accidental hypothermia and low reading thermometers. *Br. med. J.*, *1*, 1284.

Maclean, D., Murison, J. & Griffiths, P. D. (1973) Acute pancreatitis and diabetic ketoacidosis in accidental hypothermia and hypothermic myxoedema. *Br. med. J.*, *2*, 757–761.

Maclean, D. & Emslie-Smith, D. (1977) *Accidental Hypothermia.* Oxford: Blackwell Scientific.

Magbagbeòla, J. A. O. (1973) The effect of atropine premedication on body temperature of children in the tropics. *Br. J. Anaesth.*, *45*, 1139–1142.

Marcus, P., Robertson, D. & Langford, R. (1977) Metallised plastic sheeting for use in survival. *Aviat. Space environ. Med.*, *48*, 50–52.

Miller, D. L. & Oliver, T. K. (1966) Body temperature in the immediate neonatal period: the effect of reducing thermal losses. *Am. J. Obstet. Gynecol.*, *94*, 964–969.

Miller, R. D. (1973) Complication of massive blood transfusions. *Anesthesiology*, *39*, 82–93.

Miller, R. D. & Roderick, L. L. (1977) Pancuronium induced neuromuscular blockade and its antagonism by neostigmine at 29, 37 and 41°C. *Anesthesiology*, *46*, 331–335.

Moritz, A. R., Henriques, S. C. & McLean, R. (1945) The effects of inhaled heat on the air passages and lungs. *Am. J. Path.*, *21*, 311–331.

Morris, R. H. (1971) Operating room temperature and the anesthetised paralysed patient. *Archs Surg., Chicago*, *102*, 95–97.

Morris, R. H. & Kumar, A. (1972) The effects of warming blankets on maintenance of body temperature of the anesthetised, paralysed adult patient. *Anesthesiology*, *36*, 408–411.

Morris, R. H. & Wilkey, B. R. (1970) The effects of ambient temperature on patient temperature during surgery not involving body cavities. *Anesthesiology*, *32*, 102–107.

Naito, H., Yamazaki, T., Nakamura, K., Matsumoto, M. & Namba, M. (1974) Skin and rectal temperatures during ether and halothane anesthesia in infants and children. *Anesthesiology*, *41*, 237–241.

Newman, B. J. (1971) Control of accidental hypothermia: occurrence and prevention of accidental hypothermia during vascular surgery. *Anaesthesia*, *26*, 177–187.

Noguchi, H., Takumi, Y. & Aochi, O. (1973) A study of humidification in tracheostomized dogs. *Br. J. Anaesth.*, *45*, 844–848.

Pflug, A. E., Aasheim, G. A., Foster, C. & Martin, R. W. (1978) Prevention of post-anaesthetic shivering. *Can. Anaesth. Soc. J.*, *25*, 43–49.

Prys-Roberts, C. (1968) Post-anaesthetic shivering. In *Clinical Anesthesia: Common and Uncommon Problems in Anesthesiology*, ed. M. T. Jenkins, pp. 358–369. Philadelphia: F. A. Davis.

Radford, P. & Thurlow, A. C. (1979) Metallized plastic sheeting in the prevention of hypothermia during neurosurgery. *Br. J. Anaesth.*, *51*, 237–240.

Roe, C. F. (1970) Temperature regulation in anaesthesia. In *Physiological and Behavioural Temperature Regulation*, ed. J. D. Hardy, A. P. Gagge & J. A. J. Stolwijk, pp. 727–740. Springfield, Ill.: Charles C Thomas.

Roland, S. I. (1956) Hypothermia induced by cystoscopy. *J. Urol.*, *75*, 1006–1010.

Russell, W. J. (1974) A review of blood warmers for massive transfusion. *Anesth. intensive Care*, *2*, 109–130.

Scott, S. M. (1967) Thermal blanket injury in the operating room. *Archs Surg., Chicago*, *94*, 181.

Shanks, C. A. & Marsh, H. M. (1973) Simple core rewarming in accidental hypothermia. *Br. J. Anaesth.*, *45*, 522–525.

Shanks, C. A. (1974) Humidification and loss of body heat during anaesthesia, ii: effects in surgical patients. *Br. J. Anaesth.*, *46*, 863–866.

Shanks, C. A. (1975a) Heat balance during surgery involving body cavities. *Anesth. Intensive Care*, *3*, 114–117.

Shanks, C. A. (1975b) Control of heat balance during arterial surgery. *Anesth. Intensive Care*, *3*, 118–121.

Simpson, J. M. (1970) Environmental temperature and response to premedicant drugs. *Anaesthesia*, *25*, 508–517.

Smith, N. T. (1962) Subcutaneous, muscle and body temperature in anaesthetised man. *J. appl. Physiol.*, *17*, 306–310.

Soung, L. S., Swank, L., Ing, T. S., Said, R. A., Goldman, J. W., Perez, J. & Geis, W. P. (1977) Treatment of accidental hypothermia with peritoneal dialysis. *Can. med Ass. J.*, *117*, 1415–1416.

Staples, P. J. & Griner, P. F. (1971) Extracorporeal hemolysis of blood in a microwave warmer. *New Engl. J. Med.*, *285*, 317–319.

Tsuda, T., Noguchi, H., Takumi, Y. & Aochi, O. (1977) Optimum humidification of air administered to a tracheostomy in dogs. *Br. J. Anaesth.*, *49*, 965–977.

Vale, R. J. (1969) Post-operative accidental hypothermia. *Anaesthesia*, *24*, 449–452.

Vale, R. J. (1973) Normothermia: its place in operative and postoperative care. *Anaesthesia*, *28*, 241–245.

Vivori, E. & Bush, G. H. (1977) Modern aspects in the management of the newborn undergoing operation. *Br. J. Anaesth.*, *49*, 51–57.

Wagner, J. A., Robinson, S. & Marino, R. P. (1974) Age and temperature regulation of humans in neutral and cold environments. *J. appl. Physiol.*, *37*, 562–565.

Wallace, C. T., Baker, J. D. & Brown, C. S. (1978) Heated humidification for infants during anaesthesia. *Anesthesiology*, *48*, 80.

Walker, A. K. J. & Bethune, D. W. (1976) A comparative study of condenser humidifiers. *Anaesthesia*, *31*, 1086–1093.

Wessel, H. U., James, G. W. & Paul, M. H. (1966) Effects of respiration and circulation on central blood temperature of the dog. *Am. J. Physiol.*, *211*, 1403–1412.

Whitby, J. D. & Dunkin, L. J. (1968) Temperature differences in the oesophagus. *Br. J. Anaesth.*, *40*, 991–995.

Whitby, J. D. & Dunkin, L. J. (1970) Oesophageal temperature differences in children. *Br. J. Anaesth.*, *42*, 1013–1015.

Whitby, J. D. & Dunkin, L. J. (1971) Cerebral, oesophageal and nasopharyngeal temperatures. *Br. J. Anaesth.*, *43*, 673–676.

General and regional techniques of altering body temperature

INDUCED HYPOTHERMIA: TOTAL BODY COOLING

Generalized cooling has been used to control fever, i.e. to normalize body temperature. Cooling to induce hypothermia is indicated for certain cardiac and neurological operations which require cessation of the heart beat, but the application of induced hypothermia is not limited to cardiovascular or neurological surgery: profound hypothermia has been used for hepatic lobectomy in a 10-week-old infant (Ward et al. 1977).

The physiological changes during hypothermia which have been described previously accompany induced hypothermia and an understanding of them is necessary for the safe intraoperative and postoperative management of the patient. The general considerations described below are therefore stressed.

Tissue Oxygenation

General Tissue oxygen requirements (Civalero et al. 1962; Abbot 1977) decrease exponentially to 40–45% of basal at 25°C and 20–25% of basal at 20°C. The heart, liver and brain have a higher oxygen uptake than other tissues at all temperatures. The greatest fall in oxygen requirements occurs from 37°C to 30°C; below this level there is a gradual reduction to 20°C below which the decline is minimal (Blair 1964). On rewarming, the reverse occurs with a gradual increase in oxygen consumption as the body temperature rises. At temperatures above 27°C oxygen consumption is higher for a given temperature than during cooling.

Shivering should be avoided, since it increases the metabolic rate and lactic acid production in hypoxic muscle. Dill and Forbes (1941) found that the metabolic rate can rise to five times basal during shivering. It also raises the intracranial pressure.

Alterations in the activity of drugs due to reduced metabolic activity and lowered temperature will affect not only the operative technique but also the preoperative preparation and postoperative management of the patient.

Central Nervous System   Hypothermia protects the brain and spinal cord against hypoxic damage. The cerebral demand for oxygen is halved by general anaesthesia and moderate hypothermia (30°C). The significant difference, however, in the two techniques is the rate of ATP depletion, which is considerably slower with hypothermia (Mitchenfelder & Theye 1970). Also, there is no narcosis during moderate hypothermia. During circulatory arrest at low body temperatures, the brain is protected from irreversible damage in three ways:

1. The normal metabolic rate is reduced.
2. The quantity of oxygen in the body may be increased because oxygen is more soluble in the tissue fluids at low temperatures Abbott (1977).
3. Metabolism is maintained anaerobically.

A lactic acidosis can be interpreted as having been produced by an excessively long period of anaerobic metabolism. Abbot (1977) found that a severe lactic acidosis was not produced in infants cooled to 20°C and arrested for varying periods (30–75 minutes) but that oxygen uptake following circulatory standstill was initially four times that expected for the body temperature, falling to normal levels in ten minutes. This quantity of oxygen is equivalent to the tissues stores of oxygen. Brain stores of oxygen in animals have similarly been found to be replenished within ten minutes at 20°C (Nilsson & Busto 1976).

Cerebral metabolic activity should be monitored if circulatory arrest is contemplated. The multiple leads of an EEG are cumbersome and require expert interpretation (Clutton-Brock 1959); other methods based on a general assessment of electrical activity may be used, such as the cerebral function monitor (CFM). Schwartz et al. (1973) found that predictions of neurological outcome were possible with this method.

The CFM passes signals from a pair of parietal electro-encephalograph electrodes into an amplifier and then through a filter which allows only frequencies in the range 2–15 Hz to pass through. The average, maximum and minimum peak-to-peak amplitudes are recorded on slow-moving paper (Maynard et al. 1969). During hypothermia for cardiac operations Branthwaite (1973) observed that there was no change in the recorded signal until the temperature reached 30°C, but at nasopharyngeal temperatures of less than 25°C marked reduction in activity occurred. Since temperature only affects the CFM record to any significant extent in deep hypothermia, this type of monitor of cerebral electrical activity can detect undesirable complications, e.g. cerebral embolisms, which occur during cardiopulmonary bypass and moderate hypothermia.

Myocardium   Myocardial oxygenation is at risk during cardiac operations for a number of reasons of which the following are examples:

1. Cardiac arrest may be precipitated before hypothermia or cardio-pulmonary bypass is properly instituted.
2. During aortic surgery, cross-clamping the aorta will stop coronary blood flow.
3. Coronary artery surgery will necessitate obstruction to coronary artery blood flow.
4. Perfusion pressures from cardiopulmonary bypass machines may be low.
5. Emboli of air or particulate matter may obstruct coronary flow.

The oxygen consumption of the non-contracting heart is about 20% of that of the beating heart. Basal oxygen requirements are those essential for the maintenance of electrical activity and the integrity of the cell membrane. Braunwald (1971) reviewed the various determinants of myocardial oxygen consumption and found that the major factor was the velocity of the contraction. It is assumed that myocardial oxygen consumption can be reduced by arresting the heart during hypothermia and venting the left ventricle. However, Nelson et al. (1977) found ischaemic changes in dogs following profound topical hypothermia of the myocardium for 60 minutes at 16°C, whereas cardiopulmonary bypass at normothermia for the same time showed minimal ischaemic charges. In the bradycardic, hypothermic heart Cooper et al. (1977) found that an artificial increase in heart rate can produce subendocardial ischaemia. Tachycardia, ventricular fibrillation and augmented myocardial contractility with inotropic agents will increase myocardial oxygen consumption and reverse the expected beneficial effects of hypothermia on the myocardium.

Brazier et al. (1977) have shown in dogs that, although myocardial hypothermia to 28°C reduces myocardial oxygen uptake by 52% from the value at 37°C and 100 mmHg perfusion pressure, the left ventricle is not protected against subendocardial ischaemia if the perfusion pressure falls to 50 mmHg, a level which frequently occurs during clinical open-heart surgery. Myocardial hypertrophy will exacerbate this situation. The effect of lowering perfusion pressure in the normo-thermic beating heart is to dilate the coronary arteries (McConnell et al. 1977). Compensatory vasodilatation is inadequate in hypothermic hearts and at 50 mmHg there is a 44% reduction in subendocardial flow, leading to anaerobic metabolism and histological ischaemic changes. However, Goldman et al. (1971) consider that the data from animal experiments may not be strictly related to the human heart: they found that the capacity of the human heart to withstand ischaemia appeared to be significantly greater.

When the heart arrests at normothermia, the available oxygen reserves are initially used to supply energy (Scheuer 1967). These reserves can be increased by a high arterial oxygen tension, but this is only of transient benefit. A progressive functional deterioration then begins with the decline of energy-rich phosphate stores and, secondarily, a reduction in adenosine triphosphate (ATP). Creatine phosphate is not detectable after seven minutes and after ten minutes half the stores of ATP are depleted. Breakdown products of these high-energy compounds pass out of the myocardial cells and are unavailable for the regeneration of ATP.

When the levels of ATP fall glucose is taken up by the cell and in the absence of oxygen, is metabolized extremely ineffectively. Beyond a certain point the reduction in available high-energy phosphates becomes critical in the re-establishment of effective myocardial contractility. Hypothermia can slow down the loss of phosphates by reducing myocardial oxygen consumption, but abnormalities in regional perfusion and bad technique in cannulating and venting the heart limit its effect. The results of this can be seen when rewarming starts and the myocardium is unable to sustain an adequate ventricular output despite adequate surgical correction of the cardiac deformity.

An intensive study of cardiopulmonary bypass in humans by Goldschlager et al. (1972) compared aortic cross-clamping (intermittent ischaemic cardioplegia) and continuous direct coronary artery perfusion and attempted to relate excess lactate production to ECG evidence of ischaemia. A surface ECG was found to be normal despite lactate production and arrhythmias were usually of sudden onset. Intermittent aortic cross-clamping during moderate hypothermia was associated with a fall in oxygen extraction which may be related to cellular ischaemic injury. The continuously perfused myocardium increased lactic acid production and was not the ideal method of maintaining adequate myocardial oxygenation during moderate hypothermia. This type of study is difficult to perform under standard conditions in the operating theatre.

Hedley-Brown et al. (1974) compared the methods of intermittent ischaemia and coronary perfusion in dogs. They concluded from enzyme and histochemical studies that intermittent ischaemia at moderate hypothermia is not as effective for maintaining myocardial cellular integrity as continuous perfusion at normothermia.

The clinical justifications for moderate hypothermia are firstly that when the body's temperature is lowered accidental problems are tolerated for longer and, secondly, that it is often difficult to achieve adequate coronary blood flow by coronary artery cannulation (e.g. atheromatous arteries, malformations).

It does seem that the arrested, perfused heart is in a healthier state than the fibrillating heart, but the mechanisms and effects of cardioplegia (chemical or cold) require further evaluation in humans. At the moment the decision as to which method can best preserve the myocardium must be made by the cardiac surgeon on an individual basis (Maloney & Nelson 1975).

Carbon Dioxide and Oxygen

As body temperature is lowered the metabolic rate falls, carbon dioxide production decreases and the blood solubility of carbon dioxide and oxygen rises so that the gas tensions are reduced by factors which depend on the temperature and the pH (Severinghaus 1958). In the dog, Severinghaus et al. (1957) found that a fall in temperature of 10°C lowered Pco_2 by 2 kPa (15 mmHg). If the Pco_2 is less than 2 kPa (15 mmHg) cardiac output is reduced, severe cerebrovascular vaso-constriction and hypoxia can occur (Granholm & Siesjö 1969) and cardiac dysrhythmias increase. Burton (1964) administered carbon dioxide in concentrations of up to 5% in the inspired gases to maintain normocapnia during surface cooling. Johnston et al. (1974) recommend up to 10% carbon dioxide during cooling bypass. The resulting increase in P_aco_2 causes a minimal shift to the right of the oxygen dissociation curve. A reduction in inspired minute volume is not helpful in maintaining normocapnia because it predisposes to atelectasis.

The effect of changing temperature on gas solubility affects blood cooling with an extracorporeal circuit. The warming process must be completed before oxygenation in order to prevent bubble formation.

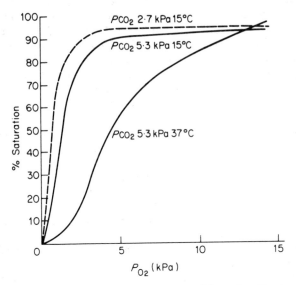

Fig. 36. Oxygen Dissociation Curves of Haemoglobin when Temperature and Pco_2 are Varied (after Callaghan et al. 1961)

Oxygen supply to the tissues may fall because of vasoconstriction and the shift to the left of the oxygen dissociation curve which occurs with hypothermia and a low $P_a co_2$ (Figure 36) (Severinghaus 1958; Callaghan et al. 1961). During rewarming the $P_a co_2$ rises, reaching a maximum early in the rewarming phase.

Acid–Base, Electrolyte and Fluid Changes

The interpretation of in vitro measurements of pH, Po_2 and Pco_2 can be confusing. Some early workers performed their in vitro tests at the core body temperature of the patient (Burton 1964). Nowadays, measurements are usually performed in vitro at 37°C and related to the patient's core temperature by a nomogram (Kelman & Nunn, 1966).

Metabolic acidosis occurs during rewarming because of inadequately cooled, poorly perfused tissues. Respiratory acidosis also develops which reflects the $P_a co_2$ levels. Serial measurements of acid–base status are essential during rewarming, and there is a tendency to administer 100% oxygen during this period to prevent unnecessary tissue hypoxia. Usually there is a spontaneous correction of the metabolic acidosis providing tissue blood flow and oxygenation are adequate, especially to the liver, and the premature administration of sodium bicarbonate can lead to post-operative metabolic alkalosis.

Liver blood flow is important for citrate metabolism and when impaired may cause acidosis in the presence of large blood transfusions. For this reason some anaesthetists prefer fresh heparinized blood. Hypothermic patients compensate poorly for blood loss (Cooper & Ross 1960).

Electrolyte changes can affect myocardial performance. Cardiac tissue loses potassium and gains sodium and cooling below 32°C, or abnormal cardiac pathology, exacerbates this problem (Geevarghese, 1977).

Glucose metabolism is also impaired and the use of a 5% dextrose solution may cause hyperglycaemia. A urinary catheter and nasogastric tube are essential to control fluid balance.

Coagulation Disturbances

Although coagulation of the blood is reduced at low temperatures, heparin is required to prevent coagulation during cardiopulmonary bypass. A 'heparin rebound' may occur if heparinized blood is returned from previously vasoconstricted tissues.

Haemodilution is important to avoid sludging and the packed cell volume should be adjusted to 25–30%. For deep hypothermia, Subramanian (1977) suggests a non-blood prime in the extracorporeal circulation and fresh frozen plasma appears to give satisfactory results. It may be employed before or at the time of starting the extracorporeal circulation. Dilution of fresh heparinized blood has been used by Johnston et al. (1974) in the oxygenator prime. Their patients were transfused fresh blood as necessary after the bypass. Low molecular weight dextrans have been used to reduce viscosity but they have not achieved universal acceptance.

The Stages of Induced Hypothermia
The lower limit of temperature for induced hypothermia is debatable and depends on the pathological circumstances of the case and the age of the patient. Patients of all ages can tolerate mild and moderate hypothermia for the length of time specified below, but profound whole body cooling is only applicable to infants: older people are at risk from cerebral damage and other complications. The following terminology is employed by Cooper and Ross (1960) in distinguishing between different degrees of hypothermia:

Mild hypothermia (31–35°C) reduces tissue oxygen requirements so that if the circulation is accidentally interrupted, hypoxic damage of major organs is less likely to occur than at normothermia.

Moderate hypothermia (28–30°C) is used to protect essential tissues during an ischaemic arrest or when it is necessary to interrupt the extracorporeal circulation. It allows lower flow rates to be used during cardiopulmonary bypass but is seldom used without a pump oxygenator.

Deep (*profound*) *hypothermia* (less than 25°C) is used where total circulatory arrest is necessary, e.g. operations on the aorta and neonatal cardiac surgery. Deep hypothermia has been used successfully without cardiopulmonary bypass (Mohri et al. 1969) but such a technique is now of historical interest only.

Period of Circulatory Arrest
The effect of low temperature on the heart's action limits safe surface cooling to 30°C. When the cardiac output is maintained artificially by means of pumps, cooling can be taken to almost any depth. At temperatures below 30°C physiological flows (2·2 litres/m²) can be reduced and at 25°C short periods of circulatory arrest can be tolerated while delicate stages of the operation are performed. Hypothermia can reduce the flow of blood needed from an oxygenator to maintain tissue oxygen supplies: this will reduce trauma to the red blood cells. Table VII indicates the period of time for which total circulatory arrest can be tolerated at various body temperatures.

General Techniques in Induced Hypothermia
Anaesthesia Usually a simple method of providing general anaesthesia is used (Subramanian 1977) with muscular relaxation, intermittent positive-pressure ventilation with humidified gases and supplementation with an opiate or inhaled agent. This technique can prevent shivering and excessive vasoconstriction but in profound

Table VII: Maximum Safe Period of Circulatory Arrest at Various Body Temperatures

37°C	4 min
30°C	6 min[1]
25°C	15 min[2]
20°C	20 min[3]
15°C	30 min[4]
10°C	56 min
5°C	100 min

1. Botterell et al. (1956).
2. Lougheed & Kahn (1955).
3. Bigelow et al. (1954).
4. Drew et al. (1959).

hypothermia the phenothiazines (e.g. chlorpromazine) are usually administered to facilitate heat loss. At temperatures below 28°C anaesthetic agents can be reduced. During rewarming and in the postoperative period vasodilator drugs may be indicated in order to prevent peripheral tissues remaining cold and vasoconstricted. Shivering should be prevented.

Temperature Monitoring

Apparatus Temperature. The temperature of the heat exchanger and the arterial blood returning to the patient should be monitored.

Body Temperature. The rectal temperature can be misleading in induced hypothermia because of the proximity to the warming/cooling blanket (Steward et al. 1974) and is not used in many cardiac centres (Macdonald 1975). Oesophageal and nasopharyngeal temperature should be carefully measured every minute during surface cooling and rewarming. Once surface cooling is completed cerebral temperature needs to be monitored either by the nasopharyngeal or external auditory meatus routes. One probe to measure muscle temperature may be useful to assess temperature gradients.

General Care. Ileus is the most common complication and a nasogastric tube should be passed when blood coagulation is normal. The pressure points over bony prominences require attention and should be massaged frequently. Alternatively, a suitable mattress (e.g. one which ripples) or a sheepskin bedcover may be used.

Postoperative Care. Cardiorespiratory problems are dominant and myocardial and respiratory support is often needed for a few hours. Intensive nursing care is mandatory for at least 24 hours and the highest mortality occurs in this period. Neurological complications such as convulsions may require treatment and continuation of preoperative monitoring is necessary, combined with EEG and electrolyte monitoring (Subramanian 1974).

Techniques of Induced Deep Hypothermia
Oxygenation of the blood during cardiac operations which require profound hypothermia can be achieved using a cardiopulmonary bypass machine with a pump and oxygenator or using the patient's own lungs. Use of the lungs requires extra cannulation of the pulmonary artery and left atrium. This is troublesome in small children and impossible in cases of Fallot's tetralogy.

Blood Stream Cooling. This is used preferentially in cardiac surgery because major vessels are easily exposed and the rate and depth of the temperature drop can be readily controlled. A variety of methods are available to suit the particular indications for the technique:

1. Arteriovenous cooling (femoral artery to femoral vein) is used in neurosurgery (Geevarghese et al. 1977) because a thoracotomy is not necessary. Although in humans the shunt is large, it reduces during hypothermia. This is a slow method of cooling and the viability of the leg may be at risk as a result of the shunt.
2. Venovenous cooling (superior vena cava to inferior vena cava). A pump is required as well as a heat exchanger, but the patient's systemic and pulmonary circulations are maintained by the heart. It follows that this technique has a limited use and should not be employed at temperatures less than 30°C.
3. Venoarterial cooling. The following arrangements are available:
   a. Right atrium to pulmonary artery and left atrium to femoral artery
   b. Right atrium to aorta bypassing the lungs
   c. Left atrium to left femoral artery. This technique has a limited usefulness in surgery of the descending aorta.

Surface Cooling. The advantages of preliminary surface cooling are that it decreases the total time required on bypass (Steward et al. 1974), it slows the heart rate and enables vessel cannulation to be performed more easily. It also reduces oxygen consumption in an irritable myocardium. Passive cooling, using ambient air, is slow. There are various active methods that can be used, singly or in combination. The most rapid method of surface cooling is cold immersion in water and ice. The ice is added to the bath after the patient has been adequately anaesthetized. This allows a large area of heat exchange to be available, including the back. The patient's head is supported by a sling.

A large 'after-drop' may occur, i.e. the temperature will continue to fall after cooling is discontinued. In addition, the technique is cumbersome, monitoring may be difficult and if temperature gradients are allowed to occur between the limbs and the body sudden movement may empty cold blood into the central circulation and cause myocardial disturbances. Limbs should, therefore, either be kept still or massaged in order to prevent stagnation.

Methods which can be combined in cooling the patient include partially wetting the body with cool water and using fans to assist evaporation, placing ice packs (or iced alcohol) around the neck, axillae and groins and the use of a cold water blanket underneath the patient. Vidne and Subramanian (1976) describe the development of a 'hypothermic chamber', with an ambient temperature of −10°C, but wind tunnels and chambers are associated with problems such as frostbite and lack of visual assessment.

Deep Hypothermia without an Oxygenator

This method, shown diagrammatically in Figure 37, was pioneered by Drew et al. (1959) and was used to induce pharyngeal temperatures of 13–15°C in infants undergoing cardiac surgery (Drew & Anderson 1959). It is well described by Benazon (1964). The right and left atria were cannulated. Blood from the right atrium was pumped into the pulmonary artery and oxygenated blood returning from the lungs was pumped through a heat exchanger and via a cannula into the femoral artery. This allowed ideal operating conditions with easy access to the still, bloodless heart for one hour. In theory at least, surgery could be more accurate, blood trauma from the oxygenators could be avoided (Lee et al. 1961) and the incidence of air or particulate emboli could be reduced. However in practice the operator was limited to a fixed operation time and myocardial or other abnormal pathology (e.g. cerebral) would have reduced the time available for circulatory standstill.

Deep hypothermia without an oxygenator is time-consuming and the cannulation of major vessels can lead to permanent damage. Where there is already pulmonary hypertension the method is strongly contraindicated (Björk & Hultquist, 1962). Overdistension of the ventricle in a steadily failing heart before induced cardiac arrest may

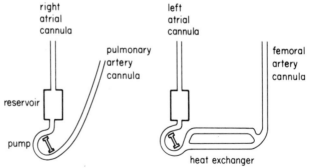

Fig. 37. Drew's Method of Cooling and Rewarming

produce postoperative myocardial dysfunction. Postoperative pulmonary complications are common. Macdonald (1975), in a survey of contemporary practice, reported that this method was going out of use.

Deep Hypothermia with an Oxygenator

Surface cooling may be employed to lower the temperature as far as 30°C. Below this temperature cardiopulmonary bypass is used to support the circulation because of the danger of ventricular fibrillation. Johnston et al. (1974) suggest that the development of ventricular fibrillation during the initial surface cooling is related to a decrease in plasma potassium level, especially in digitalized patients. Commonly, a pump oxygenator is used to induce profound hypothermia (Macdonald 1975). The technique was pioneered by Barratt-Boyes et al. (1971) and is now used for correction of complicated congenital cardiac defects in the first year of life (Bailey et al. 1976; Subramian 1977; Caldwell et al. 1977; Wakusawa et al. 1977). Deep hypothermia allows early correction of congenital defects and reduces the morbidity associated with palliative procedures (Stark 1976). It may be superseded by refinements in cardiopulmonary bypass techniques.

Rewarming

Rewarming essentially follows the pattern described for accidental hypothermia. Spontaneous rewarming takes a period of six to eight hours during which deep sedation is continued. Active rewarming by surface methods, using water at 42–46°C, has been abandoned. When an extracorporeal heat exchanger is used it is important to warm as fully as possible before bypass is discontinued, and the transfusion of cold, stored blood is to be avoided. On completion of the operation the patient should be transferred to a warm bed: this allows spontaneous rewarming to supplement more active measures.

Local Cooling as an Adjunct to General Cooling

Where mild general cooling is required for a long period, e.g. with hyperpyrexial infants, local cooling of body cavities may be employed in addition to other active external measures to reduce body temperature (Dundee & King 1959). Intragastric cooling has been used by Khalil and MacKeith (1954) to reduce body temperature. They ran fluid at 5–7°C through a balloon in the stomach at a rate of 750 ml/minute. The same technique has been employed by Barnard (1956). Cooling induced by washing the pleural or peritoneal cavities with cold fluid is a slow process and it can take up to three hours to reduce the temperature from 37°C to 30°C. Fluid and electrolyte imbalances may result if the dialysis which occurs in both cavities is not properly controlled.

BODY TEMPERATURE IN NEUROSURGERY

General Body Temperature Control

In neurosurgery, temperature monitoring should be used at all times with children and for any procedure of more than two hours with adults (Geevarghese 1977). Postoperative temperatures should be monitored in comatose patients. It is also necessary to control shivering with its concomitant increase in cerebral oxygen consumption (Barker 1973).

Hypothermia

A survey of British neurosurgery by McDowall (1971) shows that the use of hypothermia in neurosurgery is declining, presumably because its advantages are limited in relation to the complexity of the technique. However, surface-induced hypothermia to 30°C has been used (Hellings 1958) to reduce the hazards of a reduced blood flow to the brain during major arterial occlusion. Barbiturates and other anaesthetics may also offer some protection of the ischaemic brain (Smith 1975) and this effect may be augmented by hypothermia induced at the time the drug is administered (Michenfelder 1978).

Hypothermia also reduces cerebrospinal fluid pressure (Rosomoff 1968) but cerebral oedema at normal temperatures occurs after rewarming. It may be caused by uneven cooling of the brain during hypothermia, especially if the brain is retracted or temperature gradients are produced by irrigating fluids (Bendandi & Galletti 1963). Moreover, the technique of surface cooling is time-consuming and does not result in profound hypothermia of the brain. Safe profound hypothermia demands cardiopulmonary bypass, which requires a team of experts in this field as well as the neurosurgeons. This limits its application.

Hypothermia is indicated in the following situations:

Vascular Lesions: Aneurysms and Angiomas. The major problem of intracranial aneurysms is rupture of the aneurysm prior to clipping. This may be prevented by keeping the arterial pressure within the aneurysm low by either hypotension or hypothermia. However, McKissock et al. (1965) found that ischaemic damage to the brain consequent to rupture of an aneurysm was not prevented by hypothermia. There also appears to be an increased incidence of arterial spasm especially when the operation is performed early in the post-haemorrhagic period and Sellery et al. (1973) recommend that hypotension rather than hypothermia is used when anaesthetizing patients with intracranial aneurysms. For the same reasons hypothermia is not the method of choice for the surgery of arterial malformations.

Carotid Artery Surgery. Reconstructions of the carotid artery can be complicated by postoperative neurological deficits which the operation was designed to prevent. Bland et al. (1970) found that the supposed reduction in cerebral metabolic rate produced by hypothermia did not in practice protect the brain against neurological damage during carotid occlusion. Enthusiasm for the technique has waned.

Head Injury and Cardiac Arrest. Prolonged mild hypothermia (34°C) may reduce brain damage due to hypoxia but pulmonary complications (Popovic & Popovic 1974) and skin pressure necrosis may complicate recovery. Hypothermia beyond 48 hours duration can itself induce cerebral oedema (Bloch 1967). Induced hypothermia may be essential where hyperpyrexia complicates brain stem lesions.

REGIONAL HYPOTHERMIA

Regional hypothermia has been used for many hundreds of years to assist surgery. It has controlled haemorrhage from the extremities and from the stomach (Herman et al. 1964), it has enabled amputations to be performed in the Napoleonic Wars (Davison 1959) and it is now routinely used to protect the kidney from hypoxic damage during operations on these organs (Hanley 1970).

Local cooling would appear to be a preferable technique for localized procedures where problems of general hypothermia can be avoided. Crampton et al. (1964) emphasize that local cooling may lead to general hypothermia and steps should be taken to prevent this.

Gastrointestinal Tract

Stomach. Historically, gastric cooling is associated with the treatment of peptic ulcers. At temperatures less than 30°C, gastric secretion is markedly reduced and blood flow in the arteries supplying the stomach is similarly depressed. This may be the major mechanism in the control of upper gastrointestinal bleeding (Wangensteen et al. 1958). Reduction in portal blood flow during hypothermia may explain the cessation of bleeding from oesophageal varices when this technique is used. Hermann et al. (1964) found that the method provided temporary relief of haemorrhage. Complications of local cooling included gastritis, gastric rupture and aspiration of stomach contents (Barker et al. 1964). Gastric cooling can be used to prepare a patient for surgery (Hubbard 1966) where upper gastrointestinal bleeding may threaten life.

Colon and Rectum. Haemorrhage from diverticulitis has been treated with a rectal balloon irrigated with cold fluids (Barker et al. 1964).

Nervous Tissue

Brain. Local cooling of the brain does not protect the myocardium, spinal cord or kidneys from hypoxia. Carotid artery perfusions of cold solutions require additional major surgery. Negrin (1971) used subarachnoid and intraventricular infusions of cold fluids postoperatively after removing brain tumours and Sôurek and Trávniček (1970) reported a reduction in epileptic seizures following mild general hypothermia and local cooling of the subarachnoid space. Barker (1973) outlines the use of preferential cooling of the brain following a cardiac arrest, but the technique is only experimental. Cooling may be difficult to control because of poor thermal conduction by cerebral tissues.

Spinal cord. Hypothermic subarachnoid saline injection for the relief of chronic pain was first attempted in 1967 by Hitchcock. It has been further evaluated by Raskind et al. (1972) who found that it was only useful in neoplastic disease and that out of 23 patients, one had a *grand mal* convulsion and another a transient respiratory disease associated with the injection. Its effects may be related more to the hypertonicity of the solution than to the effect of its temperature on the spinal cord (Matthews & Pace-Floridia 1970).

Peripheral Nerves. A cryoprobe utilizing nitrous oxide at a minimum temperature of −60°C has been applied locally under direct vision to peripheral nerves to produce a reversible nerve block. Analgesia persisted for a mean duration of eleven days (Lloyd et al. 1976).

Myocardium

Topical hypothermia (below 16°C), producing cardioplegia, is an effective means of myocardial protection during aortic cross-clamping when no coronary perfusion is set up. The heart requires venting and thermal gradients in the myocardium should be avoided. Occasionally left phrenic nerve paralysis occurs postoperatively if the nerve is not protected during its pericardial course. This is directly related to cold injury which is reversible but causes postoperative pulmonary dysfunction (Marco et al. 1977). Coronary perfusion permits aortic cross-clamping before myocardial cooling is complete but Urschel and Greenberg (1959) found that haemodiluted blood was necessary for the perfusion because of the increased viscosity of whole blood at low temperature.

Urogenital Tract

Kidneys. The kidney may be cooled, intra- or extravascularly to prevent blood loss during the operation of pyelolithotomy, as an adjunct to surgery on the aorta above the renal vessels, or when required for transplantation.

Complete stone clearance during a pyelolithotomy ideally requires a bloodless field. Hanley (1970) has developed a cooling system using the principle that if a gas under high pressure is allowed to expand its temperature will be reduced. Pressurized nitrous oxide is passed through a narrow orifice and then allowed to expand into coils of a size suitable to surround the kidney. The temperature inside the coils is measured electrically and a thermostat controls the rate of gas flow into the system. The kidney can be cooled to 23°C in ten minutes by keeping the pads at 7°C. Heat exchange needs to be prevented between the coils and the abdominal tissues. Once cooling is achieved, and providing the arterial supply to the kidney is clamped, the kidney temperature will remain below 25°C for about 30 minutes. Recooling requires further application of the coils. The anaesthetist should monitor body temperature closely once the cooled kidney is perfused again.

Bladder. Massive bleeding from carcinomas has been controlled by an intravesical hypothermic balloon (Barker et al. 1964). Cold bladder irrigations have not been used to induce hypothermia, but rectal temperatures in young infants have been observed by Roland (1956) to reach hypothermic levels following cystoscopies.

Liver
Local cooling of the liver for partial hepatectomy has been attempted in animals by Huggins and Carter (1957) but no recent developments have occurred in humans.

INDUCED HYPERTHERMIA
Heat has been used to destroy cancer cells. It appears to act by more than one mechanism. Selective direct damage of the malignant cells is achieved at temperatures of 42–43°C. Raising the temperature may augment the action of radiotherapy and some cytotoxic drugs: work with animals in this area is being applied to patients. Dickson (1979) has reviewed the methods of heat production which are available. These are:

Local Heat
Regional hyperthermic perfusion of limb sarcomas at 43°C for up to eight hours can not only reduce the tumour mass but also cause regression of metastases. In rabbits this is associated with an enhanced immune response.

Total Body Heating
This has not been as successful as local heating.

Diathermy
There is limited experience with this technique. It is based on the hypothesis that differential heating of the normal and abnormal tissues occurs because of the difference in blood supply; while normal tissues increase their blood flow to dissipate the heat load the tumour tissue is unable to do so.

Combination Therapy
Hyperthermia and irradiation affect different phases of the cell cycle and their effect can summate.

References

Abbott, T. R. (1977) Oxygen uptake following deep hypothermia. *Anaesthesia*, *32*, 524–532.

Bailey, L. L., Takeuchi, Y., Williams, W. G., Trusler, G. A. & Mustard, W. T. (1976) Surgical management of congenital cardiovascular anomalies with the use of profound hypothermia and circulatory arrest. *J. thorac. cardiovasc. Surg.*, *71*, 485–492.

Barker, C. F., Nance, F. C. & Peskin, G. W. (1964) Regional hypothermia for massive bleeding. *Surgery, St Louis*, *56*, 624–627.

Barker, J. (1973) Induced hypothermia: its place in modern hospital practice. *Anaesthesia*, *28*, 236–252.

Barnard, C. N. (1956) Hypothermia: a method of intragastric cooling. *Br. J. Surg.*, *44*, 296–298.

Barratt-Boyes, B. G., Simpson, M. & Neutze, J. M. (1971) Intracardiac surgery in neonates and infants using deep hypothermia with surface cooling and limited cardiopulmonary bypass *Circulation*, Suppl. I, 25–30.

Benazon, D. B. (1964) Profound hypothermia. *Int. Anesthesiol. Clin.*, *2*, 941–966.

Bendandi, G. & Galletti, G (1963) Temperature distribution in the brain during profound selective cooling and anoxia of central nervous system. *J. cardiovasc. Surg.*, *4*, 65–71.

Bigelow, W. G., Mustard, W. T. & Evans, J. G. (1954) Some physiologic concepts of hypothermia and their application to cardiac surgery. *J. thorac. cardiovasc. Surg.*, *28*, 463–480.

Björk, V. O. & Hultquist, G. (1962) Contraindications to profound hypothermia in open-heart surgery. *J. thorac. cardiovasc. Surg.*, *44*, 1–12.

Blair, E. (1964) *Clinical Hypothermia*, p. 22. London: McGraw-Hill.

Bland, J. E., Chapman, R. D. & Wylie, E. J. (1970) Neurological complications of carotid artery surgery. *Ann. Surg.*, *171*, 459–464.

Bloch, M. (1967) Cerebral effects of rewarming following prolonged hypothermia: significance for the management of severe cranio-cerebral surgery and acute pyrexia. *Brain*, *90*, 769–784.

Botterell, E. H., Lougheed, W. M., Scott, J. W. & Vandewater, S. L. (1956) Hypothermia and interruption of carotid or carotid and vertebral circulation in the surgical management of intracranial aneurysms. *J. Neurosurg.*, *13*, 1–42.

Branthwaite, M. A. (1973) Factors affecting cerebral activity during open-heart surgery. *Anaesthesia*, *28*, 619–625.

Braunwald, E. (1971) Control of myocardial oxygen consumption. *Am. J. Cardiol.*, *27*, 416–432.

Brazier, J. R., Cooper, N., McConnell, D. H. & Buckberg, G. D. (1977) Studies of the effects of hypothermia on regional myocardial blood flow and metabolism during cardiopulmonary bypass. III: Effects of temperature, time and perfusion pressures in fibrillating hearts. *J. thorac. cardiovasc. Surg.*, *73*, 102–109.

Burton, G. W. (1964) Metabolic acidosis during profound hypothermia. *Anaesthesia*, *19*, 365–375.

Caldwell, T. B., Blunk, J. N. & Escobar, A. (1977) Experience with deep hypothermia and elective circulatory arrest for cardiac surgery in infants. *Sth. Med. J., Nashville, 70*, 681–685.

Callaghan, P. B., Lister, J., Paton, B. C. & Swan, H. (1961) Effect of varying carbon dioxide tensions on the oxyhemoglobin dissociation curves under hypothermic conditions. *Ann. Surg., 154*, 903–910.

Civalero, L. A., Moreno, J. R. & Senning, A. (1962) Temperature conditions and oxygen consumption during deep hypothermia. *Acta chir. scand., 123*, 179–188.

Clutton-Brock, J. (1959) Some details of a technique for hypothermia. *Br. J. Anaesth., 31*, 210–216.

Cooper, K. E. & Ross, D. N. (1960) *Hypothermia in Surgical Practice*. Philadelphia: Davis.

Cooper, N., Brazier, J. R., McConnell, D. H. & Buckberg, G. D. (1977) Studies of the effect of hypothermia on regional myocardial blood flow and metabolism during cardiopulmonary bypass. IV: Topical atrial hypothermia in normothermic beating hearts. *J. thorac. cardiovasc. Surg., 73*, 195–200.

Crampton, R. S., Cali, J. R., Yerys, P., Buetow, G. W. & Glaubitz, J. P. (1964) Experience with gastric hypothermia for active upper gastrointestinal tract hemorrhage. *Surgery, St Louis, 55*, 607–611.

Davison, A. M. H. (1959) The evolution of anaesthesia. *Br. J. Anaesth., 31*, 134–137.

Dickson, J. A. (1979) Hyperthermia in the treatment of cancer. *Lancet, 1*, 202–205.

Dill, D. B. & Forbes, W. H. (1941) Respiratory and metabolic effects of hypothermia. *Am. J. Physiol., 132*, 685–697.

Drew, C. E. & Anderson, I. M. (1959) Profound hypothermia in cardiac surgery. *Lancet, 1*, 748–750.

Drew, C. E., Keen, G. & Benazon, D. B. (1959) Profound hypothermia. *Lancet, 1*, 745–747.

Dundee, J. W. & King, R. (1959) Clinical aspects of induced hypothermia. *Br. J. Anaesth., 31*, 106–133.

Geevarghese, K. P. (1977) Anesthesia for neurological surgery. *Int. Anesthesiol. Clin., 15*, 36.

Geevarghese, K. P., Shields, C. B. & Gray, L. A. (1977) Anesthesia for neurological surgery. *Int. Anesthesiol. Clin., 15*, 333.

Goldman, B. S., Trimble, A. S., Sheverini, M. A., Teasdale, S. J., Silver, M. D. & Elliot, G. E. (1971) Functional and metabolic effects of anoxic cardiac arrest. *Ann. thorac. Surg., 11*, 122–132.

Goldschlager, N., Gerbode, F., Osborn, J. J., & Cohn, K. E. (1972) Patterns of myocardial oxygen and lactate extraction in patients undergoing cardiopulmonary bypass. *Am. Heart J., 83*, 167–178.

Granholm, L. & Siesjö, B. O. K. (1969) The effects of hypercapnia and hypocapnia upon the cerebrospinal fluid lactate and pyruvate concentrations and upon the lactate, pyruvate, ATP, ADP, phosphocreatine and creatine concentrations of cat brain tissue. *Acta physiol. scand., 75*, 257–266.

Hanley, H. G. (1970) An improved system of local renal hypothermia. *Br. J. Urol., 42*, 540–544.

Hedley-Brown, A., Braimbridge, M. V., Darracott, S., Chayen, J. & Kasap, H. (1974) An experimental evaluation of continuous normothermic, intermittent hypothermic and intermittent normothermic coronary perfusion. *Thorax, 29*, 38–50.

Hellings, P. M. (1958) Controlled hypothermia. Recent developments in the use of hypothermia in neurosurgery. *Br. med. J., 2*, 346–350.

Hermann, G., Karsh, H. B. & Kauvar, A. J. (1964) Gastric cooling in the management of massive upper gastrointestinal haemorrhage. *Gastroenterology*, *47*, 513–516.

Hitchcock, E. (1967) Hypothermic subarachnoid irrigation for intractable pain. *Lancet*, *1*, 1133–1135.

Hubbard, T. B. (1966) A method of gastric hypothermia. *Surgery, St. Louis*, *59*, 670–672.

Huggins, C. E. & Carter, E. L. (1957) Partial hepatectomy employing differential hypothermia. *A.M.A. Archs Surg.*, *74*, 189–200.

Johnston, A. E., Radde, I. C., Steward, D. J. & Taylor, J. (1974) Acid-base and electrolyte changes in infants undergoing profound hypothermia for surgical correction of congenital heart defects. *Can. Anaesth. Soc. J.*, *21*, 23–45.

Kelman, G. R. & Nunn, J. F. (1966) Nomograms for correction of blood Po_2, Pco_2, pH and base excess for time and temperature. *J. appl. Physiol.*, *21*, 1484–1490.

Khalil, H. H. & MacKeith, R. C. (1954) A simple method of raising and lowering body temperature. *Br. med. J.*, *2*, 734–736.

Lee, W. H., Krumhaar, D., Fonkalsrud, E. W., Schjeide, O. A. & Maloney, J. V. (1961) Denaturation of plasma proteins as a cause of morbidity and death after intracardiac operations. *Surgery, St Louis*, *50*, 29–39.

Lloyd, J. W., Barnard, J. D. W. & Glynn, C. J. (1976) Cryoanalgesia. A new approach to pain relief. *Lancet*, *2*, 932–934.

Lougheed, W. M. & Kahn, D. S. (1955) Circumvention of anoxia during arrest of cerebral circulation for intracranial surgery. *J. Neurosurg.*, *12*, 226.

Macdonald, D. J. F. (1975) Current practice of hypothermia in British cardiac surgery. *Br. J. Anaesth.*, *47*, 1011–1017.

Maloney, J. V. & Nelson, R. L. (1975) Myocardial preservation during cardiopulmonary bypass. *J. thorac. cardiovasc. Surg.*, *70*, 1040–1050.

Marco, J. D., Hahn, J. W. & Barner, H. B. (1977) Topical cardiac hypothermia and phrenic nerve injury. *Ann. thorac. Surg.*, *23*, 235–237.

Matthews, G. J. & Pace-Floridia, A. (1970) Intrathecal cold saline for the relief of intractable pain. *Can. med. Ass. J.*, *103*, 1143–1146.

Maynard, D., Prior, P. F. & Scott, D. F. (1969) Device for continuous monitoring of cerebral activity in resuscitated patients. *Br. med. J.*, *4*, 545–546.

McConnell, D. H., Brazier, J. R., Cooper, N. & Buckberg, G. D. (1977) Studies of the effect of hypothermia on regional myocardial blood flow and metabolism during cardiopulmonary bypass. II: Ischaemia during moderate hypothermia in continually perfused beating hearts. *J. thorac. cardiovasc. Surg,*. *73*, 95–101.

McDowall, D. G. (1971) The current usage of hypothermia in British neurosurgery. *Br. J. Anaesth.*, *43*, 1084–1087.

McKissock, W., Richardson, A. & Walsh, L. (1965) Anterior communicating aneurysms. *Lancet*, *1*, 873–876.

Michenfelder, J. D. & Theye, R. A. (1970) The effects of anesthesia and hypothermia on canine cerebral ATP and lactate during anoxia produced by decapitation. *Anesthesiology*, *33*, 430–439.

Michenfelder, J. D. (1978) Hypothermia plus barbiturates. *Anesthesiology*, *49*, 157–158.

Mohri, H., Dillard, D. H., Crawford, E. W., Martin, W. E. & Merendino, K. A. (1969) Method of surface-induced deep hypothermia for open heart surgery in infants. *J. thorac. cardiovasc. Surg.*, *58*, 262–270.

Negrin, J. (1971) Hypothermia of the central nervous system *Trans. N.Y. Acad. Sci., U.S.A., 33*, 557–563.

Nelson, R. L., Goldstein, S. M., McConnell, D. H., Maloney, J. V. & Buckberg, G. D. (1977) Studies of the effect of hypothermia on regional myocardial blood flow and metabolism during cardiopulmonary bypass. V: Profound topical hypothermia during ischaemia in arrested hearts. *J. thorac. cardiovasc. Surg., 73*, 201.

Nilsson, L. & Busto, R. (1976) Brain energy metabolism during the process of dying and after cardiopulmonary resuscitation. *Acta anaesth. scand., 20*, 57–64.

Osborn, J. J., Gerbode, F., Johnston, J. B., Ross, J. K., Ogata, T. & Kerth, W. J. (1961) Blood chemical changes in perfusion hypothermia for cardiac surgery. *J. thorac. cardiovasc. Surg., 42*, 462–476.

Popovic, V. & Popovic, P. (1974) *Hypothermia in Biology and Medicine*, p. 198. New York: Grune and Stratton.

Raskind, R., Weiss, S. R. & Huertas, J. (1972) Hypothermic subarachnoid saline injection as a method of pain control. *Am. Surg., 38*, 142–144.

Roland, S. I. (1956) Hypothermia induced by cystoscopy. *J. Urol., 75*, 1006–1010.

Rosomoff, H. L. (1968) Cerebral oedema and brain swelling. Acta anaesth. scand., suppl., *29*, 75–90.

Scheuer, J. (1967) Myocardial metabolism in cardiac hypoxia. *Am. J. Cardiol., 19*, 385–392.

Schwartz, M. S., Colvin, M. P., Prior, P. F., Strunin, L., Simpson, B. R., Weaver, E. J. M. & Scott, D. F. (1973) The cerebral function monitor. *Anaesthesia, 28*, 611–618.

Sellery, G. R., Aitken, R. R. & Drake, C. G. (1973) Anaesthesia for intracranial aneurysms with hypotension and spontaneous respiration. *Can. Anaesth. Soc J., 20*, 468–478.

Severinghaus, J. W., Stupfel, M. A. & Bradley, A. F. (1957) Alveolar dead space and arterial to end-tidal carbon dioxide differences during hypothermia in dog and man. *J. appl. Physiol., 10*, 349–355.

Severinghaus, J. W. (1958) Oxyhaemoglobin dissociation curve correction for temperature and pH variation in human blood. *J. appl. Physiol., 12*, 485–486.

Smith, A. L. (1975) Effect of anaesthetics and oxygen deprivation on brain blood flow and metabolism. *Surg. Clins N. Am., 55:4*, 819–836.

Sòurek, K. & Trávníček, V. (1970) General and local hypothermia of the brain in the treatment of intractable epilepsy. *J. Neurosurg., 33*, 253–259.

Stark, J. (1976) Debate on congenital heart disease. *Adv. Cardiol., 17*, 51–72.

Steward, D. J., Sloan, I. A. & Johnston, A. E. (1974) Anaesthetic management of infants undergoing profound hypothermia for surgical correction of congenital heart defects. *Can. Anaesth. Soc. J., 21*, 15–22.

Subramanian, S. (1974) Early correction of congenital cardiac defects using profound hypothermia and circulatory arrest. *Ann. R. Coll. Surg., 54*, 176–187.

Subramanian, S. (1977) Deep hypothermia. *Johns Hopkins med. J., 140*, 163–169.

Urschel, H. C. & Greenberg, J. J. (1959) Differential hypothermic cardioplegia. *Surg. Forum, 10*, 506–509.

Vidne, B. A. & Subramanian, S. (1976) Surface induced profound hypothermia in infant cardiac operations: a new system. *Ann. thorac. Surg., 22*, 572–577.

Wakusawa, R., Shabata, S. & Okada, K. (1977) Simple deep hypothermia for open heart surgery in infancy. *Can. Anaesth. Soc. J., 24*, 491–504.

Wangensteen, O. H., Root, H. D., Jensen, C. B., Imamoglu, K. & Salmon, P. A. (1958) Depression of gastric secretion and digestion by gastric hypothermia: its clinical use in massive hematemesis. *Surgery, St. Louis*, *44*, 265–274.

Ward, C. F., Arkin, D. B. & Benumof, J. L. (1977) The use of profound hypothermia and circulatory arrest for hepatic lobectomy in infancy. *Anesthesiology*, *47*, 473–474.

Appendix:

Correction factors for pH, Po_2 and Pco_2
during hypothermia

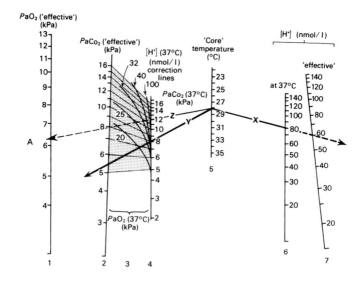

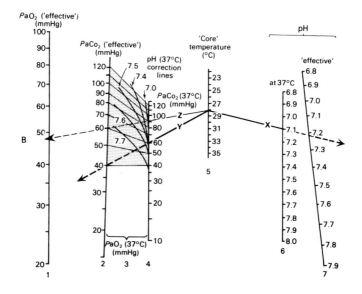

Fig. 38. Nomograms for the determination of the 'effective' arterial pH, PCO_2 and PO_2 values at low core temperatures during accidental hypothermia from their values measured in the laboratory at normal body temperature (37°C). In A, the values are expressed in SI units, whereas in B conventional units are used.

pH: The 'effective' pH at the patient's core temperature is easily obtained by first drawing the straight line X from the appropriate point on scale 5 to the point on scale 6 that corresponds to the measured pH (i.e. the *core temperature—pH at 37°C* line) end then extending it (broken part) to intersect scale 7. This latter point of intersection gives the effective pH value sought. Thus, in the example shown, that of a patient at 28°C, the measured pH (80 nmol/litre in A and 7·1 in B, when corrected to take the hypothermia into account, assumes a new value of 60 nmol/litre in A and 7·22 in B.

PCO_2:   The 'effective' PCO_2 is similarly easily derived by first drawing the *core temperature—PCO_2 at 37°C* line Y between scales 5 and 4 and then extending it (broken part) to intersect scale 2. In the example shown, the measured PCO_2 (8 kPa in A and 60 mmHg in B), when corrected to take the hypothermia into account, assumes a new value of 5·4 kPa or 40 mmHg.

PO_2:   Before the *core temperature—PO_2 at 37°C* line Z can be drawn, however, it is necessary first to determine the point that represents the PO_2 value (as measured at 37°C) after it has been corrected to take into account the modifying effect of pH (also as measured at 37°C). In the shaded area of each diagram, scale 3 is represented by a series of straight lines that connect scales 2 and 4; the PO_2 (at 37°C) value that corresponds to each of the lines that constitute scale 3 has the same numerical and unit values as do the points on the two PCO_2 scales (*at 37°C* and '*effective*') that form its ends. Thus, for example, the 12 kPa in A or 90 mmHg in B 'measured' (at 37°C) PO_2 line is the one that connects the 12 kPa (or 90 mmHg) points on scales 2 and 4, and so on. These PO_2 (at 37°C) lines are intersected by a series of curved [H^+] (A) or pH (B) lines (also shown in the shaded area of each diagram); the points of intersection correspond to PO_2 values (at 37°C) corrected to take into account the modifying effect of [H^+] or pH (measured at 37°C). The 'effective' PO_2 at the patient's core temperature is thus determined by drawing the *core temperature—PO_2 at 37°C corrected for* [H^+] (*or pH*) *at 37°C*—line (Z) and then extending it to intersect the effective PO_2 scale (scale 1).

In the example shown, the measured PO_2 (at 37°C) of 12 kPa (A) or 90 mmHg (B) is effectively 6·3 kPa or 48 mmHg at the patient's core temperature (28°C). The measured [H^+] or pH (at 37°C) therefore determines the point on the PO_2 (at 37°C) line through which line Z is drawn and therefore it has an important influence on the calculated effective PO_2 value for the patient's core temperature.

(Reproduced from Maclean, D. and Emslie-Smith, D. (1977) Accidental Hypothermia. Oxford: Blackwell Scientific)

INDEX